SAP Project Management Pitfalls

How to Avoid the Most Common
Pitfalls of an SAP Solution

Jayaraman Kalaimani

Apress®

SAP Project Management Pitfalls: How to Avoid the Most Common Pitfalls of an SAP Solution

ISBN-13 (pbk): 978-1-4842-1390-2

ISBN-13 (electronic): 978-1-4842-1389-6

Managing Director: Welmoed Spahr
Acquisitions Editor: Celestin Suresh John
Technical Reviewers: Naveen D'Souza, Rahul Navandar, Gurusom Rath
Editorial Board: Steve Anglin, Mark Beckner, Gary Cornell, Louise Corrigan, James DeWolf, Jonathan Gennick, Robert Hutchinson, Michelle Lowman, James Markham, Susan McDermott, Matthew Moodie, Jeffrey Pepper, Douglas Pundick, Ben Renow-Clarke, Gwenan Spearing, Matt Wade, Steve Weiss
Coordinating Editor: Rita Fernando
Copy Editors: Laura Lawrie, Sharon Wilkey, Tiffany Taylor
Compositor: SPi Global
Indexer: SPi Global

Distributed to the book trade worldwide by Springer Science+Business Media New York, 233 Spring Street, 6th Floor, New York, NY 10013. Phone 1-800-SPRINGER, fax (201) 348-4505, e-mail orders-ny@springer-sbm.com, or visit www.springeronline.com. Apress Media, LLC is a California LLC and the sole member (owner) is Springer Science + Business Media Finance Inc (SSBM Finance Inc). SSBM Finance Inc is a Delaware corporation.

For information on translations, please e-mail rights@apress.com, or visit www.apress.com.

Apress and friends of ED books may be purchased in bulk for academic, corporate, or promotional use. eBook versions and licenses are also available for most titles. For more information, reference our Special Bulk Sales–eBook Licensing web page at www.apress.com/bulk-sales.

Any source code or other supplementary material referenced by the author in this text is available to readers at www.apress.com. For detailed information about how to locate your book's source code, go to www.apress.com/source-code/.

I would like to dedicate this book to my family

Contents at a Glance

Contents

About the Author

Jayaraman Kalaimani graduated in 1996 from the department of mechanical engineering at the University of Madras. He is an SAP professional with over 20 years of experience in the industry. He has worked with various clients in the United States, European Union, and the Asian Pacific American Coalition with successful ERP implementations, upgrade, and rollout projects. He currently is a Senior Project Manager-SAP at Capgemini in India and a frequent blogger in the SAP Community Network, helping clients to achieve their project management goals.

About the Technical Reviewers

Gurusom Rath is has over 18 years of experience in SAP/Supply Chain Management and has played many roles in this journey. He started as an Analyst and worked his way up. He is now managing his own supply chain boutique firm and is serving clients in various industrial sectors.

Naveen D'Souza is an SAP MM Certified Consultant with overall experience of 17 years and over 7 years of SAP consulting experience. He has handled end-to-end full-cycle implementations, rollouts, support, and up-gradation projects. He has worked on site Go-Live (Hyper Care) Support and Offshore Production Support. He has also provided SAP consulting to diverse business environments, including retail, tobacco manufacturing, oil and gas, trading and dealership, and chemical manufacturing. He has international experience and has worked with clients around the globe, including in Oman, the United Arab Emirates, Singapore, and Jordan.

Acknowledgments

I would like to thank Apress for the opportunity to share my experiences with the world of SAP consultants and project managers. It is a journey and SAP is still evolving as a cutting-edge technology. It will remain as the pioneer ERP with simple solutions to complex client requirements.

I would like to thank my family, friends, and colleagues. A book of this size would not have been possible without the support of them all. I would like to give sincere thanks to my team for the review and proofreading throughout the stages of this book. I would also like to thank Sultan Golighar, SAP BW consultant, for contributing to the Analytics chapter, Amjad Jamadhar, SAP TM consultant, for contributing to the SAP transportation management chapter, and Sivakumar, Natarajan, Associate Director-SAP, Capgemini for their kind support.

I would like to thank all of my colleagues for their enthusiasm and support for this project, and, finally, to the Divine Space, thank you—for everything.

Introduction

This book is designed to help you manage SAP implementation projects. It is a compilation of implementation techniques, notes, and tips that I have learned.

Often, the volume of SAP embarrasses me and how the massive structure of SAP adapts to various enterprises is a wonder. Hence, it is easy to get lost in the maze without knowing what to learn and how to implement an SAP project. The objective of this book is to present quick artifacts of implementation software upgrade projects to help you to succeed as a project manager or consultant.

After compiling the information that I had collected into a coherent structure, I was approached by numerous friends and colleagues to share this information with them. Thus came the decision to publish this book. You will find it a valuable source of trustworthy advice given in an easy-to-access format, with direct answers.

This book is directed at project managers and consultants implementing SAP, but is also a valuable tool for the IT/IS department to make decisions with deeper knowledge and understanding of the product.

As you read this book, you will enhance your knowledge of SAP projects through the implementation guides, time-saving tips, and information on the do's and don'ts to keep in mind when implementing SAP projects. Most implementation projects fail due to lack of understanding the technology, lack of skills, lack of seasoned project manager, and/or lack of understanding customer requirements. The SAP project manager is the key person, the captain navigating the ship.

SAP Project Management Pitfalls will help you to understand SAP ERP from an end-to-end perspective, to help you manage ERP implementation projects completely from R/3 and ECC evolution to SAP HANA DB. However, without practicing these steps, it will be of no use. Hence, I recommend that you install SAP IDES (Training/Demo system) to practice exercises, set up projects, create orders, and so on. This will help you to get acquainted with the system.

If you're a beginner, read this book completely and ensure that you run through the system to familiarize yourself with the concepts. Each topic discussed in this book will explain the background info regarding the concepts and processes. You can refer to the SAP website (`https://training.sap.com/us/en`) for any additional information. This book is not a replacement for regular training, but it will help you to understand SAP ERP structure and effective tips provided via the real-time case studies.

CHAPTER 1

■ ■ ■

Introduction to SAP Enterprise Software

The key objective in project management is to complete a project successfully by avoiding common pitfalls. You're responsible for implementing SAP as a Project Manager or Consultant, by understanding the ERP software from an end-to-end solution perspective. One of the common pitfalls is the lack of knowledge of the software itself. This handy list of 12 common pitfalls will help you to avoid some of the problems that plague SAP implementation projects:

- Lack of basic ERP software knowledge
- Lack of end product vision
- Lack of goals
- Lack of risk management
- Lack of steering committee support
- Lack of proper planning
- Scope is unrealistic
- Poor communication
- Lack of skills
- Lack of milestones, without proper schedule
- Lack of change control
- Unrealistic resource levels

In this chapter, you'll learn about the first common pitfall, Lack of Basic SAP ERP knowledge. This chapter will cover the following areas:

1. Overview of SAP

2. Why ERP?

3. SAP System Architecture and WebAS

4. SAP ERP Solution Overview

5. Key Business Process/SAP Mapping (OTC, P2P)

Overview of SAP

SAP (pronounced ess-aye-pea) is the market leader in the enterprise application software, which has changed the way that clients do business with over 291,000 customers in 190 countries with annual revenue of €17.56 running their business on SAP (as of 2014; source: SAP). SAP's vision is to help the world with technology to improve the living standards. It has adopted best practices since its inception in 1972, evolved into Web-based architecture from the traditional Enterprise client server–based R/3 to the Netweaver-based Enterprise Core Component (ECC). Today, the enterprise applications are accessible in mobile applications. SAP has developed into the next generation mobile platform known as "SAP Mobile Platform" for adapting to new age enterprise mobile applications with flexible user (UX) experience. Whether it is a traditional client-server (R/3), a Netweaver-based Enterprise Core Component (ECC), or a mobile platform using SAP, the best run businesses run SAP. The SAP ERP product has evolved since 1972 based on customer requirements, transitioning from traditional client-server database software to Netweaver-based software (WebAS) with quick access to enterprise information. It has continued to evolve into enterprise mobility applications, analytics, and cloud-based enterprise.

SAP will continue to evolve in the future as it embraces changes with the advent of the SAP® HANA native database. With HANA, customers are creating major breakthroughs that solve complex and intricate problems. SAP® HANA has its footprint in industries including oil and gas, health care, real estate, retail, clinical trials, genetic engineering, biotechnology, R&D in the genome sequencing project, and oncology R&D, touching lives of millions of cancer patients with over 30 industry-specific solutions. SAP is the most exciting ERP product, available today with its robust architecture and a business suite almost for every requirement.

SAP Industry-Specific (IS) Solutions

SAP industry-specific solutions (IS Solutions) addresses almost every business scenario in the world. As you flip through the chapters of this book, you will learn about the product suite, releases with additional features, and the release plan for the HANA database, mobility, and cloud, which will support rapidly changing business requirements.

SAP is an orchestra of technology, business applications, and innovation, developed for the customer. It has been amazing to observe the evolution of the product from R/2, R/3, which indicates simple client-server architecture of the Enterprise Core Component (ECC) on the Netweaver platform with high-performance HANA database. The SAP Netweaver orchestration helps business seamlessly integrate both SAP applications and non-SAP with the middleware component known as "PI," which stands for Process Integration. In a nutshell, SAP is the best enterprise application software, adapting to almost every business requirements with its advanced integration capabilities. It will continue to evolve into mobility and cloud service offerings.

Hence, the architecture is continually changing with improved capabilities adapting to new trends. Today, we talk about quick-in-time data access to the volume of information as analytics, enterprise mobile applications, and enterprise portal. It is all available in the SAP enterprise software, which is integrated application software to help clients' succeed in digitizing 360-degree view of client's end-to-end business operations. The ease of SAP implementation is improving day by day with the advent of many tools such as SAP Solution Manager accelerators with improved methodology such as rapid deployment (RDS), in addition to SAP professional consulting services.

The massive SAP system can be configured in weeks, as opposed to the months and years of previous implementation techniques. You'll be excited to learn all about the techniques, tools, and accelerators to implement SAP software, responding to client requirements. A basic knowledge of the SAP product ecosystem, technical architecture, functional overview with SAP's future trending into HANA, mobility, and cloud will help SAP consultants and project managers to succeed in the endeavor.

Needless to say, if your system is configured correctly, you'll be able to run an SAP system within few months, with optimized consulting requirements. The evolving strategy of SAP will be leveraging the cost-effective cloud-based enterprise solution to quickly run business transactions in no time without having to procure an expensive hardware solution with recurring maintenance costs of the ERP software, hardware, operating systems, and the database. The trend is changing rapidly from hosting the solutions in-house to cloud-based enterprises with SAP's native database, known as "HANA" dB, with high performance guaranteed.

SAP Implementation Partner Expectations

As an SAP implementation partner, project manager, and/or a consultant, you're the most sought-after consultant/project manager in the world, based on the current job market. This trend will continue in the future due to the increased demand for ERP packages. If you're a client, you'll learn the solution offerings that will solve your business problems with faster implementation techniques. As an architect, you'll be able to comprehend the best of the features that SAP offers, to help clients with the simplest solution for complex business problems. It can be a simple "CRM on-cloud," which can be implemented in a few weeks with preconfigured scenarios, or perhaps an ERP solution with a plan to digitize a client's business operations from an end-to-end perspective. The flexible SAP solution integrates with existing mobile applications or legacy if need be, with interoperability. Cloud solutions are flexible and ready-to-use services offered such as "SaaS," software as a service, or hosting the ERP on the cloud platform, "PaaS," platform as a service. The solution architect is responsible for analyzing customer requirements, and for mapping the most appropriate cost-effective solution for the business. Hence, the key aspect of an ERP implementation is to understand the requirements of the business prior to providing a solution.

Most of the clients will need an expert consultant to guide them from the initiation to the successful implementation of the project. Thus, it is imperative for an SAP consultant and/or a project manager to have comprehensive knowledge of SAP Technical (BASIS), Functional (Modules) & Development (ABAP), as well as mobility, HANA DB, and cloud with an overall product ecosystem to succeed as an SAP evangelist in the marketplace. As an SAP brand ambassador, you'll need to have a complete view of SAP as a product, ecosystem, technical architecture, and functionality to implement the product successfully. Also, you should be able to gauge the complexities of client business requirements, by assessment of the required percentage that can be utilized as a standard solution, by leveraging the product to the maximum extent possible.

SAP Roadmap

The SAP's roadmap is to standardize the applications with its robust ERP architecture, by providing consumable services to help clients run their business in less time, thus eliminating year-on-year expensive software development, as well as license and maintenance costs. The advent of Enterprise Core component (ECC) on the SAP Netweaver platform has stabilized the backend with releases ECC 6.0 and above, with the focused changes to the application server (WebAS), and with the expanding solution offering bundle available in SAP with improved features in every release. These enhancements are available as packages known as "EHP" on ECC. With more and more IS-Solutions as add-ons to the ERP suite, this expands the SAP solution bundle. I believe there is no other software in the ERP world that is more exciting than SAP with its unique solution offerings.

The evolution of HANA as the native SAP database with advanced in-memory capabilities has improved overall performance. In simple terms, it helps you read volume of data in less time possible as opposed to the longer query time in a traditional RDBMS, providing advanced analytical capabilities. SAP has transformed itself to provide solutions with HANA as its core database, and this transformation will change the business. For the first time in the history, a software solution provider has transformed the way that we conduct business, instead of the traditional way of business requirements and/or clients driving changes in software applications.

Why Is SAP a Game Changer?

If you analyze the historic evidence of failures, big giants have failed due to lack of innovation after establishing its market. They had not reengineered their products, solutions, and services. As a result, these so-called giants in manufacturing hardware, developing software, database, and/or services failed to innovate, without being able to sustain changes in the customer landscape. Hence, the innovative small players had ventured into the ERP market and captured the market as small-scale desktop vendors to grow larger and larger in developing software applications for the enterprise customers. As you know, the large HW vendors had been replaced with smaller laptop/tablet vendors and this evolved to mobile manufacturers with larger disk space requirements and scalable operating systems to run the most demanding enterprise applications in the mobile platform.

SAP is a software giant that has continuously improved itself as the enterprise game changer, instead of acting like a giant. It listened to its customers, responding to continuously changing requirements. SAP reevaluated itself, thus shedding its image of a giant, and continuously rediscovered itself like a small product vendor. It has shaken itself from R/2, R/3 to ECC and has further evolved into HANA dB from its traditional RDBMS. This is definitely a step ahead into the world of enterprise mobile applications software and cloud enterprise practices. In addition, SAP has provided supplementary tools to implement its solution faster with solution manager (SolMAN) tools; accelerators implement ERP solutions in weeks as opposed to months and years. If you're unable to find a solution in SAP for the client's business requirements, this simply indicates your lack of understanding the requirements and/or the solutions offered by SAP.

Evolution of the Next Generation ERP Suite

You've chosen the right book to comprehend the values of SAP and the common pitfalls to avoid to succeed in the endeavor. It will help you to understand the evolution of the product suite from the past and present with future strategy. As a customer, you will need to analyze changing business requirements to explore different market avenues for the products and services. SAP is in the pursuit of an ERP that will help you achieve the vision of every enterprise. SAP is an ERP software with the offerings spanning into mobility and enterprise cloud. It will help you plan your production schedule, analyzing sales, inventory, and/or customer behavior. You'll be able to check your sales, margin, analyze employee retention, profit margin, balance sheet, and gross profit, and so on.

Someday, it will be possible to run your enterprise completely off-site, sitting in the comfort of your home in Los Angeles or Germany. Also, it will help you in researching alternate fuel technology and measuring the environmental pollution to help the world reduce global warming. The time-space will exist no more; you'll be able to integrate all business operations via cloud-based enterprise connecting all distributed locations across EMEA, North America, and Asia Pacific. There will be no difference between a demand generated in the United States, England, Germany, China or India, as the ERP will be able to scan and integrate products and services across geography.

Furthermore, at some point, SAP will be able to control and monitor an unmanned rocket launched toward Mars, Saturn, and Jupiter. It may be possible to fly an unmanned airplane or automatic cars, and even perform brain surgery with the help of robotics aligned with the SAP HANA dB in health care. It will be possible as the big data can store information with precision, enabled with electronic sensors/gadgets in the consumer electronics industry with services developed at the front-end to deliver a complex business solution. The entire future is mobility and cloud based enterprise architecture, which SAP is ready to change itself despite all challenges.

Indeed, the IT landscape will become leaner and leaner with the ease of maintaining the systems hosted on cloud, virtually leading to zero cost of application maintenance. As an entrepreneur, you'll be able to run all the business operations on-cloud, without much upfront IT investment. The next generation entrepreneurs will be able to procure appropriate SAP services for managing customers and suppliers with innovative products and services. These entrepreneurs will be able to think ahead by innovating their business, instead of getting bogged down by the IT complexities of running the enterprise software. Hence, there will be a continuous improvement along with the ROI generated for customers by running SAP ERP, more than any other ERP in the market.

There will not be upfront and huge investments in IT hardware, software licenses, and database and/or implementation costs, leading to the next generation digital entrepreneurs to begin manufacturing, sales, inventory, and distribution of their products with ease. This transition will take place in the market as more and more mid-tier, small, and new enterprises (SMEs) seek cost-cutting measures to implement business processes. However, as a consultant, you'll be required to develop innovative products and solutions as part of the cloud enterprise. SAP had responded to SMEs with Business by Design software, which are cost-effective solution.

The newer breed of SAP mobility services will increase in providing an ability to the enterprise running entirely on mobile devices. The ease of running an app is recognized throughout the world; hence, it will transform business transactions, as an app-based innovative solution. The ERP app-based enterprise solution will help you track sales, employees, HR functions, production plans, and MRP. The ERP app-based solution will disintegrate complex ERP-centric solutions into the service-based component model, where you'd be able to procure tangible services that you'll need to run a specific business operations, as not every business will need extensive end-to-end ERP software. Indeed, SAP provides it all for small and mid-tier enterprises.

Next time, when you walk into the nearest grocery store or a small or large restaurant, you may want to check the billing application! You may apply for a higher education, or file an insurance claim for your child, or register for an online course, or your doctor may send you SMS about your health checkup routine using SAP ERP mobile application. The RFID integrated with the ERP mobile app will raise an order automatically for replenishing stocks. These are just a few examples of SAP in consumer applications, and this will expand in the enterprise segment for managing inventory using RFID enabled to manage demand and supply with SAP HANA dB at the back-end.

A strategic move into aerospace will provide new avenues of business opportunities for SAP, from avionics to customer service on-board and offline customer services. The software giant has moved its strategy from a large scale enterprise software service provider to the simple, tangible service provider. SAP ERP is scalable, as it provides developers with the ability to build scalable software services based on native ABAP "Webdynpro" programming capabilities and/or external J2EE services that will integrate with core ERP solutions on Netweaver. In a smart home, a refrigerator could be filled by an order from the grocery store whenever stock is low.

Your car might have the adequate security to track, automatic warming solutions triggered through a mobile application, linked to GPS connected to the ERP. This security application can track anywhere real-time, to help you in case of an emergency, anywhere in the world. The predictive analysis in HANA can help in the behavioral analysis of customers. As a developer, you'll be able to do wonders by integrating with several applications such as LinkedIn, Facebook, Twitter, Pinterest, Skype, and WhatsApp to raise sales orders, and enhance customer experience by using voice apps to generate sales order.

Some day, psychologists and psychiatrists might be able to generate analytics of the brain/mind to assess a possible solution to your impending mental problems by harnessing SAP's Big Data known as "HANA." In the consumer arena, as well as in industry, these SAP ERP mobile applications will expand usability to simple and flexible solutions offered to millions of retail end-users first time in the history of software evolution leading into mobility.

SAP Next Gen Mobility Solutions

The mobility and cloud offerings are transforming the industry and the consumers. While writing about the future of SAP mobile app, I was amazed to read about a pregnancy app that helps in tracking the development and helping women coping with depression, released at the Heidelberg University hospital. It's just getting more and more exciting, isn't? The information is getting more transparent, and SAP mobile app is helping an intimate relationship with customers. The intuitive user interface helps you achieve the success with the power of back-end database SAP® HANA.

If you're an aspiring SAP consultant and/or an SAP project manager, or you are contemplating a change in your career, venturing into SAP, there is nothing that can be more exciting than SAP. Learning SAP is fun and exciting as you'd comprehend its journey from the legacy applications to SAP ECC, mobility, and cloud. You'll be amazed to understand how it solves the most complex business.

As an SAP expert, you'd have a role to play in advising clients and the future of mobility and the cloud if you're willing to be part of the enterprise game changer. The SAP HANA DB, mobile, and cloud services will provide you with a plethora of opportunities to excel and innovate as a consultant, architect, and a manager. If you're an existing SAP consultant, it's never too late to learn SAP HANA, cloud, and mobility services. SAP is the present and the future of the ERP world. I'd like to welcome you all to read the technological story of a game changer and be the game changer yourself!

The next generation business suite, known as SAP S/4 HANA, is the current breakthrough in this technology. Your organization will soon be required to upgrade to SAP S/4 HANA, a.k.a. SAP Business Suite 4 SAP HANA platform, to gear up to the challenges to leverage the best ERP business application suite in the world. Are you ready for the change? Your understanding of the ERP software will help you to avoid implementation pitfalls. This, in turn, will help you to succeed in the endeavor of a successful implementation by solving your customer's business problems.

▪ **Note**   You might have heard this before: SAP AGS was founded in 1972 in Germany by a group of young and talented engineers. They named the company Systemanazlyse and Programmentwicklung. Their objective was to address impending problems of integration, thus providing an end-to-end software package that integrated a company's myriad business functions in a manner that referenced best practices. Finally, their idea became a full-fledged product known as Systems, Applications and Products in Data Processing (SAP).

Technology Breakthrough

Gone are the days of developing application software using a traditional database design with expensive hardware and development due to the laborious efforts, large teams, huge implementation costs, schedule, quality, and maintenance involved. In today's market, customers are looking for a quick shrink-wrap product, out-of-the-mill product, one that is up and running instantly in days to implement a solution. With SAP, you can run Order to Cash (OTC) or Procure to Pay (P2P) process of manufacturing, production, manage inventory and sales, track orders, plan and execute warehouse movements, and much more. All of this can be done quickly in a span of two to three weeks, instead of spending years and months in implementing a solution.

The myriad examples of implementations across the globe indicate a transient product in the market, which adapts to the business requirements with preconfigured scenarios, which are ready to run the business. You have a product that can be configured in less than four to six weeks using the Rapid Deployment Solution, "RDS," methodology with preconfigured scenarios provided by SAP. The IS-Solution specific add-ons address industry-specific scenarios such as claims processing for insurance, patient database for hospital management, and/or enhanced supply chains for automotive and consumer products. SAP has reengineered every business process scenario across industries.

In this book, I will explain the basics of SAP architecture and help you to understand the reasons for an ERP implementation and product ecosystem. I will delve into the details of how it works as an ecosystem by helping you to configure your business requirements. The following chapters will help you to gain tremendous insights based on real-time implementation case studies of large & complex projects. I will be candid about project failures, as often these failures have not been discussed. In my view, every failure is a stepping stone to success, and this applies to your professional and personal life as well. These failed projects gave me tremendous insights into possible modes of failures, and what should be averted to achieve success. If you're able to learn the failure modes, this will lead you to success without chasing it.

SAP System Architecture

In this section, you will learn the basic architecture of SAP. It runs on a three-tiered architecture, which is further subdivided into the following layers based on respective functions:

- The Database layer, which hosts the relational database (RDBMS)

- The Application layer, which takes care of the workload allocation process using Work processors (WP)

- The User Interface layer, which is the end-user interface

Figure 1-1 shows you the SAP System Architecture in a three-tier architecture, with a core database such as SAP's native HANA DB, application layer with multiple work processors (WP), which does the workload process, and a presentation layer, which refers to SAP GUI or a mobile interface.

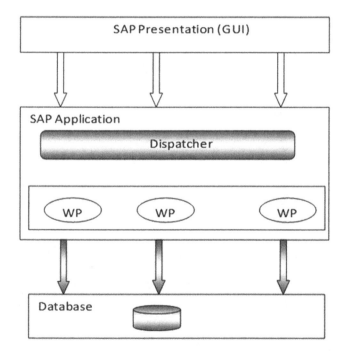

Figure 1-1. *SAP System Architecture*

The Database server hosts the relational database known as RDBMS, which can be any dB, from ORACLE, Microsoft to SAP's native HANA DB, and thus this is the storehouse of the client's data.

The Application server acts like an administrator, and it is responsible for background processing such as printing. It also manages these background requests. The Application server allows *n* number of services to run in a three-tier design.

The Presentation layer hosts the GUI; this is the interface for end users. There can be any number of front end clients to serve as an interface to access SAP. These front end clients will present the SAP screen and data output to end users. This is referred as the SAP GUI, or graphical user interface.

SAP Netweaver Architecture

Now let us understand how these SAP solutions are integrated. The SAP NW application server is the foundation for the entire SAP software stack. It hosts components such as Portal, Business Warehouse, Master Data Management, and so on. SAP NW is a comprehensive platform for development, composition, and maintenance of the enterprise software. All applications such as business process management, data warehouse, OLAP, and extending applications to mobile devices reside on the SAP Netweaver application server, as illustrated in Figure 1-2.

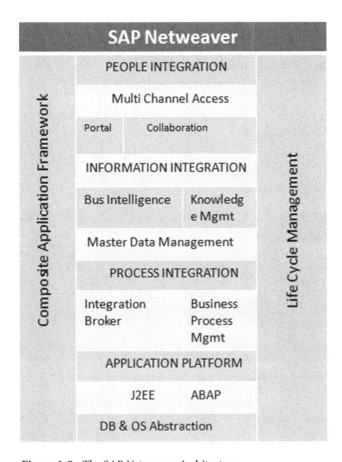

Figure 1-2. *The SAP Netweaver Architecture*

SAP NW runs a four-tier architecture:

- Application platform layer
- Process Integration layer
- Information Integration layer
- People Integration layer

SAP NW integrates Web services and Internet support within the core SAP NW Web Application Server (WebAS) platform; business applications are hosted in Extended Service architecture framework, a.k.a. "ESA." The highlight of this application is to share data via XML.

SAP NW provides the platform for integrating these application services. SAP NW is the technology foundation for ESA, which indicates SAP's Services Oriented Architecture (SOA). The SOA is a technical framework for building software applications that use services that are available from the network, such as the Web. The applications in SOA are designed to use Web services as the standard way to communicate well-defined information with an array of other applications. Let's analyze components within SAP NW architecture, as shown in Figure 1-2.

SAP NW provides an integration framework of people, processes, and information. SAP has improved the application platform with extensibility of "HANA" as the native database, SAP solution bundle, and IS-Solutions, which are capable of integrating people (business) and processes (key business operations).

The SAP NW platform has extended to the mobile space with the Fiori-based mobile platform. SAP NW platform developed with an objective of supporting heterogeneous software to provide more flexibility to a customer's solution. SAP's ESA services provide collaborative and process-centric approaches, which will respond to the services.

You'll need to understand that ESA is open and flexible architecture to consume services, and this is illustrated in Figure 1-3.

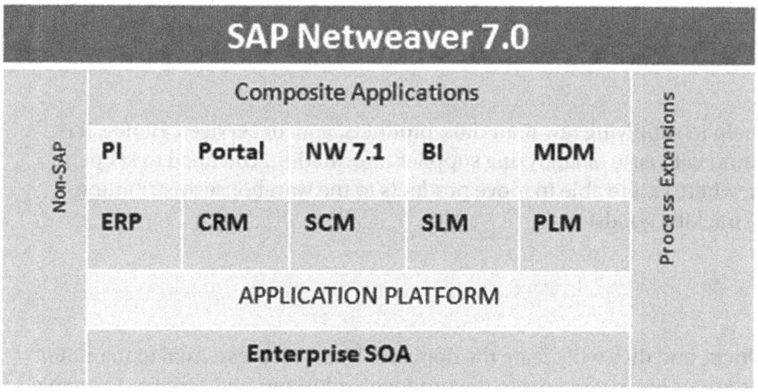

Figure 1-3. *SAP Extended Services Architecture (ESA)*

SAP NW is the technical layer for all business applications running on it. For example, you may run a Java-based application or any other homegrown customer application, which can consume SAP applications via XML as consumable services, and vice versa. You have a choice as a customer to develop your own software applications in Java (J2EE) and/or ABAP with customized solution.

■ **Note** The NW application server can extend to ABAP and Java using AS-Java and AS-ABAP. During the upgrade to Netweaver 7.1, there were challenges to segregate the application server as SAP intended to separate these two servers. SAP WAS is used for Web services and knowledge management applications using AS-Java. AS-ABAP is primarily used for applications using ABAP/4 and content management such as documentation, manuals, and training materials.

Why ERP?

Before you read through the next section of SAP ERP Components, step back and think for a moment. If you were to start up your own business, what are the key functions that you'd like to focus on? Why do you think that your business will need ERP software?

Enterprise Planning

As part of your enterprise planning, you will need to look at product design, plant maintenance, production planning, inventory, logistics execution, finance and sales of your finished products.

Products and Services

Before launching a new product, you should conduct a market survey about the existing products, competitiveness, and demand in your Analyze demand and supply, planning the production with the lean manufacturing plant to keep production costs low, the ability to schedule MRP, and so on.

Suppliers

The suppliers are the ones who'd help in supplying raw materials, products, and/or services. Hence, it is essential to store supplier information with ease of analyzing supplier information. You need to keep in mind transportation management, where you're able to move products to the warehouse, distribution centers with low-cost carriers, and tracking goods.

Customers

You'll need customers to buy products, and they will create the demand. Hence, it is essential to maintain good customer relations, with continuous improvements to the products, solutions, and services to enable a long-term liaison with customers to expand your business. In the current market environment, as customers are located globally, it is essential to build intelligence to predict customer's behavior.

Employees

There is a need to maintain employee relation within the organization to support in personnel administration, benefits, compensation, payroll, and employee self services to support various human resource functions. The market has expanded globally; hence, there is a need for HR administrative functions to support employees globally in diversified locations. The HR policies, procedures, and administration will enable a good employee-management relation, thus conducive to promote high productivity.

Finance

Of course, finance is the most important aspect as you conduct business to make profit. As an entrepreneur, you'd like to check profit/loss, general ledger, analyzing balance sheet. If you're a large corporation, then you'd be interested in analyzing the stock market to assess the scope of impact to the business. It is important to manage accounts as per the Universal standards such as GAAP accounting procedures with required taxation policy adherence, tax liability.

Production Planning

The production department produces products of high quality to ensure that sales can promise customer demand. The planner basis this on orders or even anticipates bulk orders, depending on the demand. In a complex scenario, advanced production capacity planning is required to ensure that demand is met.

Enterprise Structure

If you further drill down into the dynamics of your business, you'd want operations to be set up something like that indicated in Figure 1-4, showing a basic flow of organization functions.

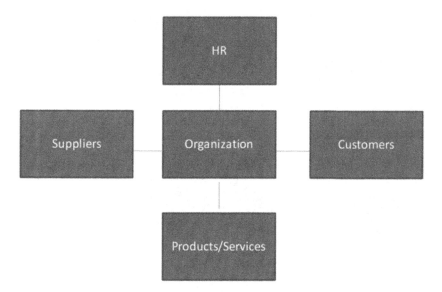

Figure 1-4. *A Simple Organization with Various Departments*

It is impossible to track each of these transactions across departments in real time with increasing demand and supply. The OLTP system helps to access data real time. For example, a sales organization in Italy might want to check the inventory in China for available products and report back to the customer in the region accordingly. Each of these departments can work seamlessly by accessing data real time. A sales engineer can check the availability of products, and/or access production data to analyze the turn-time for the products available. A production planner can forecast using the real time data such as raw material availability, and so on.

As you expand your customer base, wouldn't it be interesting to know your customer has purchased turbines with the same capacity from two different regions? This will help you get closer to the customer's thought process, to redesign your products, and to analyze the market segment. You can assess the scope of demand and ensure adequate supply with the tools such as planning optimizer in SAP.

In earlier days of developing application software, costs of application maintenance were very high due to hardware, operating system, and database licenses, in addition to software application licenses and integration issues. Every time you introduced a minor change to the application, there would be an intensive code correction, and testing would be required, which is time-consuming, labor-intensive. Most businesses increased IT investments year-on-year without much ROI.

Figure 1-4 illustrates a simple organization structure with various departments.

Organization can be even more complex, as shown in Figure 1-5.

Figure 1-5. *A Complex Organization with Various Departments*

In addition to the complexities of the business, there are stringent operational requirements such as Sarbanes-Oxley (SOX) compliance and GAAP accounting adherence required as standards. SAP can help in achieving compliance without having to go through a roller coaster ride. The ESS.MSS portal is used for employee HR core process, such as organization management, time management, recruitment, and so on, with a streamlined workflow.

Overview of an SAP ERP Solution

Now, let's explore the most exciting solution offerings from SAP. SAP Business Suite is the solution bundle provided by SAP AG for all of your business requirements. You will find that SAP Netweaver provides a platform to host the entire business suite. As a customer, you have a choice to procure it as an entire solution bundle and/or individual solution. Figure 1-6 illustrations the SAP Business Suite.

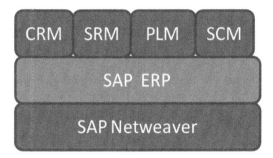

Figure 1-6. *The SAP Business Suite*

The SAP Business suite consists of:

1. SAP ERP

2. SAP Customer Relationship Management (CRM)

3. SAP Supplier Relationship Management (SRM)

4. SAP Product Lifecycle Management (PLM)

5. SAP Supply Chain Management (SCM)

As referred in Figure 1-6 SAP Netweaver is the base technical layer hosting it all. The SAP ERP is the core component, which maps the business process. You'll be able to map operative business process across departments.

The core SAP ERP solution contains the following applications:

1. SAP ERP Financials for accounting

2. SAP ERP Human Capital Management for human resources

3. Logistics, comprised of:

    a. SAP ERP Operations

    b. SAP ERP Corporate Services

SAP ECC is the core of SAP ERP. This is the online transaction process (OLTP) system, which has replaced the traditional SAP R/3. Each of these solution bundles is made up of individual components necessary to accomplish the intended needs. It's also important to note that any of these solutions can be easily customized for a specific client requirements. Table 1-1 shows a list of available modules in SAP ERP.

Table 1-1. *SAP ERP Modules*

Application	Function	Acronym
Accounting	Financial Accounting	FI
	Controlling	CO
	Financial Supply Chain Management	FISCM
	Treasury	TR
	Enterprise Controlling	EC
	Project System	PS
Human Resources (HCM)	Personnel Administration	PA
	Recruitment	PR
	Personnel Development	PD
	Payroll	PY
	Event Management	EM
	Organization Management	OM
	Time Management	TM
	Travel Management	TM
Logistics	Purchasing	MM
	Production Planning & Control	PP
	Sales & Distribution	SD
	Customer Service	CS
	Warehouse Management	WM
	Transportation & Distribution	LE
	Quality Management	QM
	Real Estate Management	RE
	Plant Maintenance	PM
	Environment, Health & Safety	EHS

▓ **Note**   For the most recent list of ECC modules list, visit SAP's Quick-Sizer link at
`http://service.sap.com/quick-sizer`.

SAP INDUSTRY SOLUTIONS (IS-SOLUTIONS)

Every industry is unique. Hence, SAP has designed solutions specifically for different industries. For example, the oil and gas industry is different from the consumer products industry. IS solutions combined standard processes with special requirements and functions for an industry. SAP offers the following IS-Solutions:

  i. Manufacturing Industry

   • SAP for Automotive

   • SAP for Aerospace & Defense

  ii. Processing Industry

   • SAP for Oil & Gas

   • SAP for Chemicals

iii. Financial Services

- SAP for Banking

- SAP for Health Care

- SAP for Defense & Security

iv. Services Industry

- SAP for Utilities

- SAP for Retail &

- SAP for Consumer Products

There are over 30 IS-Solutions available and the list is expanding every year.

SAP for Small & Mid-Sized Enterprise (SME)

SAP supports small and mid-sized enterprises (SMEs) with the following solution offerings:

- SAP Business One—This solution is easy to configure in days, and customers have a choice to select specific business functions to map such as financial, human resources, and materials management. There is no need for SAP Business Suite, which might be costlier for a small enterprise.

- SAP Business All-in-One—This is the IS Solutions for small and mid-sized enterprises offered by SAP. It also provides different SAP Business Suite as required.

- SAP Business ByDesign—This is an on-demand solution hosted by SAP. Customers can select the functions applicable to them. The applications are managed at SAP's data centers. The user can access the required functions using a browser via VPN connectivity, firewall settings, and so on. Figure 1-7 illustrates this setup.

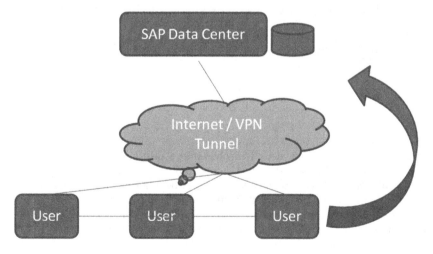

Figure 1-7. *Business By Design—System Infrastructure*

SAP Cloud Enterprise

SME concepts of Business by Design extended into Cloud Enterprise and mobility where companies decide to outsource their IT (hardware, software, data) to external providers on a lease basis for a certain period of time.

Key Business Process

Order to Cash (OTC) and Procure to Pay (P2P) are the key business processes. Let's look at how you would map into SAP ERP software.

Order to Cash (OTC) Business Process/SAP

The OTC Cycle involves the following steps to execute the business process to completion (see also Figure 1-8):

1. Create Sales Order

    a. Run Credit and Availability checks

    b. Confirm Order

2. Delivery and Goods Issue

3. Generate Invoice

    a. Send invoice to the customer and receive confirmation

4. Account for the sale in Finance as receivables

Figure 1-8. *OTC Business Process*

A typical OTC process cycle consists of these four steps. It involves sales & distribution, finance, and production planning modules. Let's say a dealership orders for 100 cars from a car manufacturer. It is general practice to conduct credit and availability checks for the customer and provider information, whether the order can be released or not. There is no financial posting yet! In order to fulfill the customer order, you'll need to know the timeline required for production. When the car (good) is ready for delivery, then it is issued with financial postings. The next step is to generate the invoice and send it to the customer, and accounting entry is posted in accounting books in the receivables.

■ **SAP Modules**   Sales & Distribution (SD), Finance (FI)

Now, let's talk in SAP. The SAP allows for an execution of integrated scenario of this business process as highlighted in Figure 1-9.

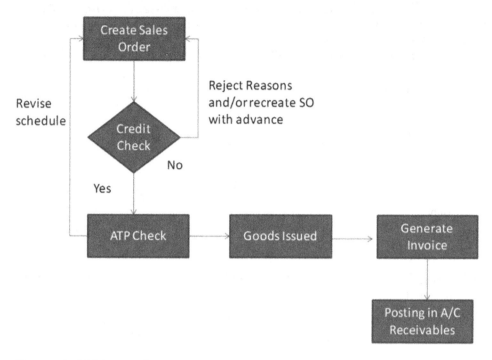

Figure 1-9. OTC Process Flow in SAP

Step 1—The credit check is initiated as soon as the customer order is entered to provide information on the order fulfillment

Step 2—The Available to Promise (ATP) module in SAP helps in analyzing the production schedule prior to promising in the customer and the order is confirmed to the customer

Step 3— Goods are issued when ready for delivery. Step 4—The invoice is also generated and sent to the customer right away, and corresponding accounting entry is also posted in books

The account receivables posting is done in the background process. The sales/delivery staff will enter the necessary details for shipments/deliveries and the accounting entries happen in the background. The next step is receipt of the cash from the customer for the order fulfilled, which is accounted for against the account receivables. There are additional processes provided in SAP to handle bank transactions such cash, checks, and/or wire transfer received by the banks, as well as for the bank statements posted into SAP.

As you observed, most of the steps are automated with less manual intervention only needed to fix issues. The turnaround time for OTC process is reduced between the order fulfilled and the cash received. I had an opportunity to conduct six sigma QA analysis of defects for one of the largest consumer & industrial organization. It resulted in analyzing transactions in SAP which proved high customer satisfaction in the Order to Cash process based on the customer survey. It helps in building transparency in order flow. The integration of credit management with the OTC process scenarios helps in tracking delays in payments.

Procure to Pay (P2P)

In a typical scenario, an organization might want to procure some material to fulfill its sale order request by a customer. For example, a customer raised an order for a diesel variant car to sales organization, which was not available in stock. Hence, the purchasing organization will create PR/PO to procure required raw material to fulfill the order.

The P2P Cycle involves the following steps to execute the business process to completion, as illustrated in Figure 1-10:

1. Create Purchase Requisition (PR)

   a. Approve PR

   b. Create Purchase Order (PO)

   c. Approve PO

2. Purchase Goods

3. Receive Goods

4. Receive Invoice

   a. Verify invoices and approve for PO, GR quantity/value matches

5. Issue payments and account for the purchase in the Finance module in accounts payables

Figure 1-10. *P2P Process Flow*

The cycle consists of the following steps with interim verification as highlighted in Figure 1-11.

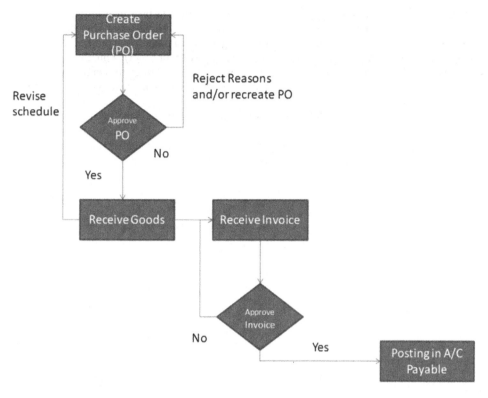

Figure 1-11. *P2P Process flow in SAP*

In step 1, a purchase order is created by the purchasing department as soon as the PR is created & approved. Then, the PO will go through the verification process and will be approved in step 2. In step 3, goods will be delivered by the supplier and received by the purchasing organization. There is no finance entry up to this point. Finally, the supplier sends the invoice, which is verified against the goods delivered by the customer with final settlement, and, payments are made for the specific invoices. There might be some exceptions, such as invoice not matching with goods receipts or PO.

■ **SAP Modules**   Materials Management MM, Finance (FI).

The purchase requisition step creates requests for Purchase, which would lead to the creation of the Purchase Order. There are subsequent Approval steps in MM module in SAP. After the supplier receives PO, and delivers the goods, the liability is created for the goods received. The supplier sends invoices and accounted for the payments completed.

Organization Structure

Now, let's understand how to create a simple organization structure in SAP. Let's take an example of a DCM International Car company. The DCM Company has three plants, two in the United States, strategically located in Texas, Houston, and Michigan, and the other one in England for the European market. A subsidiary warehouse is subdivided into finished products and quality assurance (QA). A purchasing department is responsible for the procurement for all plants across the group through the centralized purchasing channel. Now, having understood the basic purchasing organization of a customer, it is easy to map in SAP.

You'll need to use SAP IMG for configuration. You can create and assign the organization units through Customizing. Once this assignment is done, it is difficult to change. You may need several organization units.

After you map organization units into SAP, it will look like the Figure 1-12, which describes the organization units of DCM International in the SAP system (Purchasing Area).

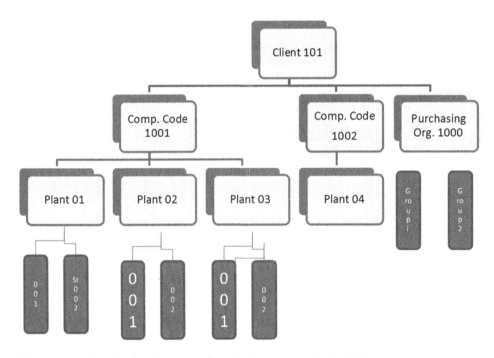

Figure 1-12. *Organizational structure from Logistics perspective in SAP*

The Client 101 is the Enterprise structure in SAP. It refers to the corporation headquarters and is topmost in the organization structure hierarchy. Company codes 1001 and 1002 are located below the client and represent the companies in the United States and England. There are three plants for each company code, namely, Plant 01, 02, 03 for company code 1002; there is only one plant for company code 1001, assigned plant 04. The purchasing organization is not assigned to a company code. Each plant has its storage locations. The purchasing groups under purchase organization 1000 deals with purchasing and is not assigned to any other organization element directly.

Client

Client is the highest Organizational unit in the system. You can select the client to log in. All settings that are applicable for the client applies to the subordinate units.

Company Code

Generally, accounting is mapped at the company code level. A client may contain multiple company codes; however, a company code is unique across the client. The key for the company code has four digits.

Plant

A plant produces goods or sells services. It is the central unit of an organizational unit of logistics. A plant can be used for:

- Production facility

- Sales Office

- Issuing storage location

A plant is assigned to a company code.

Storage Location

A storage location is assigned to a plant. It helps you to differentiate material stocks within a plant. For the storage location, the quantities of materials are relevant.

Purchasing Department

The purchase organization can be central or a decentralized.

Purchasing department as indicated in Figure 1-12, which maps the purchasing department in the system. It can be mapped to a specific company code, or a cross company code.

Purchasing Group

Typically a purchasing group is a team of employees. The purchasing group is not assigned to any other organization unit.

The following menu path indicates the navigation sequence in SAP:

Menu Path: IMG--[Materials Management] - [Purchasing] - [Purchase Order] - [Create] - [Vendor/ Supplying Plant]

When you raise a PO, you'll need to indicate the purchasing organization.

How do we map a sales process in the SAP system? As you know the sales process consist of Inquiry, Order, Delivery & Good Issues and Billing as depicted in Figure 1-13.

Figure 1-13. *Sales Order Process as Mapped in the SAP System*

First, a customer inquires about a product and its price and availability:

1. The customer places the order

2. Your enterprise executes the order and confirms a delivery schedule to the customer

3. Your internal sales organization checks availability of inventory, creates ATP, and then informs the customer. The sales organization will check schedule delays due to zero inventory. In this case, the purchasing organization will confirm the schedule based on the purchasing department schedule and the production capacity planning. Final goods are issued and delivery completion is confirmed

4. Customer is billed and accounts received

■ **SAP Modules**   Sales & Distribution (SD), Warehouse Management (WM), Materials Management (MM), Inventory Management (IM)) and Finance-Account Receivables (FI-AR), Invoice verification (SD-IV).

Concluding Remarks

Let's recap what we have discussed in Chapter 1:

- Overview of SAP ERP

- SAP Netweaver Architecture and WebAS

- Why SAP ERP?

- Organization Structure and Master Data

- Critical Business Process Mapping/SAP (OTC/P2P)

- Overview of SAP ERP Business Suite

Exercise

If you're relatively new to SAP Projects, I would recommend logging on to the test system and familiarizing yourself with the SAP GUI options, easy access, and transactions:

1. Navigate in SAP and various GUI options, familiarize yourself with the SAP ERP software ecosystem with improved features

2. Perform tasks using transaction code, familiarize yourself with IMG settings

3. Create a user profile, favorite folder, and move transactions

4. Familiarize yourself with business process flow mapping in SAP

5. Create an organization structure in SAP

In Chapter 2, you'll get an in-depth view of the modules in SAP and New Dimension Product suite (NDM) products.

▪ **Note**   For detailed solution briefs by industry, LOB, product categories, and solution spotlights, refer to:

`http://go.sap.com/solution.html`

■ ■ ■

Implementing SAP with ASAP 8 Agile Methodology

In this chapter, we will discover how ASAP 8.0 with Agile adapts to frequently changing business requirements to avoid pitfalls caused by a lack of product release planning.

SAP ASAP 8.0 Agile Implementation Strategy

Let's explore the quick implementation strategy offered by SAP combined with Agile and Scrum industry standards. The Scrum methodology influences the rapid build pattern of the custom code with basic principles of enhancements using SAP packages. In other words, Scrum is the methodology for implementing a simple, workable solution known as sprint releases to solve complex customer problems.

These are the latest trends in project management: implementing projects in quick time using rapid implementation methods with an iterative approach instead of waterfall method. In a traditional waterfall method, every step is well defined, and changes that occur during the course of the project would derail the phases. Hence, it takes longer to implement.

Finally, when the project hits the user acceptance test phase, end users might realize that the product doesn't meet requirements, derailing the entire project. Typically, customers tend to change their requirements unless you show them tangible solutions as a prototype with incremental releases. It's like manufacturing a hatchback with a well-defined plan, even if the customer adds a few additional variants such as designer tail lamps.

In the end, all integration points fail, leading to a failed implementation project. Now, let's assume your customer is good and helps you by providing feedback on a regular basis, don't you think, the end product would be matching their expectations, as you wouldn't spend time in developing a software that they don't agree upon. With all these caveats, you'd build a house brick by brick by showcasing every smaller unit to the customer, in the end, customers will be happy and pay for the complete construction. The same analogy goes here as well in the software development. You'll need to be transparent, not in terms of just a report or with graphical slides to woo your customer. You must provide value by showcasing, their critical business process such as "Order to Cash" or "procure to pay." At least one cycle, you should be able to run for them, in an end-to-end perspective. Otherwise, you'd be talking on the air, and customers would expect something. What is the point in developing accounting software without being able to consolidate it accurately! The end product would be confusion!

The evolution of Agile/Scrum method is to provide additional transparency, flexibility for changes, small workable product, and incremental cycles. Hence, the risks of failures are minimized. These are the features to ensure a successful implementation of the project packaged into SAP ASAP 8 methodology with tons of accelerators, rapid deployment solutions for quick and easy implementation. It is not just a metric at a high level and/or a process model to draft on paper from a management perspective, and the team fails to implement.

This is for each of you implementing a solution. It helps programmers (ABAPers) to quickly adapt to reusable components, build object-oriented coding into shippable software in multiple releases. We will discuss key SAP ABAP programming benefits in Agile by using latest ABAP development environment known as Eclipse for SAP, in the later sections to cover task level implementation techniques using Agile best practices.

Now, customers are requesting for mostly fixed bids for implementing solutions in less time and the partner organization has to live up to the expectations without exceeding the budget and/or surprising the client with too many change requests (CRs) at a later stage, to avoid pitfall of schedule slippage. The Agile Scrum methodology helps in defining the requirements, with conditional changes, by setting the right expectations by showcasing the incremental developments using rapid implementation techniques, thus averting a major disaster during the integration phase of the project.

Let's explore the power of SAP ASAP 8 combined with Agile methodology to succeed in implementing projects quick, on budget, leaving both customer and the partner as happy campers! You'd be able to achieve faster results by delivery of the products as sprint release comprising of two to three weeks each. The benefits are summarized as indicated below:

- 80-20 Rule: Now, it's easy to prioritize critical business processes

- As explained earlier, showcasing products in workable mode would enable trust and transparency with the customer

- Risks are identified, mitigated in every step throughout the process to avoid a major pitfall due to lack of risk management

- Increased flexibility as partner can adapt few additional changes as increments, which can be released subsequently to avoid pitfall due to lack of change control

- Enhanced communication with the customer by engaging them early, and throughout the process to avoid pitfall due to poor communication

- Bilateral commitment as both the partner and customer "agree" on deliverables and empower each other in terms of review, feedback, and so on to avoid pitfall due to lack of stakeholder's responsibilities

- Can respond to changes per "sprint," continuous configuration and delivery of software, can take account of insight into the business

---

■ **Note** The Agile SAP ASAP 8 Methodology is the latest and standard implementation best practices by leveraging the Agile add-on available in SAP Solution Manager to define work products, combining the power of SAP ASAP and Agile.

Creating Business Value

New Age project managers have realized the "Design Thinking" concept, which is the Agile Development strategy to implementing business requirements, unlike classical development. This concept prioritizes the business value and the integration of systems, and end users early on in the development process. The Agile design thinking is a methodology for practical, creative resolution of requirements and gaps that looks for an improved future result.

It is solution-focused thinking that starts with the goal. Then, by focusing on the inputs, various parameters of the problem and the solutions are explored.

The six basic steps of design thinking are illustrated in Figure 2-1.

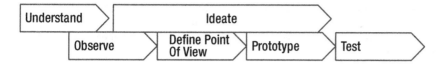

Figure 2-1. *Design Thinking*

The key tenets of Agile include:

1. Iterative delivery of business value

2. Simplicity and elimination of defects

3. Improved visibility of projects

    a. Development iterations

    b. Frequent inspection

    c. Working software as measure of progress

4. Flexibility—which means to change is anticipated and software is flexible enough to handle the situation

5. Engagement with business users—A very close interaction with the business users is imperative throughout the process of design, development, and validation of a solution.

The partner team adhered to these Agile principles to succeed in the implementation. Table 2-1 illustrates specific conditions that will challenge implementation projects using Agile methods.

Table 2-1. *SAP Agile Scrum Challenges*

Conditions that challenge Agile	Risk	Mitigation Plan
1. Implementation projects with complex system landscape with interdependent applications	High	Consider integration plan
2. Deployment in regulating Industries	High	Consider usage of Scrum
3. Initiatives that require long-term planning due to Organization dependencies	Medium	Follow the guidelines with large Scrum deployment window aligned with an organization
3. Physically separated large teams		
4. Lack of high performance teams with decision making abilities	Low Medium	

Overview of Scrum

Scrum is the best Agile software development methodology today. You'll need to understand what this product offers for managing projects. The Waterfall methodology goes through several months to build the product, then testing, reviewing, and eventually deploying the product. This may end up building a product that doesn't meet customer requirements. Often times, the project fails due to lack of planning and this cycle happens every time. Whenever there is a problem, this can lead to fixing bugs in the code and re-testing as a repetitive process, which is time consuming.

In Scrum, the process is broken into multiple subprocesses. First, the plan is to develop something tangible to the customer, thus deploying one process that is acceptable. This process is repeated to planning to development, thus reducing the development cycle. This incremental release cycle is called sprint.

There are three key factors in Sprint:

a. In the planning phase, the product owner, the Scrum master, discusses the product backlog items that are working product during the sprint cycle

b. The daily scrum is the daily standup meeting to discuss tasks completed the previous day, and elaborate on any impediments

c. Sprint review is a retrospective analysis to demonstrate the work done to the product owner. The objective of the review is to discuss the goal, agree on it, and negotiate to deliver a portion of the product requirements most relevant to the goal by the end of the Sprint.

Figure 2-2 illustrates the Scrum process from defining the product catalog, which is the business requirements, then sprint planning session with discussions on the product backlog items to prioritize and deliver product incrementally.

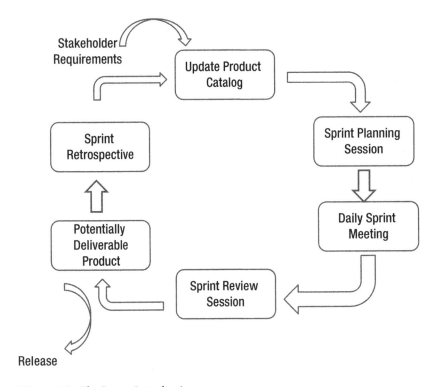

Figure 2-2. The Scrum Introduction

A Scrum team consists of one person or. A Scrum Master is a project manager, responsible for the project schedule, delivery, and removal of any issues, whereas a product owner is responsible for product acceptance from an end-user perspective. Also, you should be familiar with the proposed solution (product), Scrum backlogs—which simply indicates a list of customer requirements. Each of these backlogs can be drilled down into release backlogs. Each Sprint cycle is a milestone, with tangible deliverables. Finally, the burnout chart indicates executive analysis of the project on-track or not, with additional release features delivered. It is an iterative process and every release will be bundled with features as prioritized and agreed with the customer. Hence, the customer will see their features implemented gradually in every release, thus final product meeting all customer requirements. Even if there is change request, as insisted by the customer, it will be possible for the Scrum team to implement the changes in the respective sprint release.

Why Agile?

One of the primary reasons for using Agile methodology is to avoid communication issues, lack of understanding the product limitations or incorrect sizing of complexities and/or solution architecture. If you're familiar with the Use case design and the traceability matrix, often times, Project managers have agreed unanimously that the traceability of requirements vs. the actual product implemented has been totally different. This is staggering as 50-60% of the projects goes through a mindless approach till it crashes due to pitfalls such as lack of well-defined customer requirements. You'll need a pilot to take-off the plane, navigate and ground the plane safely isn't? The pilot may use visuals, technology to fly the plan in auto or manual or whatever is conducive based on his expertise in flying for safe navigation.

Now, this analogy goes well with Agile, it's like managing a project with a proper navigation system. Without this navigation system, several projects have been scrapped in the past due to the factors indicated above. The solution is to provide a tangible software methodology to help you implement solution as an incremental approach with milestones achieved, rather than a big bang & fail. This method will increase transparency within the Organization to avert any disaster. I believe with appropriate control measures with simple and transparent method, you can deliver a project successfully without major issues. If Scrum method is as simple as helping you in approaching a problem such as "planning a wedding", it can be adapted to technology as well. There is no doubt "ASAP with AGILE" would be the "winning deal" for both customers and the partner implementing a solution. As a matter of fact, the customer wants a solution that works, whilst implementation partners wants an application that runs as expected by the business to avoid burn-outs with increased transparency. Hence, there is an urgent need to deliver capability at an early stage of a project by solving customer problems with tangible benefits.

Now, let us compare traditional software development methods such as waterfall vs. Agile custom code development (ABAP) in SAP. Now, let us analyze the SAP Custom code Development processes in detail by leveraging Agile best practices. As you know there is a clear shift in software development to provide value to the customers. A successful implementation project will rely on its key aspects such as project management, resources, tasks and of course the goal influence the success of realization. The waterfall method compared to an agile development process is structured, but not flexible way of Design thinking as explained. Agile method is based on results and the rapid solution. Now, let's visualize a traditional custom code development using a waterfall methodology as illustrated in Figure 2-3.

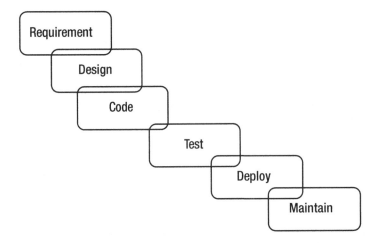

Figure 2-3. *Custom Code Development Using Waterfall Methodology*

As discussed Waterfall methods represent the most structured implementation methods. From requirements, analysis, design, coding/configuration, and testing in a strict, preplanned sequence. Each phase has predefined quality gates and checkpoint to be controlled. Each phase can be long or short, depending on the complexities of the project. There are always constraints, such as Time, Scope and costs, which are managed across phases.

One of the common pitfalls is unrealistic scope, due to this there is always a risk of missing goal, even if all phases were completed successfully. The explanation is simple and easy to understand. The final product may not meet the requirements as users come in at a later stage and the software may not fulfil the expectations of a customer. Hence, software development transformed itself to Agile's flavor of adaptive, iterative and evolutionary development.

The Agile Manifesto is based on twelve principles:

- Improve Customer Satisfaction by the use of rapid implementation techniques to avoid pitfall of schedule slippage

- Provide flexibility in changing requirements, even later in development stage to avoid pitfall of lack of change control

- Deliver working software packages as releases in weeks

- Metrics driven based on the working software to avoid lack of planning the schedule pitfall

- Sustainable development, able to maintain a constant pace

- Intense coordination between IT and business teams throughout the process to avoid lack of communication pitfall

- Improved communication, most preferably with face-to-face teams

- Empower teams to make decisions to avoid pitfalls due to setting unrealistic expectations to the team

- Provide Continuous attention to technical excellence and good design to avoid pitfall of lack of end product vision

- Simplicity—the art of maximizing the amount of work not done—is essential

- Self-organizing teams

- Adapting to the changing environment to avoid pitfall of lack of change control

These principles lead to new concepts like scrum teams or Kanban board. It is not in scope to describe all these concepts in this document. The experiences with agile development allow us to recommend agile development. It is essential to define clearly RACI (roles) matrix with assigned ownership of the development process. "Eclipse" is an easy to use development tool which successfully extends the ABAP development capabilities of SAP to the Eclipse development environment (including the SAP NetWeaver Developer Studio environment).

As a core method of Agile, tasks are broken into small increments and iterations are short time frames known as 'time-boxed.' The overall ASAP Realization will encompass multiple sprint cycles, which may be required to release a product or features with changing requirements. The teams are empowered to make decisions. A Project Manager / Product Owner must emphasize scrum methodology, by leveraging the accelerators provided by SAP such as SAP Eclipse for Development, SAP Code re-use of code from libraries. A product owner must provide scoring technique to custom development. Now, let's see how SAP has integrated Agile core principles in the software development (ABAP).

Traditionally, Waterfall method uses a structured approach, whereas Scrum provides the flexibility to adapt changes, throughout the product evolution cycle with an iterative and incremental work product approach as described in Table 2-2 showcase differences between Waterfall vs. Agile methodology.

Table 2-2. *Waterfall versus Agile Methodology*

Description	Waterfall	Agile	Comments
1. Structured Approach, but not very flexible with design, development, testing and go live	Yes	No	Waterfall provides a structured & inflexible approach from Requirements to Implementation
2. Iterative approach	No	Yes	Agile provides changes at every stage as incremental product development
3. Productivity is measured by deliverables in every phase	Yes	No	Productivity is measured by working functions or products
4. Quality gates	Yes	No	As per the Quality gate review plan to measure completion of each phase
5. Time, scope, and budget constraints are managed across phases with fixed targets with additional change requests	Yes	No	Moving targets are welcome in Agile, this is the flexibility it provides to the customer with no additional costs
6. Documentation efforts	Yes	No	Mostly Agile capture system generated document

In summary, there is no flexibility in the Waterfall method, when compared to the flexibility provided by the Agile methodology to avoid pitfall of lack of change control. No customer can completely envisage a product without actually looking at it, hence waterfall is not flexible enough for adapting changes as highlighted above. Agile methodology provides flexibility in adapting to the customer requirements, assuming that they're valid. The entire project in broken down into smaller increments, with iterations of short time frames. There might be multiple ("n") iterations required to achieve a product. Finally, progress is measured with the working functions and/or work products.

Agile methodology will help you to avoid the following common pitfalls:

- Lack of basic ERP software knowledge
- Lack of end product vision
- Lack of goals
- Lack of risk management
- Lack of steering committee support
- No proper planning
- Scope is unrealistic
- Poor communication
- Skills are not available
- Lack of milestones, without proper schedule
- Lack of change control
- Unrealistic resource levels

Agile addresses each of these common pitfalls in the following ways:

- Scope is realistic and manageable, with the inclusion of incremental model, there is less scope for ambiguity, thus helping you avoid pitfall of unrealistic scope
- Team is high performing with the Sprint meetings such as standup meetings to ensure the team is aligned, high performing and agile. Thus, it helps you avoiding a major pitfall due to lack of skill requirements and unrealistic resource levels by leveraging the teams effectively
- Stakeholders are responsible, with the inclusion of Product Masters working closely with the customer stake owners. Thus, it helps you avoid a common pitfall of lack of steering committee support
- The schedule is manageable by breaking down the complexities into sprint releases. There are no major surprises in the end. Thus, it helps you avoid a pitfall of schedule slippage
- Risks are mitigated. By the usage of the iterative approach, risks are identified early and mitigated. Thus, it helps you avoid a pitfall due to lack of risk management
- Improved communication as customer gets a workable solution demo. Managing change request is part of the Scrum methodology, hence there is no major approval cycle required. There is intense communication throughout the cycle of the project. Thus, it helps in avoiding a pitfall due to poor communication
- Ability to deliver the project on budget, due to highly disciplined product implementation by avoiding a major pitfall of lack of milestone plan, without proper schedule

SAP ASAP 8 with Scrum

Now, let's understand the usage of scrum combined with SAP ASAP 8 methodology. The SAP ASAP 8 methodology comprises of six phases as highlighted in Figure 2-3, which is a disciplined approach to managing complex projects, organizational change management, solution management, & industry specific implementations. The SAP ASAP 8 methodology is the enhanced Delivery model with templates, tools, questionnaires, and checklists, including guide books and accelerators. ASAP 8 empowers project teams to utilize the accelerators and templates built in to SAP solutions. The Agile add-on is available in SAP Solution Manager. Figure 2-4 explains various phases of SAP ASAP 8 Methodology.

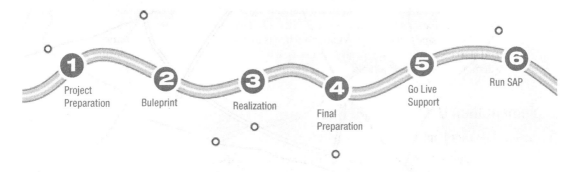

Figure 2-4. *SAP ASAP 8 Methodology*

- Project Preparation—This phase encompasses the entire project preparation and planning activities with infrastructure, hardware/network sizing requirements completed. It involves setting up the infrastructure, team, project goals, charter, and agree upon schedule, budget, risk baseline, proof-of-concept planning if applicable with implementation sequence. The project manager on the ground will discuss with the customer project manager to identify risks early on with a mitigation plan. The PM will be responsible for drafting a high level project plan with all milestones with a detailed task level plan chalked out with critical dependencies. Each phase deliverable should be agreed between both parties. Finally, a project organization, steering committee is organized with assigned resources.

- Blueprint—This is the most crucial phase of the project for a project manager as he just about to steer the ship, like a captain. The objective of this phase is to be on a common platform on how the company plans to run SAP for their business operations. Thus, a PM is responsible for analyzing the project goals and objectives and revise the overall project schedule if required. In simple terms, it is the critical requirements gathering phase, A PM might use appropriate tools to collect requirements with required traceability. The result is the Business Blueprint, which is a detailed flow of business process AS-IS, how they run the business operations with a TO-BE mapped in SAP, on how these business operations will run in SAP. Depending on the implementation complexities, number of business process, Blueprint workshops might span for a few days or weeks or even months, in a complex environment. The output of this phase is the baseline configuration in SAP with detailed custom code requirements analysis done.

- Realization—In simple terms, realization is the actual development phase of the project, where you'd configure, develop custom code and conduct required testing. It involves coding-unit testing-integration testing-User acceptance testing (UAT). As per the business blueprint and mapping the SAP system as agreed with business, all the business process requirements will be implemented. In reality, there are two major work packages: (a) Baseline (major scope); and (b) Final configuration (remaining scope). The success of any implementation project relies on how closely you're able to develop custom code, test and release it to the UAT phase, in order to support adequate testing by the users. Also, the challenge is to adopt changes as indicated during the UAT. This phase is resource intensive and the team is at peak team size to ensure all deliverables are met and sign-off. Often times Integration fail due to lack of test data, and testing in a "PRD" like environment to be able to test all critical business scenarios. A good practice is to copy a "PRD"-like environment and start testing if the system already exists. If it is GreenField environment, ensure adequate test data is available to test it rigorously.

Implementation Best Practices

This list explains some implementation best practices:

- Solution Manager is configured with Solution Landscape integrated

- Custom code developed and unit tested in the Development environment

- End to end testing completed in the Quality system to ensure all business process testing is completed with required data

- Solution readiness to be released to PRD

- Ensure delivery of training with "Train the Trainer" approach to the customer users with required training content

- Ensure completion of data migration and data archival planning if required

- Perform necessary regression, performance testing in the respective environment

1. Final Preparation—The main objective of this phase is to complete the final preparation such as system readiness check, final rehearsal and the Organizational readiness to go live. It is typical to conduct one or more rehearsals to ensure smooth business operations during the Go Live. The Final Preparation phase also serves to resolve all critical open issues. A PM must ensure cut over plan is accurate, with all necessary tasks for the cut over captured. A successful completion of the Final preparation will indicate read to Go Live as scheduled.

2. Go Live Support—Now, you're in the crucial stage as the entire business community is awaiting for a final Go Live, which means, expecting to conduct business using SAP. Isn't exciting? The purpose of this phase is to migrate from the project environment to the production environment. Some of the key elements will include plans for support, system monitor, and optimize.

3. Run SAP—The main objective of this phase is to ensure operability of the SAP solution implemented. The primary goal of this phase is to further optimize and automate the operability of the solution. Typically, customers will ask for 60-90 days of hypercare support or more to ensure IT systems are operating without major issues with systems availability and required performance levels.

SAP ASAP 8 Scrum Methodology

The ASAP 8 Scrum methodology helps you accelerate the solution implementation, some of the key benefits include, reusability, solution demo, iterative builds and parallel services with the advent of RDS methodology. Each of these techniques are explained here:

- Reusability—As it indicates, these are reusable components such as assets from projects, best practices and pre-configured scenarios to help you speed up the solution implementation.

- Solution Demo—This indicates early visualization of the project, with possible iterative method without disturbing the project bottom-up.

- Iterative Build—As it indicates, it is strategy to perform an incremental build and test cycle as part of the scrum best practice

- Parallel Services—It indicates usage of rapid deployment services (RDS) using pre-configured scenarios. You'd select the respective mapping scenarios and implement it using RDS pre-configured business configuration ("BC") sets.

Benefits of the ASAP Methodology 8 include:

- The ASAP methodology helps you in Implementation, Upgrade and enhancement of SAP software by combining the power of the Agile/Scrum methodology.

- TCO of Implementation is reduced due to acceleration techniques and pre-configured and tested scenarios, which take less time to implement

- It combines the power of Agile/Scrum methodology to accelerate solution implementation

- Provides accelerators, templates, WBS, RDS templates, and guides

- Transparent value delivery through consistent reflection of the business case

- Provides templates of project governance, quality management, and guidance for Agile implementation projects, Business Process Management

- Overall, it combines business process, IT centric and operations management

- Cover end to end implementation and support using solution manager.

Now, the Agile SAP ASAP 8 methodology helps you demonstrate each of the above tenets of building an iterative and rapid prototype as explained above. Figure 2-4 becomes slightly altered by the inclusion of Agile methodology, which looks improved, as illustrated in Figure 2-5.

Figure 2-5. *SAP ASAP 8 with AGILE Methodology*

In simple terms, in addition to the standard accelerators, best practices, SAP has adopted an Opportunity phase ahead of the realization phase to enable an accelerated approach by breaking the processes in simple tangible processes. Typically, an SAP Project Manager will discuss the "best practices" and pre-configured scenarios in SAP to map with the corresponding business scenarios. For example. An SAP Project Manager will go through a detailed checklist of best practices to accelerate implementation timelines. Thus, the above methodology combines the power of ASAP with Agile to really accelerate product implementation in simple and tangible incremental method to succeed.

The SAP ASAP 8 Agile implementation combines the power of ASAP and Agile as explained above. It consists of two phases: Baseline and Sprint Realization. The framework of SAP ASAP 8 applies to the additional techniques of the Scrum methodology. The actual sprint cycle would start during the ASAP Blueprint phase, where you'd showcase pre-configured scenarios to map business scenarios. You're already in Agile/Scrum during the Blueprint phase to establish scrum baseline phase. Thus, the sprint cycle starts with analysis, realization, documentation and testing. When the project moves into SAP ASAP 8 Realization, you'd have already established the baseline and now the actual sprint release cycle starts based on the product backlog, which are the requirements from the Blueprint phase. Thus, you'd have accelerated two phases by actually showcasing the preconfigured scenarios such as Order to Cash (OTC) or Procure to Pay (P2P) scenarios. Now, in the subsequent sprint release cycles, you'd implement the backlogs, in other words, these are the additional customization requirements known as features. Every release would encompass a set of release features and it's flexible to change as required by the business.

Once you move into the SAP ASAP Final Prep, you'd have completed required releases, with the final product release planned. This will be your final go live. You can change the release duration, plan for number of go lives depending on the complexity of the business. Perhaps, you can internally plan the sprint cycles, whilst aligning to the overall SAP GO LIVE. Either way you can leverage Scrum methodology as a hybrid approach or an end to end approach to benefit from rapid implementation techniques. The main objective is to break down the complexities into tangible sprint release cycles and manage features for every release, based on the backlogs. These backlogs are vetted by the product owners to ensure feasibility. Further, SAP ASAP 8 provides you with tons of template, project artifacts that you can benefit from. Hence, implementing SAP using ASAP 8 / Agile-Scrum methodology is the proven and best practices to drive a successful Implementation of the project.

The sprint release cycle encompass the following:

- Analysis

- Realization

- Documentation

- Testing

Figure 2-6 illustrates the Sprint release cycle.

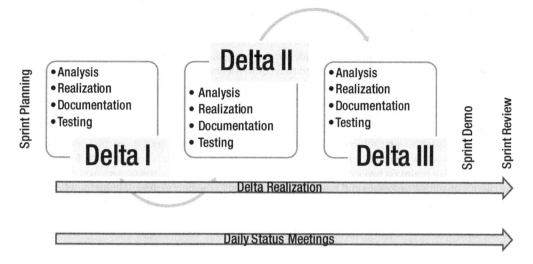

Figure 2-6. *SAP ASAP Agile-Sprint Plan*

As illustrated in Figure 2-6, you'll be implementing sprint release cycle I features after the initial analysis, by mapping the business process in SAP using preconfigured scenarios. Then testing and documentation is an integral part of the sprint release cycle, as it is primarily automated. Further usage of the Solution Manager accelerator, Eclipse development for ABAP helps you integrate best practices. For all custom code development and testing, you'd be leveraging the best practice tools provided by SAP such as Eclipse development environment for standardization. You're not going to keep the ASAP Realization as a huge "black" box, that is, unknown for months, instead you'd find the above four tangible phases. Once the sprint release cycle kicks off, then the customer will see their business process in SAP, one after the other. There is a closer feedback required from the product owner and the customer to ensure the required features are bundled as per the priority of the business. There are Quality Check points to ensure required standards are met in every sprint release cycle to ensure high quality deliverables are met.

A product backlog in Scrum is the actual list of custom requirements with priorities. First set of backlog's can be achieved with the baseline configuration using the standard configuration. The SAP ASAP 8 Project Preparation phase will finalize scrum roles & responsibilities, documentation standards and hardware requirements are discussed. All critical elements such as master data, conversions, security, authorizations and interfaces will be analyzed carefully. During the Blueprint workshops, Business SEM's and SAP Functional SME's work closely, to finalize the scope of the project. Thus, a functioning Baseline System is established by the team with the standard SAP configuration. The SAP implementation team will finalize usage of ASAP 8 templates, accelerators combined with Agile/Scrum method.

SAP ASAP 8 Blueprint (Scrum Evaluation)

Further, during the evaluation state of the blueprint phase, business will determine the priority of the additional requirements and functionalities, the so-called delta list, in order of business value. A production owner will be responsible to identify "must haves" versus "nice to haves." The implementation team will be able to estimate the efforts based on the agreed set of product backlogs. At the end of this phase you will be able to identify the key processes that can realized using the standard SAP, with the delta customization requirements. Thus, a project team will come up with an initial estimate of the effort from the team, which will be the basis for a release plan.

The SAP Agile is based on a short implementation cycle and high speed, which requires constant feedback from the business process owners. These Process Owners will set the priorities for the product with good technological preparation. A Process Owner will be responsible for coordinating internally and communication with the various business stakeholders concerning the requirements and priorities;. In this way the Process Owner represents the customer and the requirements and links these to the implementation team. Also, the process owner will administer the delta list, which is the difference between baseline and additional features to be customized. A process owner gives a clear indication of the delta features required in the respective sprint releases, based on the priorities.

Finally, it is crucial that the availability of the product owner is frequent enough during the project. If the implementation is large with multiple stake owners, then you'd probably need more than one several process owners, however, you can ask for one chief product owner, who is the decision authority for the business. It is essential to maintain inventories of requirements and priorities for the project. You should explore the client's operating processes and functionalities desired in the new system. It helps in defining scope clearly. Especially, if the project priorities are established on the basis of the most added value for the organization, which forms the base of the Sprint releases.

As illustrated in Figure 2-7, during the Agile blueprint, scoping is based on the priorities of the business, the process owner will define the priorities. Once it is agreed, the respective process owner(s) will discuss with IT team for the business process mapping in SAP software.

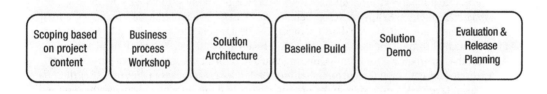

Figure 2-7. SAP Agile Business Blueprint

The IT team will be responsible for an end to end solution architecture from technical landscape and functional process hierarchy. Thus, after one or more blueprint workshops, teams will agree on a set of features to implement as baseline and subject features released as sprint cycles. The solution demo will encompass baseline configuration with the system configured to the business. Finally, the evaluation will include the analysis additional delta customization requirement with an agreed number of sprint release cycles planned. As you know, Agile is an iterative process, hence the release cycles might be informed based on the complexity of the business process.

Table 2-3 indicates deliverables in each stage gate of Agile implementation methodology.

Table 2-3. *SAP ASAP 8 Agile/Scrum Methodology*

Purpose	Deliverables	Milestones and Key Decisions
a. Align business process to the SAP business model	Lean Process and Solution Design	Completed and Signed Off Process Design
b. Documents the TO-BE process models	Business Process Hierarchy and Design	Completed and Signed Off Solution Design
c. Describes the Solution Design	Value Association on Process Level	Delta List
d. Identify function gaps	Solution Design	Phase Quality Assessment
e. Obtain business sign-off the design	Gap Identification and Resolution	Communication
f. Provide early confidence for the SAP solution	Solution Landscape and Architecture	Final Backlog—Prioritized
g. Plan for releases and sprints	Scoping—Plan for Sprint Cycles	Sprint Definition
	Baseline Build	
	Project Backlog	

Sprint Planning

The objective is to develop a shippable software in an incremental mode. Figure 2-9 indicates the Sprint realization phase and how each sprint release tasks are executed as part of the overall SAP ASAP 8 methodology. Sprint for ABAP Custom Code. This guideline considers the different phases of a complete Custom Code Lifecycle. Normally, development guidelines concentrate only on the Build phase of the Custom Code Lifecycle.

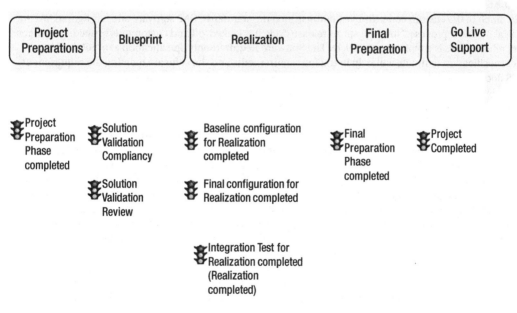

Figure 2-8. *Agile/Scrum Realization Phase*

Table 2-4 illustrates the simple R-A-C-I responsibility matrix.

Table 2-4. *Sprint Release RACI Responsibility Matrix*

Phase	Deliverables	Responsible
a. Project Preparations	Project plan, charter, landscape design, standards conduct workshops, finalize baseline	Process Owner, Client Manager Process Owner, Scrum Master, SMEs
b. Blueprint		
c. Realization	Break it down to multiple sprint release cycles unit, integration testing	Process Owner, Scrum Master, SMEs
d. Final Prep & GO Live	Trial runs, Cut Over Plan	
e. Operate	Knowledge transfer, operating manual	

A real Sprint release cycle kicks in during the ASAP Realization phase of the project. The blueprint phase will lay the foundation of the baseline configuration, post the solution demo, review and agreement with the client. The hybrid Scrum approach will merge with the ASAP as part of the overall realization phase, which incorporate several sprint release cycles. Finally, Go Live is achieved. The option is to break it further into multiple Go Live(s) or one GO Live, depending on the complexity of the system implemented.

Now, let's analyze the SAP Custom code development (ABAP Programming) using ASAP 8 Agile methodologies.

SAP Custom Code Development Using Agile

One of the common pitfalls is the lack of change control in the custom code, resulting in defects identified during the realization phase. As discussed in the various phases of the scrum, a baseline is established without much of the custom code. You've demonstrated the standards, SAP software and configured SAP for the critical business process. Now, the sprint release cycle has kicked-off and customer is expecting changes in every release. This is a typical sprint cycle. The Software Requirements Specification aka "SRS" with a product specification template will help in tracing requirements and the software meeting the requirements. The SRS document will help with design, and it serves as a basis for estimating project costs. It also serves as a basis for enhancement as it provides a foundation for continued production evaluation.

A good practice is to leverage current assets, custom code from a similar project with minimal efforts to recreate from the scratch. In case of writing code from the scratch, ensure coding standards are adhered and do it only if required, for example. A feature not available in the standards. Also, try to create online notes with SAP software team to understand the changes that could potentially impact in the future, as part of the feasibility analysis. Avoid trying to implement product features from legacy! You'd inherit the same issues from legacy design. In case of unavoidable requirements, you may want to copy the standard code as a clone, which is clearly a deviation from the best practices. In such cases, use your own discretion along with the support of SAP product support to ensure, it does not malign the overall integration of the software. Also, you should indicate to the customer about the Custom code, which would need additional maintenance and every SAP software release upgrade, would possibly impact the code. Hence, it is imperative to realize all these issues while increasing the custom code developments. There should be adequate rounds of testing to ensure robustness of the SAP software, from an end to end perspective.

We have evaluated Agile best practices from a project methodology, now let us examine SAP custom code process using Agile best practices and how it helps during the realization phase of the project.

Basic Development Environment

Now, let's examine some of the basic development and how does the SAP system landscape look like as part of the sprint release cycle, which is the realization phase of the project

Custom Code Documentation

As you know, any implementation project's technical and functional specifications are frequently changed due to changing requirements. Hence, it is necessary to keep it up-to-date and meaning to refer it back during the software upgrade and minor changes are not captured in the document. Otherwise, you'd be reinventing the wheel over and over again. The documentation is kept to minimal as progress is measured based on the working product and/or feature delivered.

One of the breakthrough's in the documentation process was the advent of SAP Eclipse for standardizing ABAP custom code development. The technical documentation focuses mainly on the interfaces and how the code was implemented in the corresponding development language. Depending on the history of creation the document will be outdated as soon as the first change request is implemented. It becomes an even more daunting task to correct user training manuals, due to the changes to the screen flows, add-ons, and so on. SAP provides integrated software development environment for custom code known as "Eclipse," which encompasses documentation introduced in the code itself. It helps in building the Maintenance documentation in combination with an operational handbook, easy to create and most sustainable form of a documentation. In the best case this documentation is integrated in the code itself. Thus, SAP has managed to provide a real integrated development environment to ease maintenance of documentation, version control and standards.

Recommendation ABAP Doc

The ABAP source code editor provides options for additional documentation within the program itself. This is the way the important information about the application should be documented. After an incident the first look is always into the application. ABAP Doc comments consist of a single comment line or a coherent block of several comment lines. In the source code editor, they can be placed in an empty line directly in front of a declarative statement like data declarations, method definition, class definitions, and so on. This is an example of how ABAP Doc can be used. For example. ABAP Doc comments can be added in ABAP classes, ABAP interfaces, ABAP programs, or ABAP function groups to describe functionality in the code element. In addition, you can generate ABAP Doc by importing the existing descriptions of global classes and interfaces, including their attributes, methods, parameters, and so on.

Development Workbench/ABAP in Eclipse

SAP offers two development workbenches (IDE). This is the well-known in SAP NetWeaver integrated development workbench and the new ABAP in Eclipse Workbench. ABAP in eclipse is available for SAP Systems NW 7.31/7.03 and NW 7.40. The integrated development workbench (Transaction SE80) provides all necessary features for a classical ABAP development project.

For new product enhancement like HANA the switch to the ABAP in Eclipse development workbench is necessary. Eclipse is a development workbench used for several development languages like Java and C. These development languages are part of the standard education in universities and new employees know how to work with eclipse. It is recommended to switch to the ABAP in Eclipse development workbench as soon as technically possible. ABAP in Eclipse offers you the following benefits compared to the classic ABAP Workbench.

- Modern UI

- Enhanced look and feel

- Integrated documentation as explained

- Plugins for code quality, code patterns and external reuse library

- Plugins for code inspections, clone detections, and so on

- It is the only workbench supporting new NetWeaver tools like Core Data Service, SQL Monitor, Dynamic Log-Points, ABAP Doc, Runtime Check Monitor, and so on

With the latest release a full integration into the ABAP Test Cockpit inclusive exception handling. Now, let us observe a custom code development using SAP Eclipse development environment as sprint release cycles.

At the end of the Sprint, the team reviews the Sprint with stakeholders, and demonstrates what it has built. People obtain feedback that can be incorporated in the next Sprint. Scrum emphasizes working product at the end of the Sprint that is really "done"; in the case of software, this means code that is integrated, fully tested and potentially shippable. Now, let's see how the scrum method helps in a SAP custom code development as illustrated in Figure 2-9.

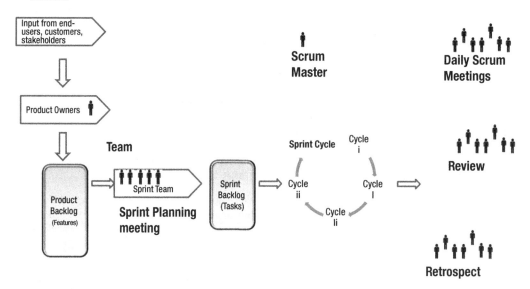

Figure 2-9. *Custom Code Development Using Scrum Methodology*

The product owner(s) will be responsible for the product backlogs (tasks), prepared based on discussions with various stakeholders and the acceptance of the release. A Scrum master is responsible for sprint backlog analysis and assess the number of release cycles required, based on the complexities of the project. The review team will conduct frequent Quality audits. In the following example, the ABAP Doc comments, indicate ease of adding a comment on the declarative statements. If you display the ABAP Element Info view in the ABAP perspective and select the method name in the source code editor, the corresponding ABAP Doc comment is displayed.

Also, you'll need to understand enhancement points, which are options to include your logic as an extension without disturbing the overall flow of the software. The enhancement spots are used to manage explicit enhancement options. Enhancement spots carry information about the positions at which enhancement options were created. One enhancement spot can manage several enhancement options of a Repository object. Conversely, several enhancement spots can be assigned to one enhancement option as illustrated in Figure 2-10. It simply indicates the ease of writing your custom specific code without altering the main program. It's easy to implement code and test it as part of the switch framework implementation.

Program a1.
```
WRITE Hello 'World'.
```

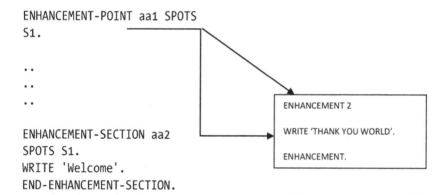

```
ENHANCEMENT-POINT aa1 SPOTS
S1.

..
..
..

ENHANCEMENT-SECTION aa2
SPOTS S1.
WRITE 'Welcome'.
END-ENHANCEMENT-SECTION.
```

```
ENHANCEMENT 2

WRITE 'THANK YOU WORLD'.

ENHANCEMENT.
```

Figure 2-10. *Enhancement Points in ABAP*

The Switch Framework controls the development objects at runtime. A switch framework in SAP manages custom code development, it acts as a package that can be turned on or off, depending on the usage and the application. It is integrated and helps customers to identify changes over a period of time and switch back to standard software, if there is an option in the future release. As a Project Manager, you might have observed custom code changes in every software release upgrade or EHP upgrade, however, with the advent of SAP switch framework, it is possible to revert back to the SAP standard programs.

As illustrated in Figure 2-11, how you'd implement changes in SAP using Enhancement points. A simple analogy of using a framework is like an additional accessory for your car. Perhaps, a GPS add-on to track your vehicle for security as an extension, however, without disturbing the standard car mechanism.

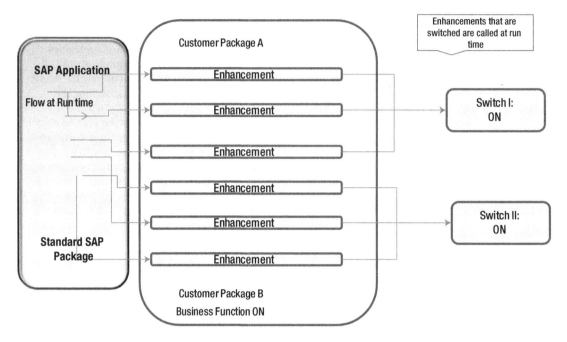

Figure 2-11. *SAP Switch Framework*

In similar terms, you will be able to add enhancements to the standard SAP software using enhancement points, that are governed by a switch framework. These enhancements can be unplugged at any point depending on the usage. Traditionally, in most of the customer SAP landscape, the custom code increases over a period of time and the maintenance becomes a huge challenge, especially during the software upgrade, these enhancements will be impacted. This additional switch framework would help in retiring old enhancements, by leveraging the standard software provided during software release upgrade. Thus, it helps in minimizing customizations, redundancies and maintenance. Over a period of time, your system would remain stable and standardized. Only the enhancements that are switched on are called at run time as illustrated above.

The Structured packaging of custom code with a Package Concept can be used to structure the custom code instead of using a kind of naming convention for the objects. The package structure is used in tools to organize and analyze the software. It is a best practice to use a package hierarchy concept, for every business functionality uses a dedicated enclosed package. Interfaces to external systems shall be managed in a dedicated interface, package separated by interface partners (e.g., by systems). Global functionality in global reuse packages. Separate business behaviors in packages with the main goal to replace or delete each package.

IMPLEMENTING SAP USING AGILE METHODOLOGY

A major utility company with approximately five thousand employees in over 10 countries, with head office in Denmark Reduced Implementation timelines to 6 months from initiation to roll out in 12 countries. They saved up to 20 percent compared to the traditional approach.

The project scope involved: HR module.

Implementing Organizational Management, Personnel Administration, Performance Management, Employee Self Service, Manager Self Service. The following figure highlights the implementation plan using Scrum/ASAP.

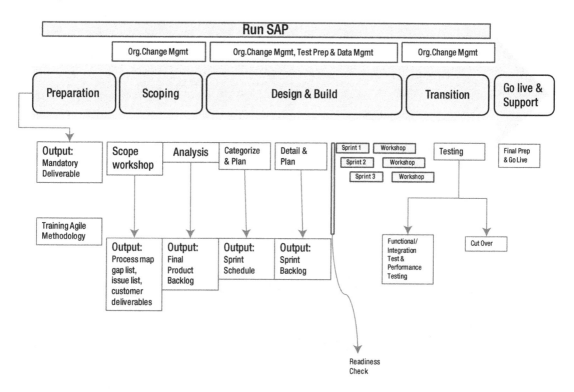

In summary, Agile comes in handy to support both the customer and the implementation partner. Finally, Agile is not a silver bullet that helps you achieve anything; a careful review of the project, customer situation, landscape, overall systems, and complexity analysis is required to ensure usage of Agile. The correct Scrum application will definitely help you to avoid common implementation pitfalls.

Refer to https://service.sap.com/asap-business-add-ons for more details about ASAP 8.0 methodology.

CHAPTER 3

Implementing SAP using Tools, Methods, and Accelerators

SAP Implementation can get tricky with increased complexity of the landscape, schedule, cost constraints, and large teams involved. With the right usage of tool, methods, and accelerator, it is easy to implement projects. A standard discipline using tools such as SAP Solution Manager, combined methodology using ASAP & Agile will yield a successful implementation.

In this chapter, you'll learn about SAP project management tools, methods, and accelerators, earn value management (EVM) used in SAP for a successful implementation, and common pitfalls to avoid such as scope, budget, and schedule. Today, SAP project managers have several tools available to effectively monitor, engage, and execute the projects to a successful conclusion. However, the real challenge is to assess each of the available tools and utilize them to benefit the organization. Therefore, it is imperative to assess tools that can help you in managing projects effectively, without getting bogged down with the tool itself. A simple PMO tool that is easy to use and easy to monitor through the project is what you'd require. In this chapter, you will see what the tools available for PMO that could be used effectively to benefit the organization. SAP is vast, and there have been a number of product enhancements in every quarter; therefore, it is essential for a Project Manager to study the latest development tools available to support the SAP project management. Gone are the days when it took years to implement an SAP project; rapid implementation can be achieved in a matter of weeks and months. It is important to leverage tools, accelerators, and methods to implement SAP from initiation to ensure successful implementation of the project.

Understanding Project Management

A good project manager will need to understand the client landscape, stakeholders, proposed solutions, and risks to mitigate. Hence, it is essential for an SAP project manager to know the solution suite available in SAP and how he/she can drive the team to identify the best possible solution mapped in SAP. Moreover, the project manager should understand the tools and accelerators available, and also should insist that the team uses SAP SolMan and/or standard tools for monitoring progress. Otherwise, there will be no way to measure success.

Most projects fail as a result of a lack of thinking through the end product. As a result, the team loses its focus without being able to develop a solution. I have observed projects fail because of a lack of thinking from an integration perspective, as well as from a lack of understanding how systems work within the SAP product ecosystem and/or external systems. If your team does not possess the right skills, your project will be at risk. Seasoned consultants need to be able to discuss options with the client to provide a solution.

Understanding Solution Manager

Solution Manager 7.1 (SolMan) is a robust platform that helps to manage solutions throughout the entire lifecycle of a project from blueprint and realization to support. If you're managing projects as part of the client team, it's better to get certified in ITIL (IT Service Management), which provides guidance in terms of IT services and how to get the best out of these services. In addition, SDLC (Software Development Lifecycle) will help you implement best practices in your organization, such as "configuration management" for managing the releases effectively in a heterogeneous landscape.

If you're a PM managing as part of the consulting organization, PMP certification will help you to gain a solid foundation into project management practices. If you're a consultant, a good understanding of using tools such as SolMan will help you to accelerate your tasks in order to manage client expectations. In my experience as an SAP consultant and/or PM, I have seen SAP help to incorporate these best practices into the package software. The PRINCE (Projects in Controlled Environments) certification will help you if you're managing projects in the UKI region. Project management is an art; when combined with people, process, and technology knowledge, you will be able to excel with a simple commonsense approach.

Project Management Process

There are five basic project management processes:

- Project initiation

- Project planning

- Project execution

- Project monitoring and control

- Project closure

However, SAP follows a standard ASAP implementation practice with the above core principles of PMI practices. If you map these phases into ASAP, initiation and planning are essentially part of project preparations, whereas execution is ASAP-blueprint, realization, final prep, go live, and support. Monitoring and control indicates the operate/run phases, with an additional phase of closure indicated at the end of the operate phase (Figure 3-1).

Figure 3-1. *Project Management Process Mapping in SAP ASAP*

How Do Tools Help in the Project Plan?

The primary objective of tools used is to help in planning, scheduling, and estimating at every stage of a project. For example, a Gantt chart, milestone chart, network chart, and so on are typically used to analyze critical path, tasks completed, and dependencies. These tools can be used to create a task and assign and create interdependencies with resources assigned to the task. Most project managers use a simple Microsoft project plan (.mpp) to develop a project plan with tasks and assign resources to each of the tasks with estimated duration and effort. Most PMO tools have the following features, based on the project management principles:

- Create a project and subproject

- Build a plan with start date and end date

- Create tasks, generally referred to as "WBS" (work breakdown structure)

- And link with dependencies

- Effectively track the efforts planned against consumed for each task

- Manage the resource allocation

- Ability to do resource scheduling and assignment

- Overall viewing of real-time project status, costs, and budget reports

- Ability to generate Earned Value reports

Remember, your objective is to deliver high-quality deliverables on time, on budget, and on cost. The real challenge is mainly because in every consulting partner organization, the solution is worked on by one team, whereas delivery is accomplished by a different team. Therefore, there is no cohesiveness in terms of effort. One of the best practices is to benchmark projects based on the available data points of similar projects to implement a project successfully.

In many consulting organizations, the original literature shared between clients and the solution team is not readily available to support the delivery organization, resulting in lots of miscommunication. A simple rule of thumb is "Honesty is the best policy." If you start right, everything will happen, if you start with an escalation with the customer, no one will be happy in the end

In a good project environment, both partners and the client teams will work as one unit to achieve common goals. There will be a political situation from time to time, which must be handled diplomatically to diffuse the situation. It is prudent to start involving all members of the organization at an early stage. The internal partner organization must be aware of the project manager's activities at the client site to mitigate risks. In some cases, this might involve getting a work visa, identifying resources, validating the solution by in-house SMEs; SAP could be a challenge. Most of these issues could be sorted out with appropriate planning and support from the partner organization's upper management.

SAP Project Management

Project management is a framework of organizing, planning, controlling, executing, budgeting, and managing the overall project to achieve project goals. The core objective of project management practice is to achieve high-quality deliverables on time, on budget, and on quality. Project management practice is the a backbone of an organization, and it helps you to succeed. Many organizations set up COE (center of excellence) models to build technical expertise with core functionality and technical strengths. The PMO is responsible for setting up the guidelines, benchmark projects, and ensuring success of the organization at a program level. The PMO also helps by establishing standards, methods, and tools to use based on project complexity and technology used. It helps by reaching out to SME's group, during the respective phases of the projects, to mitigate risks.

How Do You Measure a Project's Success?

There are few core factors that you should be aware of while planning a project:

- Business objectives and goals
- Project scope
- Risks and mitigation plan
- Efforts and timeline
- Budget
- Resources
- Infrastructure

A good project management practice is to balance the scope, schedule, and costs without compromising on any of these points as illustrated in Figure 3-2.

Figure 3-2. *Project Triangle with Three Critical Factors*

Earn Value Management (EVM) metrics will help you to assess each of these parameters to succeed in a project. A good PM will manage scope changes diligently; however, the manager must ensure that the end-product vision or impact of the software ecosystem is not altered.

It is essential to have a good implementation process and quality standards. The solution team must evaluate the core business process and the business problems prior to proposing a solution to the customer. The project discussion artifacts must be recorded and handed over to the project delivery teams to ensure continuity of requirements. A good estimation practice is required to identify tasks and the required efforts for every single task at a unit level to avoid budget overruns at a later stage. Avoid "guesstimates," as these can disrupt the chances of a successful implementation. Solution experts must be prudent during the concept stage to analyze technical challenges in the project and build enough contingency to mitigate risks. SAP projects depend on in-depth knowledge and good skills.

A good communication plan is required for the team for business achievement, priority, and scope. There are tools available to manage the key factors of a project. MPP is a Microsoft project tool that helps you to build a robust project plan. It will help you to assign key dependencies on the critical path and risks can be maintained in a risk register. The PM must ensure that milestones are met with the desired quality. This is a continuous process. The most up-to-date leaders talk about "upward thinking," a concept geared toward enhancing client relationships and fostering a good working environment with the customer.

Defining Project Objectives and Goals

Project goals should be clear and precise to the stakeholders and the business leaders. The project must ensure business objectives are met. Every goal has some objectives. These objectives should be "SMART" (Specific, Measurable, Attainable, Relevant, and Timely). If you're able to break this down in the simplest terms, it will be easy to achieve your end goals. ASAP 8 helps you to achieve each of these subgoals with detailed steps for implementation. During the phase of ASAP 8 SAP project preparation, the overall project is planned. It is absolutely imperative to outline the required information during project planning.

One of the key elements of successful project management is to have good stakeholder relationships and involve them through the project by providing reports succinctly. It's essential to publish goals and how much you're able to achieve during the various phases of the project. The communication curve should be very high and interactive during the initial phase of the project, and it will decline as you start working with the client teams. It is imperative to remain in sync with the customer. Your team's communication must be sharp and articulate in every business communication to ensure accuracy.

Typically, a good project manager will spend time with the client as well as with the team to ensure that both parties know what is going on and that everyone understands the overall solution to ensure detailed planning is done to meet customer requirements. A good project manager must ensure that the following points are taken into consideration:

- Good understanding of customer requirements

- Excellent knowledge of the SAP software ecosystem and solution mapping

- Optimization of the customer's critical business processes

- Enable customers to overcome day-to-day operational challenges

- Reduce process inefficiencies by improving the turnaround time of the process

- Help improve ROI

Each of these goals should be broken down into multiple sub-goals to achieve and showcase operational excellence in your project.

Defining Project Scope

Why do you need a Project scope? A project without a well-defined scope is like sailing a ship without a proper navigation system! It will help you to define the boundaries of work. It will help you to understand the customer requirements and assumptions made during the initial solution phase, and it will provide a detail description of the product or services that need to be delivered. It is essential to manage time and costs within the required budget to complete the work. A good project manager will ensure clear project scope before calculating the efforts to complete (ETC).

In addition, a defined scope will help you to mitigate risks diligently by planning, monitoring, and controlling your risks. There are two levels of the project scope:

1. Business level

2. Implementation level

The implementation level will be more detailed with a work breakdown structure (WBS).

Though Agile, it is possible to accept changes. A PM must carefully evaluate the change to ensure that the end product is not impacted significantly. It is important to review the project scope with the customer and other key stakeholders to keep your project goal aligned with the customer's expectations. The PM should be able to control scope changes and differentiate between change requests and scope change. The SAP project scope will be defined during project preparation and the blueprint phase.

Most projects fail during realization as a result of a lack of clarity in the early stages, during requirements gathering, resulting in excessive rework. It is a good practice to have a high-level scope defined as early as the RFP stage.

SAP provides extensive tools:

1. ASAP methodology (Accelerate SAP)

2. Value SAP

3. Solution Manager to implement the SAP project

Accelerated SAP and ValueSAP are external to the SAP application, whereas SolMan is built into SAP with required tools and resources available in the ASAP toolkit for accelerating implementation projects.

During the project preparation phase, you can define the initial project scope within the Enterprise Area Scope Document. This is based on the ECC reference model and can be generated using the Project Estimator. At this point, the project scope is defined by both at the business and IT. The implementation manager can further dip down to move the scope at a development level for each deliverable.

Defining Risk Management

Risk is the possibility of a threat that can occur due to chosen activity, action, or decision. Risks are of two types:

- Known

- Unknown

Unknown risks are also called an uncertainty. Both types of risk need to be avoided and controlled. A good practice is to assess risks as part of the project review to ensure that risks are identified and mitigated before they occur.

Managing IT Risks: Essential for the Success of Every Project

The risk related to information technology is known as IT risks. To manage your IT project effectively, it is important to identify your IT risks in the beginning, before the start of your project. Identifying all risks is a big challenge and is crucial for managing projects. All risks need to be documented properly in detail. It is very important to have a mitigation plan in place. These risks have to be monitored, measured, and mitigated as you progress with the project implementation.

Risks are assessed with a score, probability of occurrence, impact, and severity. Based on these factors, a risk can be evaluated as high, medium, or low. You should list all possible risks based on past projects, and then start documenting a mitigation plan for each of these risks. Often, project managers do not estimate the impact of a risk. However, if the risk escalates, you should have additional contingency built in to mitigate at an additional cost. Overall, risks might be related to the availability of resources, skills, technology, customization complexity, stakeholders responsibilities, infrastructure and/or customer support, testing, and so on. The mitigation plan should resolve these possible risks into action plan. A comprehensive risk register will help in consolidating, monitoring, and controlling risks.

Today, as more and more enterprises are global, most have a centralized in-house and/or cloud-based Disaster Management Plan (DMP) to handle any infrastructure or operational breakdown that can occur due to natural disaster, political uncertainty, war, or any other geographical disturbances. This helps to manage your delivery without any risks, even in the case of unpredictable situation. This could be a primary DMP setup in the cloud or as a hybrid approach with on-premise and an additional secondary fail-over server on-cloud as a DMP.

Major IT Project Risks

Table 3-1 shows potential risks in an SAP implementation project.

Table 3-1. Potential Risks in an SAP Implemenation Project

Risk Description	Risk	Impact	Mitigation Plan
1. Budget Risks	High	High	Due to incorrect estimates. Need to control using correct measurements and inform the customer for replan
2. Schedule Risks	Medium	High	Due to incorrect estimates and lack of skill. Ensure right skill and replan
3. Development Risks	High	High	Lack of requirements and/or misunderstanding the requirements. Need to replan with excellent skills
4. Quality Risks	Medium	High	Ensure adequate QMM standards

There are several tools available to manage your project risks. SAP AG provides standard guidelines and process for effectively managing SAP project risks. We will discuss more regarding the SAP QMMI standards in Chapter 5.

A PM must make sure that plans to succeed in an SAP Implementation are followed:

- The client business requirements and the proposed solution

- The scope of project

- The change management plan

- The risk management plan

- The business blueprint

- The cost and Schedule

- The roll out plan

The SAP implementation plan details out the strategy, deliverables with various solution details, and the information required for the business and the delivery team. It encompasses the overall process that defines the complete method, which can be executed in different phases step by step. The SAP implementation has the following ASAP 8 phases:

1. Project preparation

2. Business blueprint

3. Realization

4. Final preparation

5. Go live and support

6. Operate

The SAP ASAP 8 methodology provides a complete roadmap for your project plan. It divides project implementation into phases. Each phase further breaks down into work packages, activities, and tasks. Figure 3-3 shows the ASAP methodology with deliverables in each phase.

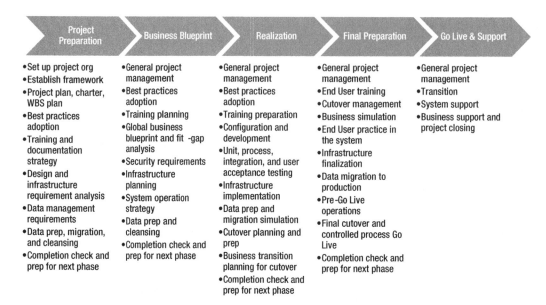

Figure 3-3. ASAP 8 Deliverables

ASAP 8 provides a standard approach to implementation projects. Each of these steps is essential for a successful project. You may choose different tools to measure, capture metrics or Agile methods implement projects. The fundamental aspects of ASAP provide a framework for a successful implementation. The steps are self-explanatory and the deliverables indicate achieving milestones in every phase. You may break it further into AGILE, but the fundamental ASAP method will help you achieve successful implementation. Typically, most of the managers use Microsoft Project Plan tools to measure WBS at task level, or you can manage projects using Solution Manager. Most functional consultants struggle to convince clients to implement best business practices.

The realization phase is very critical for a successful implementation, as you'll need to monitor baseline configuration, custom development and unit, integration, and user acceptance testing as part of the realization phase. It is better to assess the scope of each work package, assign respective resources, and monitor the schedule and completion of work. If there is a rework, ensure that the key dependencies are not impacted by the change. If you're adapting AGILE, ensure that the project plan is flexible based on the changes, however, without impacting the overall end product implementation goals.

WBS Tasks: Scheduling and Resource Assignment

WBS helps you to break things down to the task level. Task planning starts with Work Breakdown Structure (WBS). The project schedule defines the expected deadlines, specifies dependencies among the elements, and helps the PM to monitor and control the project progress.

Steps for defining the project schedule include:

1. List the tasks as identified in a work breakdown structure (WBS)

2. Define the dependencies between WBS elements.

3. Estimate the effort require for each task as per the standard guidelines and parameters

4. Determine the start date and end (finish) date based on priority or other factors

5. Assign resources for each task

6. Check the resource over allocation and the total project completion date

7. Publish your plan and generate a Gantt chart to see the graphical layout of your complete plan

You can plan the project schedule using Microsoft Excel or Microsoft project plan or can use SAP project planning board. The project planning board helps in planning and controlling the projects. It provides a graphical overview of the projects and can be managed and changed easily as per your requirements.

The project control board (PCB) is responsible for planning and monitoring until the project is complete. You can use the WBS tool to define a sequence of tasks such as dates, costs, level capacities, assigned resources, and work distribution. Additionally, you can switch to a graphical view, simulate changes, and see an overview of call logs.

Support and Maintenance Plan

During this phase, the team will provide hypercare support to ensure smooth operations. The turn-around time of completion depends on SLAs as agreed with the client. Typically, a very high priority problem will need to be resolved in under 8 hours, whereas a high priority needs to be resolved in under 16 hrs and a medium priority in under 32 hrs. During this phase, the spike in ticket volume will be closely monitored. The data will be assessed for improvements following the monitor phase. The implementation will need to ensure an adequate transition is made to the client team with detailed training and operating manuals. It is essential to ensure few training sessions by using a "train the trainer" approach. The support team will analyze if there is any additional performance enhancement requirements. The change control board (CCB) will establish a robust release framework to ensure a streamlined release process without impacting core or other implementation projects.

Typically, partner teams provide the following package service offerings to help the client post implementation:

- SAP system maintenance

- SAP application maintenance

- Configuration management

- Manage change requests

- SAP server maintenance

- Other production and operation support

The SAP AG provides standard software services that will help you to succeed in implementation and in upgrading software using specialized package offerings. You may need an additional support system to check functionally prior to Go Live. SAP supports this with 'Functional Go Live Check' and downtime analysis to assess the scope of actual downtime, and so on. You can select the services you require based on the skills that you have available as well as additional SME support that you may need. The following services are provided by SAP:

- SAP Enterprise support services

- SAP Standard support services

- Maximum support services with SAP Max-Attention

- Implementing Risk Management Services with SAP safeguarding
- Support resources
- Support for customers
- SAP HANA migration services

A key metric of PMI is the EVM (Earn Value Management), which is important to assess the status of the project. EVM is the metric used for assessing schedule, cost, and scope of a project.

There are three basic elements to understand in this process: Planned Value (PV), Earned Value (EV), and Actual Cost (AC). PV indicates the baseline value of the project and the EV is the actual work completed. You can find variance in terms of costs and schedule based on the EV.

Typically, you'd define the tasks using WBS and then assign a planned value to each of these tasks. Next, you'd define earn rules for each task and the final step is to run the project to get the earn values. Let us try to use a simple case study to assess the scope of each of these metrics and how you can benefit out of the metrics planning and execution of the project. Table 3-2 indicates key metrics for your project.

Table 3-2. *Project EVM Metrics*

SNO	Metric	Definition	Formulae
1	BAC	Baseline Project Cost	$ Value
2	PV	Planned Value	Planned % Complete x BAC
3	EV	Earned Value	% Completed x BAC
4	AC	Actual Cost	Actual Cost spent ($)
5	CPI	Cost Performance Index	EV/AC
6	CV	Cost Variance	EV-AC
7	SV	Schedule Variance	EV-PV
8	SPI	Schedule Performance Index	EV/PV
9	EAC	Estimate at Completion	BAC/CPI
10	VAC	Variance at Completion	BAC-EAC

Now, let's understand how to set up the baseline work. BAC is the sum of planned value at the completion of the project. Basically, it explains you the total budget allocated to the project. As explained Earned Value (EV) is the total work earned out of the planned value (PV). In simple terms, it indicates the planned value of work completed measured in currency. You might have completed 50% of work as planned. Total Budget is around $100,000 USD. You've completed only 50% of work, hence the Planned value (PV) = 50%*(BAC) = $ 50,000. Now, let us see an example of calculating Planned Value (PV) for a project.

Project duration: 10 months. Project Cost (BAC): $100,000 USD, Time elapsed: 5 months, Percentage complete: 50% (as per the schedule). The definition of Planned Value says that the Planned Value is the value of the work that should have been completed so far (as per the schedule). Therefore, in this case we should have completed 50% of the total work.

Planned Value = 50% of the value of the total work
= 50% of BAC
= 50% of $100,000
= (50/100) × $100,000
= $50,000

Therefore, the Planned Value (PV) is $50,000 USD

PV = Actual Work Completed X BAC = 50% x $ 50000 = $ 50, 000 USD

Earned Value is also known as the Budgeted Cost of Work Performed (BCWP). For example, you have a project to be completed in 10 months and the total cost of the project is $100,000 USD. Five months have passed and $50,000 USD has been spent, but on closer review you find that only 50% of the work is completed so far. You can clearly see that only 50% of the work is actually completed, and the definition of Earned Value says that it is the value of the project that has been earned. Hence, Earned Value = 30% of value of total work.

= 30% of BAC
= 30% of $100,000
= 0.3 × $100,000
= $30,000

Therefore, the Earned Value (EV) is $30,000 USD.

The Actual Cost (AC) is an actual cost of work if the task is 100% completed on or before the report end date. It gives you the total cost actually incurred to complete the work on specified dates. This also referred to as the Actual Cost of Work Performed (ACWP). For example, you have a project to be completed in 10 months and the total cost of the project is $100,000 USD. Five months have passed and $50,000 USD has been spent, but on closer review you find that only 30% of the work is completed so far. AC is the amount of money that you have been spent so far. And in our question, you have spent $50,000 USD on the project so far. Hence, The Actual Cost is $50,000 USD. It is used to measure Cost Variance (CV) and Cost Performance Index (CPI).

To summarize, Planned Value is the money that you should have spent as per the schedule, Earned Value is the value of the work actually completed to date, and the Actual Cost is the amount spent on the project to date.

The Cost Performance Index (CPI) shows you the utilization of your resources in the project. It reflects the ratio of actual work done against the actual cost paid for it. The CPI is calculated as follows:

CPI = Earned Value (EV) / Actual Cost (AC)
    CPI < 1 - Over Budget
    CPI > 1 - Under Budget

The Cost Variance (CV) tells you how much over or under budget your project is running. It is the difference between the Earned Value (EV) and the Actual Cost (AC) you spent for the work performed. The Cost Variance (CV) is calculated as:

CV = Earned Value (EV) - Actual Cost (AC)
    CV < 0 (Negative Value) - Over Budget
    CV > 0 (Positive Value) - Under Budget

The Schedule Performance Index (SPI) shows you the utilization of the time in the project. It also indicates you how much a project is ahead or behind schedule. The SPI is calculated as:

SPI = Earned Value (EV) / Planned Value (PV)
    SPI < 1 - Behind Schedule
    SPI > 1 - Ahead Schedule

The Schedule Variance (SV) tells you how much ahead or behind schedule your project is running. It is the difference between the Earned Value (EV) and the Planned Value (PV). The Schedule Variance (SV) is calculated as:

SV = Earned Value (EV) - Planned Value (PV)
    SV < 0 (Negative Value) - Behind Schedule
    SV > 0 (Positive Value) - Ahead of Schedule

Now, let's us observe a project performance based on the Earned Value report, as illustrated in Table 3-3.

Table 3-3. *An Example of an Earned Value Report Tool*

Activity	Planned Value	Earned Value	Actual Cost	Cost Variance	Schedule Variance	Cost CPI	Schedule CPI
Prelim Plan	100	95	220	-15	-5	0.86	0.95
Final Plan	250	210	210	0	-40	1	0.84

This Earned Value analysis indicates that the project is running over the budget (EV-AC). The trend indicates a significant deviation in the final plan as it is -40 in terms of schedule, which is 40% over the schedule, and the cost has almost doubled, as you observe in the actual cost of the final plan. To summarize, the trend is not a healthy sign, as you're overspending, and critically behind the schedule, and over the budget.

As a good practice, you must replan, an estimate based on the project situation; hence, there is no fixed plan. It will always remain dynamic with frequent changes to the plan, which can be controlled with proper diligence. You should use your past experience, benchmark standards, historical data, judgmental methods to ensure that the project can be controlled at any given point to succeed in the implementation project.

SAP Implementation Tools

Although there are several tools available for implementing SAP projects, Solution Manager is the latest, which provides required accelerators to implement a project successfully. The ASAP Roadmap is a methodology that provides you for implementing and optimizing your SAP system efficiency. It divides the project implementation process into five phases as discussed.

The SAP Solution Manager functions as a central repository to help you with tools and accelerators in every phase during project preparation, the business blueprint phase, realization, and the project analysis phase. It will help you to build business process mapping and store and execute test scripts. You can use ALM features of SolMan to support your team throughout the lifecycle of the project. The CHARM functionality is used for monitoring and controlling all change requests. The project estimator is a tool used to estimate the effort, timeline, resource requirements, and costs of your SAP implementation project. The tool is based on Microsoft Excel, which can be managed easily. The core SAP tools available to support you in implementation include:

- The Project Estimator, an SAP tool. It helps you to gauge the required number of resources, costs and time frame of SAP implementation. It helps in determining accurate scope, risk factors

  - The Concept Check Tool

  - The SAP Implementation Assistant with accelerators to support you in implementation project

- ASAP 8 Implementation Road Map

- Question and Answer Database

- Business Process Master List

- Implementation Guide

- Continuous Business Process Engineering

- Solution Manager

- Value SAP

In the following section, we will see how can use SolMan to accelerate project implementation.

Implementation using SolMan 7.1 SP26

Now, let us understand the implementation and upgrade projects using SAP Solution Manager (SolMan). You can use the SAP Solution Manager to create the following projects:

- Implementation: the implementation project helps you to create a project structure of the business processes. There are few options; either you can create a new project or you can use existing partner templates. The following options are available to create a project structure:

    - Using partner templates and/or an existing projects

    - Scenarios and configuration structures delivered by SAP

    - An existing production solution landscape

- Template Project: - most large organizations create a project template and they roll out to the subsidiaries as a global rollout. A template makes your project structure, or parts of it, with its assigned objects such as documentation, test cases, and IMG activities, available to other projects. It can be locked and managed centrally against changes when they are used in other projects. You can use templates in other systems by simply transporting it.

- Upgrade Project: this is a project structure to upgrade existing systems. In an upgrade project you have access to the following tools:

    - Upgrade customizing: Upgrade existing functions to the latest software version

    - Delta customizing: Leveraging additional functions of SAP software latest version

    - Optimization: this optimizes the flow of business processes, or the use of a software solution such as SAP System Landscape Optimization. You can use optimization projects, for example, in SAP Services.

    - Safeguarding: a project to resolve a critical situation in the implementation or use of an SAP solution. Safeguarding projects show the reasons for a critical situation and coordinate the steps required to resolve the problems.

- Maintenance project: once you implement the project, the next step is to focus on solution maintenance, such as managing changes, software updates, and so on. The release process, and all high priority changes will be taken care through this phase. The features available in Check-In/Check-Out Business Processes functionality from the Solution Directory to manage changes.

Business Process Operations Dashboard

The Business Process Operations dashboard provides a graphical display to the business users. In the Business Process Operations dashboard, end users can graphically display and monitor analytical key figures, for example throughput or backlogs, in various panels. This gives the end user an overview of the status of business processes, and he can identify current operational problems. It also helps you identify trends of your business process performance.

For example, the following end users use dashboards:

- The business process owner can manage the order process, procurement or Order to Cash (OTC), Procure to Pay (P2P) business process, and monitor and identify issues.

- A warehouse manager can identify the backlog by comparing the incoming orders.

- The dashboard administrator and the business process expert together identify the end user's information requirements, set up dashboards, and assign them to groups of end users according to their areas of responsibility.

Activities

The business process expert specifies the information requirements of various groups of end users. The dashboard administrator identifies, with the business process expert, the analytic key figures to be displayed on the dashboards, and assigns monitor objects and their analytic key figures to logical components. Monitoring objects collect data in the production system and put it in the SAP NetWeaver Business Warehouse.

MANAGING SAP IMPLEMENTATION USING SOLMAN 7.1

You will be able to succeed in a complex project implementation. As document/collaboration platform for the project, members can work directly with the organized roadmap work packages, using the accelerators and uploading their work back into the structured packages in Solution Manager. Figure 3-4 illustrates the entire lifecycle managed using SAP Solution Manager.

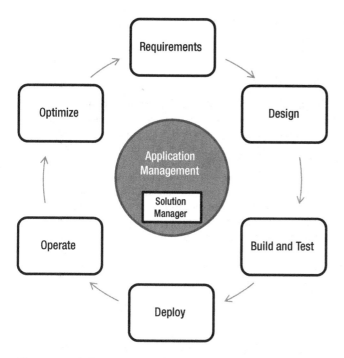

Figure 3-4. *Solution Manager for Managing the Entire Project Lifecycle*

Figure 3-5 illustrates the usage of SolMan in application lifecycle management (ALM), from gathering requirements to deployment and operate phases of an implementation project.

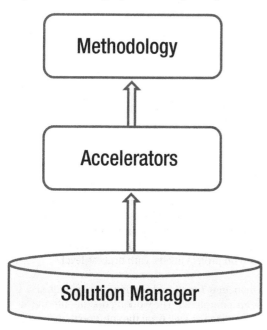

Figure 3-5. *Methodology for Projects Using SolMan*

You can map SolMan into the overall plan based on your client's PMI practices. Now, let us see how SolMan is used during an implementation project phase.

Project Blueprint Repository in Solution Manager

The key aspects of an SAP implementation include the Organization Unit, Master data setup, business scenarios, and so on. Therefore, the blueprint, configuration, development, testing, further activities, and all of the related documents can be organized on the same basis, through this process-driven approach. Within the project structure, business scenarios and processes, including standard transactions, can be pulled from SAP business process repository in Solution Manager.

For example, In the Order to Cash process, the entire business process is mapped into a project structure. During the blueprint phase, business scenarios either selected from the repository or custom made, together with the inner folders. Business processes and process steps are structured in the project. You'll be able to select a process from the repository with readily available blueprint, process document, functional process from the respective folders maintained within the project structure.

Figure 3-6 is an example of a SAP implementation project with the business process structure highlighted for a reference business process called "Assemble-to-Order Processing" with detailed step-by-step process with additional documentation.

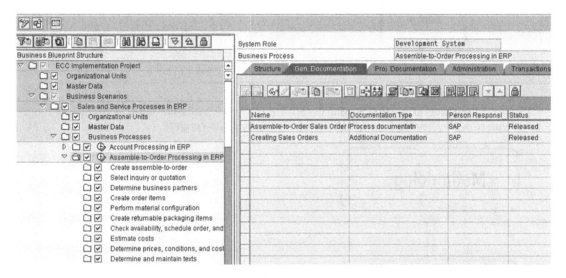

Figure 3-6. *ERP Implementation Project with Business Process (BPS) in SolMan*

The Customizable status management offers features such as Editing, released, approved status, and so on. The document template can be set as standard, for each type of new document created with history of changes in attribute of each document, including the possibility to display old files. It also offers features such as checkin/checkout functionality with additional options such as Digital signature, and so on.

There are some interesting features available in SolMan such as the Global templates copied for localization. Now, the local template can be customized based on project needs, with process level customization, business process hierarchy, and so on.

Thus, Solution Manager as a project platform helps in managing functional configuration changes; developing custom code and testing post blueprint changes are completed. The working documents and execution of configuration, development and testing can be managed as well from the solution manager project using the same business process structures.

SolMan offers a central repository for configuration, development, and testing.

Configuration: Includes configuration objects and IMG object, BC set, Dynpro application, NW content, Roles, and so on can be recorded.

Development: Includes FRICE objects, function modules and the transaction can be recorded in development.

Testing: Includes test plan, test cases, results, CATT, eCATT, and so on. From each object recorded, project members can jump directly to the object in the Development system, such as predefined system landscape, to customize their recorded IMGs, develop programs and access eCATT, and so on. Each object record also contains responsible owner together with progress status, which can be updated. This helps project management and team leads to check progress to a very detailed level.

A comprehensive test scope will include, preparing test plan, test scripts, test package, execute the package, record results, and rerun the suite, when necessary. A real challenge is to focus on business process. Solution Manager allows the business process structure with test documents or objects recorded to be pulled into the SAP standard test workbench tool. This tool manages a test plan and provides testers with a test list. Solution Manager also provides flexible options for project analysis and reporting. The detail information of status, deadlines, of selected phase or cross-phase, for cross-project or just for a project, could be extracted into the report.

Training Planning and Execution with an E-Learning Platform

Gone are the days when you'd spent a considerable amount of time in documentation and preparing the training manuals. SolMan offers features to support end-user training requirements. You can link training materials such as documents, presentations, SAP tutor recordings, and so on to processes and roles. You can create a role-based HTML training map with all of the relevant training materials inside. These training maps could be distributed to users for self-training or trainers for training sessions with end users. This approach allows a single update point for materials and all standard document management abilities, for example, status, document history, and checkin/checkout functions. The feedback functionality provides options to record the training results to communicate changes to the training team. Overall, it is easy to maintain up-to-date training documents current with changing software versions.

End-to-End Solution Operation

The SAP SolMan tool helps manage the complete application lifecycle of the solution for incident management, solution monitoring, change control management, root cause analysis, and so on. It is a consolidated repository of information required for Functional, Technical and the business. The SolMan monitoring helps you identify business problems in real time. It provides interface monitoring and most importantly, business process monitoring (BPM). BPM is focused on the business side of the solution by providing process oriented monitoring of the most critical business such as issues in OTC or P2P. You'll need to setup business processes and monitoring items mapped to them. But once it is set up, it captures the errors, triggers automatic notification, which speed up problem resolution before it becomes a lost to the business.

The System admin console is one point repository for all system admin related tasks. Administrative tasks which are mainly executed in involve system can be pre-defined as a list with recurring frequency in central administration console. This also helps to retain tailored administrative knowledge, even when the team is changed. The SLA's and report are also captured, which is a valuable source of information for managing issues. Service Desk provides an incident management engine where support messages are handled centrally inside the organization and also to SAP support. Support messages.

Solution Manager as a project platform can be created web-based or directly from problematic transaction, routed message by components to appropriate support group and level to support the organization. Change Control Management functionality controls software and configuration changes for the entire solution to ensure quality and traceability of all changes. This includes an approval process of the change requests which works on top of the service desk engine. Deployment of the change uses control over the traditional Transport Management System (TMS), or could also work over "CTS-Log" (Lodestone's enhanced TMS tool) Root cause analysis provides a diagnostic function which allows problem analysis and resolution in heterogeneous landscapes. It helps identifying the root cause problem; point out performance related problem, exceptional situations, changes in the production environment and also able to trace the problem from recorded user or process session.

QA Integration in the Implementation Process

We will talk about SAP Quality Management (QMM) practices in detail in the subsequent chapters. SAP Solution Manager can be used as a dashboard to get a status overview of the different projects. It acts as a Central administration interface for all types of transports and system landscapes and Integrates the various development workbench into a central transport and Change control system. It also synchronizes the software distribution in the different software stacks using a System Lanscape directory (SLD), synchronized changes in business processes that run in ABAP and Non-ABAP stacks, and control the quality of software changes by quality gates.

The SolMan QA cockpit helps you to understand defects raised during the realization phase. The watch list indicates the issues that deviate from the expected quality as defects, build issues, or test results. It is a complete dashboard for the quality review team as a central repository for controlling defects to produce a very high quality deliverable. It helps the QMM advisory board in your organization to have one consolidated view of defects as it increases transparency. It will help you to revise the scope of the project and revisit the plan if required by checking test results that have passed. One of the challenging tasks is to manage a comprehensive list of development transport requests for your project. Managing TR is very important in any deployment, change requests. The QA operational screen in SolMan offers change control in the Transport level as part of SolMan. You can create TR, execute a test TR to remove any inconsistencies, and release TR as a central admin tool to manage TRs in projects.

Overall, Solution Manager is a good SAP project platform considering the support of integrated document management together with a roadmap and "project" repository where business processes and all of the documents are structurally stored. It will be easy to monitor implementation, testing, and training in the later phase could be easily driven. SolMan can provide support in building test suite, execute, store results as test packages for regression, and it provides capabilities for the Change Control Management in the operation phase.

One of the daunting tasks for any project manager is to manage change requests and traceability to the original scope. SolMan offers excellent solution monitoring and administration. Service desk is a useful ticketing system for managing SAP-related issues.

Concluding Remarks

In this chapter, you've learned the best practices of SAP to avoid common pitfalls such as scope, budget, and schedule, by leveraging SAP Solution Manager, ASAP 8, and Agile methodology. In the next chapter, you'll learn common implementation challenges with risk mitigation strategy.

■ ■ ■

CHAPTER 4

Key SAP Implementation Challenges

We have discussed common pitfalls such as lack of clarity in scope, budget, schedule, planning, and lack of solution validation, stakeholder responsibilities, and skills, all of which plague SAP implementation projects. Now, let us discuss strategies and best practices on how to manage challenges that arise during an SAP implementation project with risk mitigation planning. We will also discuss various approaches to global template development plans, rollout strategies with SAP Landscape design principles, and key business process integration based on real-life lessons learned. We will examine a specific solution plan in SAP to mitigate the risks of a failed implementation with key challenges.

■ **Note**   Large SAP global implementation projects require a lot of planning and deployment strategy, as multiple sites and countries are involved. Typically, project management teams will spend a considerable amount of time discussing the rollout strategy and the site-specific challenges.

Implementation Overview

Let's start with the template approach, which indicates a consolidated business scenario. This can be used as a standard template. Global organizations follow best practices in procurement, sales, delivery, and HR. Now, questions remain as how best to leverage these common processes for a specific region with minimal customization. It's like developing a prototype of a Rolls Royce in the United Kingdom, then customizing it for the United States and other regions. The challenge is to come up with a common blueprint. Why do projects fail? They fail mainly because of a lack of planning, and also as a result of other factors such as business, end-users involvement, and project methodology, and so on. These are common pitfalls to avoid in any implementation projects.

Projects fail during the realization phase as a result of pitfalls such as lack of vision and clear-cut goals at headquarters and subsidiaries. Lack of communication is another pitfall to avoid between various stakeholders. An international SAP project becomes a daunting task as the target is always changing. It is imperative for the SAP Implementation Manager to analyze changes and manage change requests using Agile methods as discussed in the Chapter 2, without negotiating the end implementation goals to achieve and the quality of the deliverables.

Let's examine a typical case study, a large automotive enterprise implementing SAP for its end-to-end operations. Most of these implementation projects pose a huge risk related to integrating with the legacy systems in the landscape. There are major pitfalls that plague an ERP implementation project as can be seen in Table 4-1.

Table 4-1. *ERP Implementation Pitfalls*

Category	Pitfall	Mitigation
People	Lack of support from the end-users and business SMEs Lack of teamwork Lack of right skill Lack of design thinking Stakeholders responsibilities Lack of conflict resolution could lead to distress	Involve end users/business SMEs from design phase Motivate the team Hire right people/vendor Think from the end-product vision Ensure accurate reporting and ensure stakeholders participation Handle conflicts with open and honest communication to improve
Process / Project Management	Lack of process Lack of scope control Lack of project plan / WBS Lack of Agile development methods / RDS Lack of end user training leading to issues Lack of adequate Integration testing Lack of standardized estimation Lack of metrics based project environment Global/local implementation	Use standard implementation methodology ASAP/Agile with tools, accelerators, and methods Use RDS and POC to build the prototype Implement change control process approved by change control board (CCB) Implement metrics based measurements for high quality deliverables Use standard estimation techniques using benchmark standards to size a project accurately Develop baseline project plan Plan testing activities diligently including integration Plan end-user training with required time for classroom and online training sessions Plan global template with region based "wave" rollout strategy
Technology/ Method	Lack of software ecosystem knowledge and customization requirements with product limitations Lack of rapid prototype required in niche areas of Implementations Lack of global vision Lack of goal specific customizations Data migration issues	Proof of concept study Implementing global template with common blueprint can avoid costly site specific implementations Do not try to force-fit a solution in SAP, without analyzing the impact and limitations of the product If you keep customizing beyond a point, you'd be recreating a product, missing the benefits of a packaged ERP software Plan release bundles using Agile methods based on product backlogs, instead of big-bang implementation approach Understand the organization data model and challenges upfront during the blueprint and plan ahead Use accelerators, methods, and reusable assets from the past implementation projects

Above all, if you're implementing a new technology that is not yet proven in the market, this could lead to failed implementations as a result of instability of the product release. If you analyze the root cause of each of these factors, the reasons are due to both business-related and project-related challenges.

Fundamentally, if you have good project management methodology such as SAP ASAP with Agile, then you'll be able to mitigate some of the project-related challenges.

There are a few options to implement SAP as a big bang or a phased as a rollout approach for sites as bulk or individual rollout. It makes sense that this strategic commitment must be promoted throughout the entire organization because of the length of time that it can take to implement SAP. We will discuss pros and cons of each of these strategies and the best practices for a global enterprise.

Global Project Planning

There are two primary challenges in global project planning:

- You must architect an end-to-end solution in SAP, from an end-goal perspective, understanding all integration scenarios of ERP, APO/TM, BI/BO, CRM, and HR.

- You must identify complexities of the business requirements, leading to customizations. Once you identify the solution, then the next question will be, how do you implement it? Your deployment strategy might include starting with headquarters, and then roll out to the specific sites as a global template option or as a site-specific independent option or even as a bulk rollout for sites within a specific continent. Let's discuss each of these options briefly.

During the global project planning exercise and when SAP is about to be implemented in International locations, a number of issues and challenges come up, which require careful planning and preparation. These issues circle around these main areas:

- Identifying key business process and integration scenarios

- Identifying AS-IS client landscape

- Aligning with the overall business strategy

- Customization complexities, and customizing SAP beyond 20 percent and common data standards and data migration issues

I categorize issues briefly into the following categories such as: (a) people, (b) process/project management, and (c) technology. The main issue arises as a result of the lack of skill, lack of teamwork, and low morale from a people perspective. Second, process expertise in mapping complex business problems in SAP, which is the understanding of requirements, can cause failure. Finally, the technology might have limitations, which will cause problems. In addition, you might need to tweak the standard software and/ or develop your own custom application during the realization phase, altering the standard behavior of the product, causing several integration issues. In any of these cases, it might be tricky as you might change the standard behavior causing several iterations, resulting in integration-related issues. You must understand these limitations in the product and comprehend the challenges. You must be honest and reveal your discovery to the customer.

One of the common pitfalls in large global implementation is due to lack of change management and cross-cultural integration. The rollout deployment should be clear to mitigate risks from time to time. This is because the integration between headquarters and the various business functions is vital for a successful implementation. As an example, one of the large counties in the United Kingdom lost U.S. $30+ million in implementation expenses. The county scrapped ERP implementation after investing $30 million in the project, as shown in Table 4-2.

Table 4-2. *ERP implementation benchmark comparison*

Description	Benchmark	Failed ERP Implementation
Implementation Duration	15-18.5 Months	36 Months
Implementation Cost	$5-6.5 million USD	$30 million USD
Benefits Realized	35-40%	NA
Employee Satisfaction	50-60%	< 50%

The average ERP implementation was higher than the average implementation in terms of duration and costs. The satisfaction level between management and employees was lower than the benchmark standards (<50%). Figure 4-1 illustrates lessons learned from common pitfalls in failed implementations.

Figure 4-1. *Common ERP Pitfalls to Avoid*

Lack of defined goals:

- Ask yourself, why do you want to implement ERP?
- You must establish sense of purpose and goals
- Don't try to fit your business to the technology, it should be the other way around

Lack of business requirements:

- Envision the end product and be clear with your goals to achieve

- Focus on current processes (AS-IS) and mapping scenarios into SAP as TO-BE process

- Prioritize requirements as products backlogs, using Agile methods to identify core competencies

- Involve employees and key stakeholders in the process

Lack of skills:

- Build a high performance team

- Avoid too many customizations in one "go"

- Identify strengths and weakness of the implementation partner

Lack of realistic expectations:

- Once again, Agile methodology can help in identifying the product backlogs (requirements) with priority

- Benchmark with other projects to define a realistic implementation plan and budget to understand how long implementation will take in a similar Industry verticals/line of business with past performance of the project to benchmark

- Organizational change management and training

- Clearly defined business process hierarchy

- Adequate resources, timeline required for UAT and end-user training

Lack of business SMEs/end-users participation:

- Heavy user involved and business SMEs is a critical parameter throughout the implementation cycle

- Gain sign-offs at regular intervals

- Test, test, and test

- Go Live support

Lack of detailed business processes and workflows:

- Assess out-of-the-box best practices and preconfigured scenarios; however, don't assume that this can handle every single process

- Develop a configuration plan with gaps between as-is and to-be processes, focusing on opportunities to leverage best practices

- Define business process and workflows with a detailed plan

- Clearly communicate changes to employees

- Build training activities around business processes, not system transactions

Lack of scope change control:

- Identify strong internal and external project team members

- Ensure that the team has solid ERP experience

- Managing software vendor through the project lifecycle

- Consider independent oversight and validation

- Prioritize and manage software customizations

Lack of metric-based project environment:

- If you don't measure, you won't achieve it. Use earn value management and cost performance index metrics to gain meaningful insights from every milestone

- Establish postimplementation performance improvement targets, based on business case

- Conduct postimplementation audits and make adjustments as necessary

- Don't expect that all projected business benefits will be achieved right away

- Initial postimplementation audits tend to focus on working out issues in the business processes

- Continuously improve business processes where possible

In summary, most failed implementation projects are a result of business and human issues, and partially technology, as it may have limitations to the critical processes that customer has envisioned.

Now, let us study global rollout strategies in a complex implementation project.

Global Rollout Strategies

You'll need to understand the client landscape, business strategy, and complexities involved. It should provide solutions to the complex business problems, centralized and extensible in terms of addressing to the ever-expanding business needs. The ERP and IT solution provided must help clients focus on the business, while driving the innovation using IT services. The project management team and steering committee must make strategy development its highest priority. In general, there are three potential approaches for implementing SAP globally:

- Implementing individual projects

- Creating a centrally developed implementation, which is a global template design with local rollouts

- Rolling out projects based on production implementations

Each of these approaches presents its own set of advantages and challenges/risks. Combining these strategies may be the ideal strategy, in particular at larger organizations with different business units and divisions and widespread global operations. In one of the largest consumer products organizations based in Europe, we had tremendous challenges in consolidating the IT/ERP operations, as there were three huge ERP instances. Hence, there were challenges implementing new projects and/or enhancements. In addition, the change and release management was a complex task. Now, imagine the cost and schedule overruns due to region-based instances, maintained individually as a separate system. Wouldn't it be better to implement a standardized global template? This strategy would alleviate change management issues.

Primarily, there are multiple ways of deploying SAP solution, including:

- Global template with rollout strategy for site-specific region, which is the standardized approach of common business processes across headquarters and subsidiaries. Once you standardize business process, the template and subsequent rollout will be site-specific to regions and countries.

- Individual project deployments are cumbersome in a global scenario

- Rollout approach for site-specific deployments

All factors In Table 4-3 indicate that a global template is the best way forward. However, a global template is not suitable for plants with varied business processes at different plant sites.

Table 4-3. *Implementation strategy for global projects*

Strategy	Individual	Rollout	Global Template
a) Integration benefits	No	Yes	Yes
b) Maintenance Costs	High	Medium	Low
c) Uniform Process & Functions	Good	Better	Best
d) Single Central Development Costs	High	Medium	Low

An example of a global rollout can be seen in Figure 4-2.

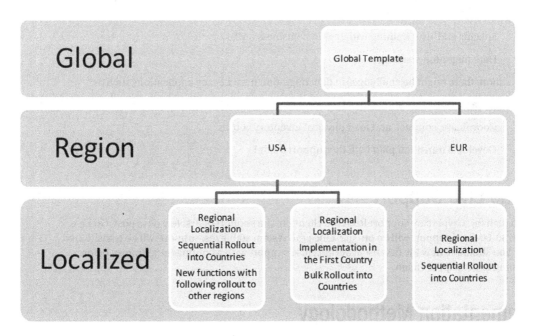

Figure 4-2. *Global Rollout Strategy*

First, you'd evolve a common business blueprint to build the global template during the common blueprint phase. The region-specific templates will be further evolved for respective regional instances, followed by a rollout to the respective countries as highlighted above with specific customizations such as tax, payroll, HR, language requirements, and so on. It can be a country-by-country sequential rollout or a bulk rollout for countries in that region, depending on specific constraints.

You'll need to test for the specific country, following ASAP 8.0 best practices to ensure that the customization for a specific country is done, such as local currency conversion, tax, payroll, and language settings. I remember a classic example of rollout to Brazil, which had a significant deviation in taxation from the standard SAP. Hence, there were additional custom developments to adapt to Brazil taxation policies. There is a strong program management required to monitor the global template with subsequent rollout for sites. The project plan should be exhaustively listing all critical paths for the site specific scenarios such as UAT, Cut Over, and Dry Run & Go Live. The RDS methodology can accelerate some of the deployments depending on fitment in the relevant process areas. In one of the projects that I had managed, there were major gaps between the global template with the local requirements, such as local specific taxation, G/L, specific SAP profiles, security, and training requirements for each region.

The PMO from HQ will be responsible for the executive oversight of the entire project; however, the respective region-/country-specific PM will be involved on a day-to-day basis to ensure that successful configuration requirements are met. There are specific challenges in commissioning site-specific infrastructure requirements such as:

- Network, access requirements for site specific, number of users and accessories such as printers, and so on

- Hardware installation, data communication acquisition, and installation

- Each site-specific UAT, Cut Over, and Go Live will need to be planned with required dry run dress-rehearsals

- Specific end-user training with regional business SMEs

- Data migration challenges

In addition, there might be challenges in data migration from Legacy applications such as:

- Extract, transform, and load data

- Coordinate, conduct, and load physical inventory counts

- Develop a transition plan with the support model

Post Go Live Support

You must plan for a hypercare support from the client on-site support of first few days post–Go Live. Typically, 30-60 days' support will be on-site. Once the system stabilizes, support will be transitioned offshore. You should review the first fiscal period close support with a contingency strategy before transitioning to the support team.

Implementation Methodology

The global rollout strategy determines the implementation project methodology to be used, as each strategy has its individual requirements for planning and executing the project (i.e., a series of subprojects). Let's analyze each of these strategies in detail.

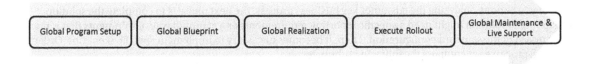

Figure 4-3. *Global ASAP Methodology*

If you're implementing an SAP solution for a small or medium enterprise, then the challenges are fewer when compared to the global implementations. Some of the common pitfalls for small and medium enterprises include:

- Lack of solution validation: The solution validation phase of the implementation project encompasses list of detailed critical business process with implementation strategy and mapping scenarios. If the specific solution such as standard order to cash (OTC) process doesn't fit the customer-specific OTC process, then every due diligence should be done to develop enhancements (exits) to adapt to customer requirements.

- Lack of UAT: Many projects fail at UAT because of a lack of acceptance from the business. I would recommend early solution validation with multiple releases of the solution.

- Lack of stakeholder support: It is imperative to discuss strategy and gain acceptance of solutions with intermediate SAP channel partners into steering committee to safeguard common interests.

- Change requests and requirements gathering: Metrics will help in traceability of the business processes implemented from the requirements.

- Lack of skill: This is the last thing that any client would like to hear. Avoid surprises to the quality of deliverables. The PM must invest time in recruiting and hiring certified candidates with experience to mitigate the risks of poor quality of deliverables.

- Lack of integration: –Integration within SAP and with respective third-party applications is very critical.

Requirements are less complex in middle-sized and small enterprises; hence, you can configure the product and showcase it to end users in regular intervals to gain concurrence to the product implementation.

SAP Organization Structure

Organization structure is the fundamental unit of SAP, with the global design can help collaborating within the organization, as well as with global customers and vendors. The key aspects of the organization structure are:

- Flexibility considering the changes in the business environment such as mergers and acquisitions

- Tight integration of business processes

- Authorization control

- Basic and master data creation and maintenance

Business Process Integration

Once you're done analyzing the customer key business process, the next phase is to complete the solution mapping. A solution might need a specific reporting requirements or a standard way of shipments that is not addressed in the standard configuration. Then, it becomes necessary to implement specific scenarios. Order to cash processes encompass the following subprocesses:

- Quotation

- Sales Order

  - Sales order fulfillment (SD)

  - Availability check (MM)

  - Credit check (FI)

- Delivery

  - Methods of goods delivery between global companies

- Billing

  - Intercompany billing

  - Credit revenue (FI)

  - Updates (FI)

Every customization will result in additional maintenance, and an upgrade of standard SAP software releases or support packs could impact the business.

Now, the key question is how to address the issues faced by customers, especially in the order management process. It is vital to develop custom objects to deliver inbound/outbound logistics management, various controls to check flow through various stages of sales order cycle, modules for RFP creation, and comparison and vendor evaluations in one-click with additional reporting for tracking sales orders and billing. The first step is to understand the key business process in order fulfillment process:

- Define Chart of Accounts, General Ledger

- Define reporting requirements

- Define archiving and authorization requirements

Key Controlling areas

- Common controlling structures

- Product-related groupwide results and budget

Key Planning areas

- Customer-related groupwide results and budget planning

- Decisions regarding common approaches to costing

- Profitability analysis and international profit

- Establishing common data standards

One of the most common pitfall is the lack of consistent global standards such as data format for each entity within the organization. If you have the same material existing in different manufacturing facilities, this could lead to data redundancy, thus resulting in missed customer delivery. Hence, an organization should strive for common global standards to support tighter integration and collaboration. Critical aspects of global data management include:

- Definition of global data structures and fields across different locations

- Consistency in authorization across client levels

- Consistency in numbering systems

- Synchronized maintenance of global customers, vendors, and products

System Landscape Design (SLD)
Centralized versus Decentralized Systems

A centralized SLD indicates a single SAP instance with single client, which means that there is one central repository for maintenance of master data. A global company like Nestlé might have one SAP instance operating from Europe as a central instance strategy or perhaps they can design SLD to have independent region specific instances for every region. SAP provides application link enabling (ALE) for decentralized processing. SAP ALE is a set of processes and tools that allow applications on different systems talk to each other, seamlessly as one unit.

One pitfall using ALE functionality is the asynchronous mode of communication, which doesn't allow communication in real time. SAP ALE is comprised of functionality and tools that address the following:

- Interface between SAP systems

- Communication protocol, monitoring, and error handling

Robust Design

One of the common pitfalls is the lack of robust design of the SAP landscape, leading to failed implementations. It is important to design the SAP landscape with the client requirements in mind, including all complexities and overall cost. In addition to the instance strategy, we would discuss how these SAP instances are hosted on a single or multiple servers, which would help you in simplifying your IT requirements. These factors form the base of decisions such as hosting on-cloud and HANA DB, which provides one platform for the entire SAP application suite.

Figure 4-4 illustrates a simple MCOD instance, which means multiple applications can be grouped as schemas in one database, the concept of HANA database.

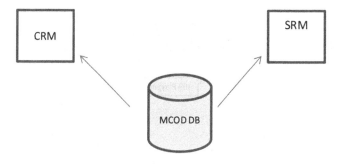

Figure 4-4. SAP MCOD DB

Multiple SAP instances can be installed and configured on a single physical server, often reducing both acquisition and systems as illustrated in Figure 4-5. The number of instances might increase over a period of time; hence, some of the enterprises would consider options such as instance consolidation, which simply indicates the consolidation of multiple instances into one global instance.

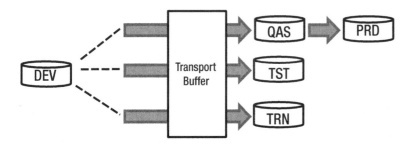

Figure 4-5. *SAP Instance Consolidation*

As discussed earlier, the SAP Landscape is made up of *systems* (also called instances) and *clients*. The SAP Client Landscape consists of the following systems (instance):

- Sandbox (SBX), Development (DEV), Quality Assurance (QAS), Training (TRN) with multiple clients as illustrated below.

- Production (PRD)

One client is designated in the production system, with other clients used for development, testing, and training, as illustrated in Figure 4-6.

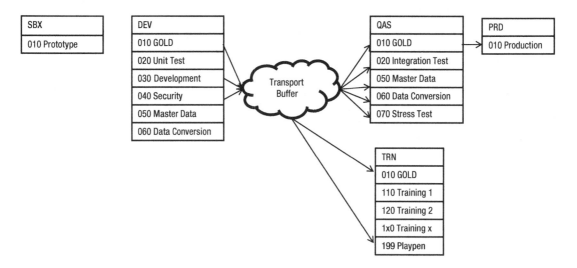

Figure 4-6. *Client Landscape Strategy*

Managing Risks

You'll need to develop a robust risk management process to mitigate above mentioned risks in the project, as illustrated in Figure 4-7. The sequence of activities indicates initiating, identifying risks based on inputs from the team and client to create a risk plan, and monitoring throughout the project realization and control. These risks are unavoidable; however, the mitigation plan to monitor and control is crucial for a successful implementation.

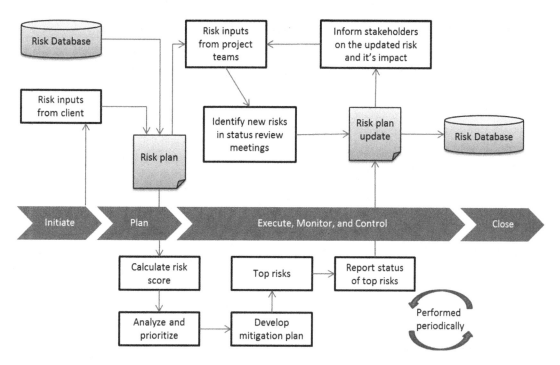

Figure 4-7. *Risk Management*

A detailed mitigation plan with the assigned risk owner will help you monitor a risk closely. If you have a risk score for each of these risks, then you'll be able to assess the impact based on the probability of occurrence. You should develop a mitigation plan to ensure these risks are monitored and controlled, with a risk plan update. A risk dB in the past implementation projects would help you monitor and plan actions early.

Concluding Remarks

International implementations are complex, expensive, and risky with major pitfalls such as scope, budget, schedule, stakeholders' responsibilities, skills, knowledge of the client's landscape, and so on. Site-specific customizations could lead to several issues. Above all, the knowledge of SAP software ecosystems, with phased and/or big bang rollout strategy and client-instance approach, is critical for success. With robust common data standards, release and change management, stakeholder's responsibilities are critical for a successful implementation. It is imperative to understand the business implications, issues, and potential problems to avoid failure.

CHAPTER 5

Approach to SAP Testing and QM Best Practices

Most of the projects fail due to common pitfalls such as lack of robust quality management practices, test skills, and scope of quality defined. One of the critical tasks in any implementation projects is to set up a robust quality control plan and execute a robust quality management process to ensure successful implementation. The quality of deliverables determines successful project implementations. The quality plan must encompass metrics, inputs and outputs measured with established baseline, and benchmark standards to develop a high quality software product. SAP provides a module "SAP QM," which is an integrated quality management for manufacturing quality analysis. This is different from the SAP software quality management best practices that we will discuss in this chapter.

This chapter will include:

- Establish quality goals and metrics

- Establish test plan strategies and execution

- Unit, system, and end-to-end integration test strategy

- Defects monitor and control

- Continuous improvement strategy with tools and accelerators to improve the quality of projects implemented

---

Note SAP provides tools and accelerators for managing quality effectively, with best practices such as integration with rational test software. These accelerators will help you achieve milestones with high-quality deliverables.

Testing and QM Overview

No one wants to buy a product that is of low quality. Everyone wants the best of the best. Your clients are demanding to get the best software product in a challenging schedule, and budget. However, there cannot be any tradeoff for quality. I recently read an article about a large well-known chocolate company in the United States that had failed in its strategic implementation project in 1999-2000, leading to millions of dollars lost in orders. This was primarily due to lack of end-to-end testing and an urgency to deploy within stipulated time resulting in a major failure. It is imperative to test, test, and test rigorously until you're not able to find any more defects. In most of implementation projects involving a wave-based rollout approach, testing should encompass site-specific requirements analysis aligned to the overall implementation schedule.

It should be the only way of deliverables to the client, either deliver 'High' quality, which is defect free or NO deliverables. If you observe initiatives such as Six Sigma, introduced by Motorola and GE, as a concept to implement defect free products, measured in parts-per-million (PPM), which is a statistical analysis to measure defects. There is no point in delivering rapidly, negotiating the quality of deliverables. Whereas scope, schedule, and cost are pivotal to a project, QM is at the center of the PMI "Iron Triangle," which indicates the importance of QM. Hence, the quality manager dons the hat of a specialist, comes up with an overall strategy, design and develop test cases, automation using tools required with defined entry and exit criteria, and so on. At the time of writing, I was working as quality lead for a major cloud migration project for a U.S. beverage company.

Let's understand the critical success factors of quality management best practices:

- Clearly agreed acceptance criteria for testing

- Documented test scenarios with clear and agreed scope

- Availability of the required test scenarios

- Defined test scenarios with the acceptance criteria

- Master data requirements for testing

- Required skills with SAP expertise

- Defined procedures and activities for test preparation and execution

- Metric-based assessment of quality such as close follow-up on timely delivery during the testing phase

- Quick resolution of defects with defect metrics

- Quick escalation and decision on test scope and defect resolution

- No technical slow down or even interruption of testing

- Test management and/or project management must take quick decisions and to control the test process where necessary

There also are other pitfalls to avoid, such as lack of skills, unclear scope, communication, stake owner responsibilities, and so on. Each of these factors will have a direct impact in the quality of deliverables.

SAP Quality Management

Now, let us understand how you'd implement a robust quality management process for SAP solutions by following the best practices of agile processes. The diagram in Figure 5-1 shows a high-level overview of a typical quality management process in an SAP-centric project. The process can be triggered by two different events:

- SAP implementation project

- SAP software upgrade or migration projects

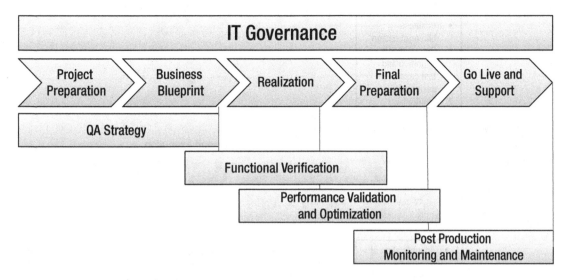

Figure 5-1. *Overview of the SAP Quality Management Process*

Figure 5-1 highlights the strategy and validation criteria established with the quality plan for optimization. You'll need to define the Quality goals at an early stage of the project, during the blueprint stage of the project. As it progresses into Realization phase, you'll be able to validate the functional solution implemented or the change and conduct validation checks on critical business process and/or performance evaluation. Once the project successfully goes live, then the Quality team will need to the process for a period of 60-90 days as a hypercare period to ensure successful transition with the process stabilization.

A detailed view of the SAP quality management process is indicated in Figure 5-2. The first step is to plan the quality strategy depending on the complexity of the project, then conduct periodic audits such as verification and optimization.

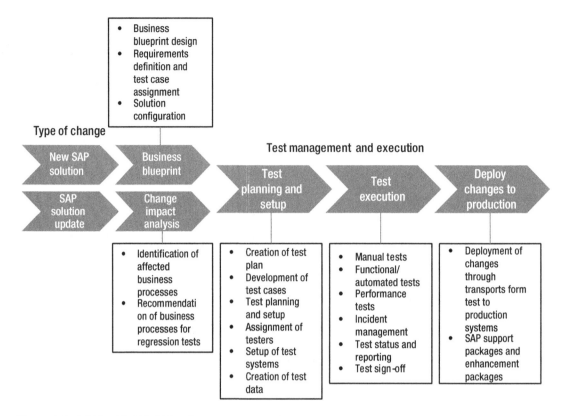

Figure 5-2. *ASAP with SAP QM tasks*

A Test Manager/Lead will be responsible to set up the team, planned at task level and define Quality goals. The following activities take place during the Test Plan, Execution and Result phase of the project as part of the ASAP-Realization phase, post developments. Now, let us see the sub-tasks involved in Test planning, Execution and Approval process. The Figure 5-3 illustrates the process flow of test planning, execution and approval process. This is the exploded view of the Realization phase of the project. If this is an implementation project, you'd define quality scope and establish benchmark standards for development.

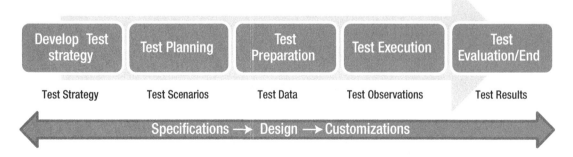

Figure 5-3. *Test Planning, Execution, and Approval Process Flow*

As you can see in Figure 5-2, which indicates an SAP upgrade project or an enhancement, there will be an additional step, evaluating the impact of a change. Let's explore detailed tasks involved in test plan, execution and control phases. Figure 5-3 illustrates a test plan and the execution and approval process flow.

A test lead will carefully evaluate complexities of the project at an early stage during the blueprint to assess the scope of testing with an execution plan. The outcome of this phase is to develop a strategy document, which includes test plan, acceptance criteria. The test strategy document will cover the test plan activities such as the unit, integration, and user acceptance test criteria, deliverables with input/output for acceptance.

Test Planning

Typically, a detailed test plan is developed for the unit, system, and user acceptance tests for large and complex projects. The documents will encompass a detailed description of the test objects and a plan, with tests to complete. The document will also include specifications of resources needed to execute the planned tests. These plans shall be approved by the supplier's project manager. Thereafter, it must be communicated to the respective test teams to ensure the right scope of the tests. The client business process/team leaders must be in sync, before the test execution, to concur on test scope. The technical and functional documentation must be available. Before starting the integration tests, the test environment must be established and tested. The test team with responsibility must be defined, and all routines and test observation procedures must be communicated to the test team. Typically, test scenarios will be provided by the client, post review by respective business process owners. After the quality control, the test scripts must be stored and communicated to the test team. This is the responsibility of the test manager. Typically, managing test data will be the responsibility of the client.

Test Execution

The tester will execute the test by using the test scenarios and the test data for the actual test stage (unit, system, and integration test). Errors are reported in the test report document. The tester will report all observations that are errors in parameters and/or user exits, or if something is not as specified in the new requirements specifications. The test manager and/or project manager will evaluate and prioritize the observed errors, and evaluate whether there is a need for regression testing after correction. The results of testing might include the following types:

- Identified errors in test data/master data

- Lack of clarity in the test scenario and/or test result

- Identified errors in the test scenarios

- Identified errors in the configuration of the test environment

- Change requests, which are not required

The SAP Application Deployment Management (ADM) team will correct errors, which are related to the setting of parameters and/or user exits, and document the process until the errors are corrected. As a test lead, you must ensure that the business requirements are identified with documented errors and communicated to the respective teams. As part of the development cycle, you'd retest wherever necessary post corrections. During the acceptance test, the user documentation will be verified and updated by the client. The focus will be on the user exits and customizing that the SAP consultants have developed, without focusing on the standard SAP functionality.

Figure 5-4 illustrates the scope of testing

Figure 5-4. *The Scope of Testing*

The following checks will be performed on custom developments to ensure integrity of the software from an end-to-end perspective:

- Check process output as per the test plan

- Check critical elements in the business processes

- Check integration points are working perfectly from end-to-end in life cycle testing

Typically, the scope of testing for the implementation partner will include testing the software from an end-to-end perspective; however, there are additional integration points, such as non-SAP software systems, which will need support from the respective partner ecosystem. For example, an inbound bank interface or HR interface will need support from the partner organization supporting the application.

Unit Test

Unit tests will be done using test scripts. Each test script is linked to a work step in client business process. The unit test will be carried out for all the work steps solved by SAP functionality. The unit tests will be executed by the development team. The unit tests will include testing of user exit programs and functional tests of processes set with parameters in the system.

System Test

The system test consists of life cycle tests, system integration tests, and performance tests. The system test will be carried out by using the test scenarios. Each test scenario is linked to a work process of key business process model. The system test will be done for all the work processes with respective functionality. A test scenario consists of a combination of test scripts used in the unit tests.

Scenario Testing

Scenario testing will include the selected scenarios such as the external integrations that are part of the customer's business processes. The test scenarios that are developed for this end-to-end process testing are based on the test script and scenarios developed in the unit and system test. As in the system test, the testers in the user acceptance test will monitor and comment on the performance of the system during acceptance testing.

Multiple Site Testing

The SAP solution is a central SAP installation that is used by many local offices at different regional locations. As part of the performance testing and verification, it is important to test from different locations in order to discover possible performance issues related to specific locations in the client environment. When executing the user acceptance test the user documentation will also be checked in order to verify that they describe client's processes in SAP.

Functional Tests

The functional tests will focus on the functional specifications of the systems. The tests will be carried out by using test scenarios. The technique is used both for the unit test, system test, and user acceptance test. The goal of these tests is to evaluate that input to the system is being processed, stored and transported as intended, and that the business logic is correctly implemented. Test objectives and methods are listed in Table 5-1.

Table 5-1. *Test Objectives and Methods*

Objectives	Description
1. Test Objectives	To verify the functionality of the test objects, including navigation, registration and processing
2. Test Method	Execution of tests based on the test scripts and test scenarios—with parameters set in the system. Test results report for system and acceptance test will be delivered at the end of test stages.
3. Test Scenario	The test scenarios will include a description of expected result in each step of the tests. Based upon this description, the tester will evaluate whether the result is correct or not.
4. Test Criteria	All planned tests are executed with relevant test data. The test environment is stable and similar to the production environment, and the quality of test data is good.

■ **Note**   Projects generally fail due to lack of test in the relevant production-like system, which causes issues at a later stage of the project during acceptance.

Performance Tests

As a test lead, you'll need to plan performance tests to ensure functional performance are included in the system and user acceptance tests. Typically, performance testing is done by using test tools for generating load on the system. The loadrunner test tool is used to create a significant load on the system. The performance test tool will be used for the following tests such as stress test, performance test, and stability test. Performance testing will be performed in two different alternative ways. The process bottlenecks in the setting of parameters and/or user-exits in processes will be monitored and controlled. In the test scenarios, there will be a check point for this activity.

Approval Criteria

The client will create, plan, and execute approval tests for each functional area. If there are errors related to the standard software, then these are not treated as development errors, and the respective service owner will raise OSS messages for response from SAP.

Before testing can start, there are a few preliminary tasks to complete:

- Test strategy/test management plan for unit, integration tests, test scripts, and test scenarios

- Relevant and adequate test data

- Test environment (not necessary for the unit tests)

- The right version of the system to be tested

- The right amount of testers with relevant skills is required for testing. Test scripts and test scenarios will be reviewed by the business process owners and the project manager. The test object is approved when the planned test scenarios are executed with errors reported and registered

- The necessity for correction of the medium and low category errors can be evaluated by the project manager. Also, the required regression test is completed. Table 5-2 indicated test deliverables that are provided to the client.

Table 5-2. *Test Deliverables Provided to the Client*

Deliverables	Description
1. Test Strategy	Over test plan document
2. Test Scenarios/Scripts	Description of the test script and the purpose of testing with the steps involved in executing the test with expected results, with statistics of completion
3. Test Results Report	Test results report for system and acceptance test will be delivered at the end of test stages. Test results will include exceptions, unplanned events, and execution results with errors

SAP Testing Automation Framework

The SAP test automation framework provides tools such as SAP TDMS for test data creation and execution using IBM Rational. In my current project, we are leveraging the Worksoft Certify tool, which is used to automate test cases for one of the major beverage manufacturers, which has around 550+ Integration scenarios with 258 Functional scenarios.

Now, let's see how we can leverage the testing best practices with the help of tools and accelerators for a successful implementation.

Let's focus on the rational software integrated with SAP Solution Manager —Rational ALM scenario. Once you create a business blueprint in Solution Manager, it can be easily transferred to the Rational software, which in turn used for creating the process hierarchy and test plan. Moreover, you'll be able to create test scripts, assign to the respective test case and execute each of these test scenarios. Once done, the test results and errors can be reported back to the SAP Solution Manager. It also helps in managing defects, which are transferred to Solution Manager as incidents to analyze in order to take care of necessary action.

Transfer a Business Blueprint

The main objective of integrating IBM Rational software with SAP Solution Manager is to build the requirements specifications and test cases, which are linked in one repository. Often times, you'd noticed that the process changes are not reflected in the business process document and/or the relevant test cases; hence as a result, it would lead to a loss of accurate information stored in the repository. Any upgrade, enhancements, or migration would result in a lot of revisions to the test cases.

You can transfer the blueprint from the SolMan to Rational software in order to create test plan and requirements set for test management. The business process content can also be extended to maintain important content for systems, interfaces, software vendors, transaction codes, training materials, and process documentation. As soon as the test scenarios are executed and the results can be transferred back to the solution manager. You can configure the Rational SAP Connector to create additional test plans and test cases. The test plans and test cases are automatically linked to the newly created requirements to ensure full lifecycle traceability.

You can review the information in the Rational requirements composer. The blueprint tree with hierarchy is maintained in the Requirements Composer project.

Test Management and Test Execution

The main activities in test management are planning the tests, defining the tests, documenting, in detail, how the tests will be executed, and executing the planned tests for a specific milestone or release. The main artifacts that result from those activities are test plans, test cases, test scripts, and test results. It is important that all artifacts provide full traceability back to the business requirements.

All requirements, test plans, and test cases are linked with Rational Quality Manager traceability features. The connector also maintains the Business Blueprint hierarchy by using the category feature in quality management. You can use the Filter by Category view to easily navigate the test cases based on the hierarchy.

These test cases are created automatically. The test cases are also linked to the requirements in the Requirements Composer that have been created as part of the blueprint push. It helps to have complete and consistent documentation and full life-cycle traceability.

Now, the next step is to link a test script to each test case. As discussed, you'll create the individual test cases. Test suites simplify the process of test execution and reduce errors such as the wrong test execution order. The Rational Quality Manager allows you to select a test plan, iteration, or a test environment. This information will be attached to the test result and is useful for reporting test progress across test plans and iterations.

The TER contains all relevant information from the test run: test case, test scripts, test environment, and, most important, the test results for each step.

The transfer of new test results from Rational Quality Manager to Solution Manager can run either automatically in a scheduled background job or manually through the Connector user interface. In either case, the test results are transferred back to Solution Manager and linked to the Business Blueprint requirements. A simple method to display the Rational Quality Manager test results in SAP Solution Manager is the Testing with IBM Rational Quality Manager option, which is accessible by calling the SOLAR_EVAL transaction directly. Select these options to reach the exact location: Project ➤ Test ➤ Test Results for Business Requirements Documents ➤ Testing with IBM Rational Quality Manager.

A tester will need to specify parameters and limit the analysis to a substructure of the business blueprint. The result of the analysis displays the project structure down to the business process step and the test results that have been transferred from Rational Quality Manager. The test results also contain information about the test case, the test execution record, the test state (Passed or Failed), and the affected test object.

One of the features that I like in Rational is the defects management, and change requests or problems and incidents. With this option, testers can quick raise defects as a result of a failed test run. The other option is to leverage the SAP Solution Manager Service Desk component to manage problems and incidents.

As discussed, you can use the Rational SAP Connector to link the rational change management system and the SAP Service Desk component. Ideally, an end user has an option to trigger a defect from Rational Team Concert, which is in turn linked to the Solution Manager. The links section of the defect form provides a menu option to add a related change request. In this example, the project is linked to a SAP Solution Manager Service Desk project.

Once you submit a defect, the defect is updated with a link to the new corresponding incident in the SAP Service Desk.

Alternately, you can also use SAP Service Desk to create an incident and align it to the Rational Team concert. You can use the External Help Desk section to select a Team Concert project and create a new defect report in the selected project.

There is an option to forward the incident to the External Help Desk, after the incident is saved. Clicking this option initiates the transfer and sends this incident into Rational Team Concert.

When the transfer is finished, the External Message ID column becomes populated with the new work ID. The ID is an active hyperlink to the new work item, and a click takes you into Rational Team Concert to see further details. An ISO 9001 certified organization is an organization will need to implement quality management system requirements for all areas of the business. The audit can be conducted by a number of different certification bodies; however, it is important to note that not all ISO 9001 auditing organization are UKAS accredited.

SAP QUALITY MANAGEMENT METRICS

A software life cycle will encompass testing as part of the inherent product development itself for continuous improvements.

Now, let's see a few test metrics critical for a successful implementation, which illustrates metrics such as the defect density, total number of requirements, pass versus fail ratio, and so on. It will help to benchmark projects and avoid repeating errors. A sample metric sheet is shown in Table 5-3.

Table 5-3. Quality Metrics

	Testing Phase	Test metrics	Definition	Purpose	Metrics Formula
			Quality Metrics		
Productivity	**Planning**	Test defect density	The number of valid defects per Raw test step	This metric is used to judge the effectiveness of test cases and quality of the product.	(Total no. of valid defects / Total raw Test steps)
		Scripting Productivity	The ratio of total Raw steps created and total man hour efforts required to write them	This metric is used to track the efficiency of the Testing Team in writing test scripts.	(Total Raw Test Steps created/ Effort in person hours)
	Execution	Test Execution Productivity	The ratio of total Raw steps executed and total person hours required to execute them	This metric signifies the number of raw test steps a team is capable of executing per hour which signifies productivity of the team	(Total Raw Test Steps * No. of pass) + Retested Raw Test Steps + Staging Raw Test Steps) /Effort in person hours

(*continued*)

Table 5-3. (*continued*)

Testing Phase	Test metrics	Definition	Purpose	Metrics Formula
			Quality Metrics	
Testing	**Planning** Review Defect Density	The effectiveness of reviews and the efficiency of writing test scripts.	This metric is used to judge the effectiveness and the quality of test scripts. Tracks the efficiency of the tester in writing test scripts.	(Total Weighted Review Defects / Total Raw Test Steps under Review)
	Effective defect density	The no. of Total *weighted defects per Raw test step	This metric is used to judge product quality considering the "weight" of defects in terms of their severity	(Total Weighted Defects /Total Raw Test Steps)
	Test Case Effectiveness	The percentage of the test cases that effectively check the requirement	This metric signifies the effectiveness of the test cases	(No. of Defects Mapped to Test Case /Total No. of valid Defects) *100
	Execution Defect rejection	The percentage of Rejected defects to the total number of defects that are opened	This metric determines the quality of the defects that are opened.	Weighted defects rejected/Total weighted defects detected)*100
	Testing Progress	Effort & schedule variance for test planning & test execution	This gives Effort & schedule variance.	Test Cases Executed vs Planned
	Defect Reported	Percentage of defects accepted as valid against total defects logged.	This metric signifies the Test team's quality in finding & reporting defects.	Total Valid defects / Total number of defects logged
	Defect Leakage	Number of defects found in production that were missed during testing execution	This metric is to determine the overall efficiency of the testing team	(Total valid defects raised in phase n+1 /Total valid defects raised in phase n + total valid defects raised in phase n+1) * 100
Product Quality	**Test Coverage** Defect without test cases vs. Total defects detected	Addresses Test scripts not executed by reasons against the Total Planned Test scripts	The purpose of this metric is to track the Test scripts not executed against the number planned for execution. Helps in analyzing the reasons for the Test Slippage.	(Test Scripts not executed /Total Planned Test scripts)

Concluding Remarks

In this chapter, you've learned about SAP testing methodology, including test planning and execution tasks, using tools such as Rational QM product integrated with SAP Solution Manager. Let's move on to the next chapter, in which we will discuss our approach on cut over plan and go live best practices.

■ ■ ■

CHAPTER 6

Approach to Cut Over and Go Live Best Practices

Now, one of the major pitfalls plaguing the SAP implementation is lack of planning the cut over and go live phase. As you'd realize, Cut over phase is the most important phase to do it right and complete a successful go live. Let's see, how you manage a successful Cut Over phase. It's not enough to getting near the finishing line, you'll need to complete it. Hence, cut over phase is extremely crucial for the team to succeed in any implementation project. There are few aspects of a cut over that you'll need to understand the key risks involved in managing cut over scope, governance, data migration, define freeze periods, interface checks and the rollback plan. As a cut over manager and/or a project manager, you'll be directly responsible for managing the cut over tasks to a successful go live phase. Let's understand the go live ecology, cut over overview, plan and templates. Now, before we dive deep into pitfalls due to lack of planning cut over ahead, let us understand the basics of cut over and the process involved during cut over. You might be a project manager, assigned to manage the cut over tasks and/or a specialist Cut Over manager, the basic objectives of cut over must be clear with defined scope, boundaries and execution plan to precision as you're going to be launching the new product soon.

What is Go live?

I hope it is not too late to ask this question, as often you're caught napping as a project and/or release manager confronted by a cut over plan and execution. Hence, it is imperative to assess the scope of cut over, assess risks with a mitigation plan to ensure a successful go live. Well. Let's analyze the basics of go live. As you know, go live is a move from one defined state to another defined state. In SAP go live ecology, a go live may indicate an SAP upgrade to the latest support pack, enhancement service pack level, and/or a Greenfield implementation where the key business process will go live in SAP. The go live is supposed to minimize on-going risks, enhance business process with several stakeholders and tasks involved. It usually involves a defined window of time for dry runs and cut over activities, along with rollout tasks if needed.

What Is a Cut Over?

A Cut Over is a process that involves execution of planned tasks by several stakeholders. There are many critical activities that a PM should take care of during the cut over period related to the infrastructure, testing, and disaster recovery plan and business acceptance prior to finalizing the cut over. A dry run is a dress rehearsal of the entire production goes live, tracked by the entire team with every single task measured diligently. There are pitfalls to avoid during a cut over such as lack of dedicated dry runs might falter a cut over plan as it evolves in dry run (i) and (ii) depending on the complexity of the implementation. Typically, as a good practices we recommend at least two dry runs to mitigate the risks of a failure. The activities of cut over will encompass final data migration, infrastructure readiness, final round of business acceptance for critical process with sanity checks and then technical cut over which is exactly the start of data migration, followed by a final business cut over, which is the actual downtime in case of an Upgrade project, whereas it refers to the actual cut off for the business migration to productive instance.

Now, let us see the cut over characteristics.

Key considerations include:

- Migrate tested functionality to production

- Performed at least once or twice to document issues and timings

- Variance from cut over for Production should be well understood

- Best practices should be implemented using lessons learnt

Characteristics of Cut Over?

It should be well planned with the following characteristics:

a. Meet customer demand and stakeholder communication

b. Ramp down business such as close open items and notify customers

c. Key decision point made by stakeholder

- Go Live or

- Rollback

d. Business ramp up

Now, let us see the different phases of cut over.

Phases of Cut Over?

A cut over consists of pre-cut over, cut over and post-cut over phases.

Pre-cut over activities

- Build production environment

- Cut over plan development

- Test cut over plan

- Dry run (rehearsal) X 1 or 2 or 3

- Finalize cut over plan

Cut over activities

- Execute cut over plan

- Perform Checks

- Go No Go Decision

Post go live support

- Transition to support team and issue management

Cut Over Plan

A cut over plan is a comprehensive document that includes all cut over related tasks with a rollback plan. Also, contains stakeholders and their tasks with decision checkpoints. It should encompass a detailed list of activities with start/end date and time for trial cut over. It should facilitate coordination between key players and stakeholders. Typically, cut over plan is owned by a project manager or a key stakeholder with the participation of the business and IT with the use of tools such as SolMan to manage the cut over process and report progress over cut over tasks. Any change to the cut over plan will need to be validated and managed by the cut over team, with the associated risks explained and contingency plan discussed. Typically, a cut over plan will consist of detailed tasks to perform, owner of the task, with description. Also, it will list rollback options in case of failures.

Cut over risks are highlighted in Table 6-1.

Table 6-1. *Cut over Risks*

Criteria	Risk Score	Assigned To
Site	High Impact	
Technology	Medium	
Training	Low	
Data migration	High	
Sustainment	Low	
Functionality	Medium	
Cut over planning	High	
Tools	High	
Resources availability	Medium	
	High	

Typically, a cut over plan is maintained in a spreadsheet with the following components:

- Document control with version control, owner, contributors, reviewers, issue list

- Properties

- Resources (with clear RACI matrix defined)

  a. Cut over escalation

  b. Post implementation Support Plan

  c. On-site/Remote Resources

- War room for an on-site period to ensure immediate attention for escalating issues and team should be one to discuss and resolve issues without impacting anything else, around the clock

- Conf. bridges

- Risk scorecard

- Cut over plan should contain task, owner, dependencies, duration, status, scores, and process improvement opportunity

- DR-Restore, which is similar to the cut over plan to restore the system to the original state

- Transition and contingency plan

- Preparations for production and production schedule: first week.

- Detailed transition plan

  a. Tasks, checklists

- Cut over contingency plan

  a. Contingency steps, upon system availability

- Preparation for production

  a. Discuss approach

- Production schedule

  a. First week

  b. Using complete infrastructure support

  c. Information system production feedback session

  d. Support status

Why Are SAP Cut Overs So Complex?

If you're spending lot of time in execution, and yet the systems are rehearsed with required number of dry runs, then there is a possible risk hidden during the cut over. It is imperative for a release and/or cut over manager to ensure that lists of transports are carefully reviewed as per the priority with necessary approvals post impact analysis and transported post trial cut over. If not, there is possible risk escalation with a potential failure.

The rollback plan is essential, if you aren't doing it early in a trial cut over, then there is a possibility of an induced risk at the time of actual cut over. Accidentally moved transports could jeopardize the entire cut over plan or blocks of missing transports cut falter the schedule. There are hosts of things that can go wrong if not planned with every task on your spreadsheet with specific tasks to accomplish. Now, the key question is to make the SAP cut overs simple and easy task to achieve.

How Do I Make SAP Cut Overs Easy?

The key task here is to effectively managing the transports. There are tools such as RevTrack to support managing the transports and keep up-to-date stock of TRs moved to production. SAP has its native SolMan ChaRM, which is intended for managing change requests, with the central tracking of transports. It's really simple to use SolMan ChaRM to manage transports without much of time spent on phone calls and/or emails. Perhaps the SAP SolMan can be used to check the conflicts during the TR import into production. SolMan gives you the overall SAP landscape. There are options in ChaRM to hold the transport requests back to the approval process. The entire list of TRs can be checked for sequence and test in pre-production systems, which would eventually save a lot of time and avoids any major pitfalls in managing transports, and the cut over itself.

In my experience of using SolMan for cut overs with various customers, the response is always the same whether we talk to the Basis team, functional and technical consultants, architects, release managers, testers or the business. You'll be amazed to use it as a simple repository for all changes required during cut over and keep track of every single change. You should leverage SolMan to ease cut over pressure by managing transports effectively, which is one of the best practices of implementation projects. Now, let us see how to plan a cut over based on a real time case study.

■ **Note**   A cut over plan is a detailed set of activities to be performed for a successful go live including data migration, transition actions with specific start and end dates, and so on.

Cut Over Strategy

Let us examine a cut over strategy based on a real-time case study.

Broadly, you'd classify the Cut over phase into pre-cut over, cut over, and post-cut over activities. The pre-cut over phases involve communicating to the various stakeholders, finalizing the exact date of cut over, system readiness, and business downtime. As stated in this case study, the pre-cut over tasks started in December for a period of four to six weeks, which includes dry run x 1 or x 2 or X 3, go live functionality checks if necessary. This is then followed by the go live.

Cut Over Approach

The cut over approach involves working alongside client IT, the local business, and third-party solution partner; we ran workshops to confirm the scope of the data migration and then developed a strategy and plan based on the SAP data migration methodology. The key activities were mapping workshops, data quality analysis, ETL development, two test cycles, data acceptance, a dress rehearsal, and then the final cut over migration. We put in place data validation and acceptance procedures and an issue management process to manage and track status during the test phases. Partner consulting put in place a structured approach to preparing and executing the cut over plan.

A high-level cut over plan will be reviewed and approved by the project team leads and stakeholders, by identifying all teams and resources involved in the cut over activities. Then the next step is scheduling and executing a series of review sessions to gather all relevant information from the team leads to develop the draft cut over plan. Presenting the plan to project stakeholders and all relevant parties to sign off.

The cut over execution phase involves managing the execution of cut over and developing a status management strategy to ensure all tasks are communicated and managed. This activity includes preparing cut over checkpoint reports, scheduling and chairing regular checkpoint meetings, managing action items and risks and issues.

The stakeholder engagement will be responsible for informing the project stakeholders of recent activity, next steps and risks and issues through summary status reports, in biweekly stakeholder update meetings. The cut over comprises of the following activities planned with specific data and time of completion as highlighted in Table 6-2.

Table 6-2. *Cut Over Task List*

Activity	From	To
End user training	MM-DD-YYYY	
Creation of master data		
Dry run I		
Go/no-go decision		
Dry run II		
Create orders		
Cut over go live phase		
Go/no-go decision		
Go live support		
Hypercare support		
Month-end support		
Handover to support team		

Preliminary Cut Over Tasks

The cut over plan is based on the following starting points, taking into account the starting points for any previous cut over activities for any other waves already been met and signed-off. All partners involved in the cut over process share the responsibility for the process; The cut over process will be planned and controlled by the cut over core team, consisting of persons from different functional and technical areas; During the cut over initial functional and technical tests will be performed by the key users and IM architects to assure the correctness of the cut over; The whole data conversion process will take place; The cut over of most transaction data will take place in the cut over "week" (including the weekend). This is the period spanning from start date to end date, the date of the official go live. Due to the fact that no shipping to and from site is expected on the sites involved from start date to end date, critical cut over activities such as the stock take and upload will be executed in this period. The key supply chain activities will be left undisturbed by the project cut over phase activities as much as possible. There will be no shipments from sites in scope between start date and end date, the official go live date. All transaction data (stocks, debtors, creditors, other balances) will be loaded with posting period.

The pre cut over checklist consists of a set of activities to check (see Table 6-3).

Table 6-3. *Illustrates Pre-Cut Over Checklist*

Activity	From	To
Finalizing transports for all workstreams	--	--
Plan for the delta transports		
Implement necessary OSS notes		
Finalize and confirm batch jobs are on hold		
Create and issue a cut over id		
Back up the entire system		
Bounce servers		
Cleanup info cubes (BW system)		

Cut Over Governance

The cut over process is monitored by several people, in particular by the cut over coordinator. The cut over coordinator will report to project management, there are different business owners involved and reporting to the steering committee on progress and issues. The cut over coordinator will work closely with all of the involved project team members in order to ensure a smooth and well-coordinated go live phase. The specific actions will be identified by the cut over coordinator, and problems encountered will be reported to him, too, so as to take appropriate actions and inform the appropriate community. Now, let us observe key SAP basis admin-related tasks as part of cut over tasks:

- Lock users

- Transport imports

- Reorg tables

- Resolve transport errors

- Assign manual tasks

- Finalize preconversion system checkout

- Identify and plan all necessary conversions

- Finalize postconversion system checkout

Post cut over:

- Unlock users

- Plan business communication readiness to the users

- Assemble the hyper care team

- Schedule all batch jobs

- Compare project plan with actual dates and freeze the plan

- Create lessons learnt document

- Reorganize team members who supported well

In the next section, we will discuss the critical technical tasks performed by the SAP basis admin during the critical cut over phase of an SAP upgrade project, with key functional activities.

A REAL-TIME CUT OVER CASE STUDY

The project involved upgrading SAP ECC EHP 4.0 to EHP 7.0. The cut over plan indicates SAPup basis preparation, checks required with dB backup done prior to the actual downtime start. The SAPup indicates the Upgrade execution phase, post which transports and manual checks are performed. Finally, the system will be released to the business users for quick validation checks, which is the actual go/no go phase. After this phase and upon acceptance, the system is available for the end users. A detailed cut over plan will define set of activities with start and end dates as highlighted below based on a real-time case study.

General preparation—During the pre-cut over period general preparations include finalizing the cut over plan and planning (cookbook) and making sure all resources required are available and instructed as per their tasks. This includes a cut over preparation session, including local implementation team and global implementation team. Now, let's examine key functional and business activities performed during a cut over phase.

As explained earlier, there is a host of activities that you'll need to take care during the cut over phase as described below in preparing the business, organization for the changes, prep for master data, and freeze period strategy. Let's review each of these tasks in detail, these tasks are imperative in a large and global implementation, and rollout projects.

Business Preparations

The regional and global business will need to prepare for the impact on both the internal organization as the impact on the external business partners (vendors, customers, etc.) and prepare the cut over activities to be performed under the business responsibility. The following activities, as a prerequisite for the cut over, are expected to come to a finalization as per the project plan.

Organizational Change Management

The preparation of organizational change will be based on impact assessment of changes brought by the new project system with the preparation and execution of the communication plan for external parties. The plan includes what will change, for example, partner numbers; material numbers; document numbers. The plan will include additionally when these changes will take effect and if testing activities, for example, for interfaces, are to be anticipated.

Master Data Preparation

This activity involves the harmonization of master data objects, cleansing of master data objects, removing obsolete objects, extraction of data for, and/or manual filling of upload data sheets with preparatory steps for stock takeover, validation of blocked stock, decision on obsolete stock items, preparation for an inventory count, and preparation for handling the system freeze period.

Determine Master Data Change Freeze Period

The following points indicate key functional components to manage during the cut over phase of the SAP implementation project.

- Determine and implement procedure for handling data changes in the freeze period

- Determine outbound and inbound shipping freeze period

- Determine manufacturing freeze period

- Determine procurement freeze period

- Determine exception procedure for handling shipment movements, manufacturing, and procurement in the freeze period

■ **Note** Strategy for handling the freeze period and takeover of open documents is indicated as part of system preparations.

In order to deliver a system ready for use by the business in the cut over execution, such as planning the system cut over activities as per detailed cut over cookbook, including alignment of third parties involved for the technical enabling interfaces. This includes both functional streams as the technical stream.

The following cut over activities include critical tasks from a business perspective.

- Business execution—Execute inventory count, manual master data creation (objects excluded from automatic data migration scope), manual transactional data creation (objects excluded from automatic data migration scope)

- System execution—Detailed system cut over activities are described in a typical cut over cookbook. Main steps include:

  - Transport configuration—Manual configuration, manual (master) data creation (subset of the total set of manual data creation)

  - Post-Cut over activities—The main post cut over activities include supporting the business organization in using the new system by Project BPSs, resolving outstanding issues resolved, and decommissioning legacy systems.

  - Support arrangements just after go live

Configuration—SAP Transports

The configuration of the SAP systems, including ECC and BI, are done by means of the SAP transportation systems. This will make sure the settings for the implementation are imported in a concise and complete way. Transports and sequence are kept as part of the SAP transport management system. Strategy is based on the following principle: All configurations in transport are transported to the NEW environment. With manual configuration is done additionally as per cookbook.

Key Functional Considerations

Now, let us observe a few key functional considerations during the cut over phase. Table 6-4 indicates key PO, GR/IR considerations during the cut over phase in a large implementation project.

Table 6-4. *Key Cut Over Considerations from the Functional View*

Situation	PO Created	GR Created	IR Created	PO Migration	FI Migration
Case I	Yes	No	No	Manual creation of PO	N/A
Case II	Yes	Yes	No	No action	Booking FI invoice upon receipt
Case III	Yes	No	Yes	Manual creation of PO	-
Case IV	Yes	Yes	Partial	No action	Book remaining FI invoice upon receipt list required

The situation of the purchase order/invoices to be received item will be looked at as of date and needs close attention. The following actions need to be performed prior to cut over date:

- Monitor invoices to be received account in legacy and ensure open accruals

- A/P items are matched/reconciled up to and including date

- Provide file with detailed invoices to be received open item information

- Download invoices to be received

- Open items into GL Upload Tool Excel template

The following tasks need to be performed during cut over of the "Invoices to be received"

- Related items

- Upload invoices to be received related items

- Check balances of total invoices to be received, then per PO reference assignment

- Sign-off upload invoices to be received items

A distinction is to be made between sales rebate agreements with an end date of final financial result known) and those (volume-related) rebate agreements that outlive this date. For open rebate agreements with a validity period to a date > estimation is made that no rebate agreements end on dates, the rebate volume needs to be updated in the rebate agreement in the SD module, so as to ensure the correct rebates/rebate levels are registered in SD, FI, and COPA. The total rebate accrual will be taken over as a lump sum balance. For this purpose, an itemization is to be kept on a spreadsheet on a customer/material level. The rebate current rebate agreement will be recreated (if not already available) in SAP; subsequently, the rebates per customer/material are manually updated on this level via the "manual accrual" functionality in the VB02 "change rebate agreement" transaction.

■ **Note** For "staggered" rebate agreements in which the rebate percentage is retrospectively dependent on the total volume sold, SAP has no automatic solution. In this case, the volume and rebate regimes should be tracked manually in a spreadsheet.

The following actions need to be performed before cut over:

- Ensure sales orders (re-) created in SAP do not constitute (part of) the rebate takeover items

- Prepare a detailed sheet of rebate agreements that are to be taken over into SAP, containing at least customer number, material number and item amount

- Ensure all rebate payouts/rebate credit notes have been processed in the legacy system before cut over

- Exclude rebates that have been paid out from the detailed rebate information list

- Create open rebate agreements that are to be taken over into SAP. The following activities need to be performed during the cut over of the rebate accruals: update historic rebate agreements with sales volume and create manual accrual per agreement/material; issue-created rebate credit memo requests for billing; check total on rebate accrual account(s), subsequently per customer; and signoff takeover of sales-related rebate accruals.

- Purchase-related rebate accruals—The purchase related rebate accruals will be taken over as a lump-sum during the G/L balance conversion. In order to enable an accurate rebate receipt processing, the rebate needs to be specified per vendor and material. The following actions need to be performed before cut over: Ensure that all rebate receipts have been processed in the legacy system before cut over, exclude received items from detailed rebate accrual list. g) Prepare list of detailed rebate information on vendor/material level with new vendor and new material code, Check total on purchase rebate accrual account(s). The actions to be performed after go live, when it has been verified that the total rebate accrual balance taken over correct, the following actions need to be performed: Perform debit/credit posting to specify the rebate on vendor/material level (for as far as the legacy information allows this), in the assignment field on the G/L account (BSEG-ZUONR) use the new vendor code to assign the rebate accrual to the vendor and material.

- Bad debt provisions—The bad debt provisions are accrued on a special account in the legacy system. Detailed information on the bad debt per customer is also kept within the legacy system. The total bad debt provision will be taken over as a lump-sum during the G/L balance conversion. Bad debts that can be written off prior to cut over will be written off. The receivables that qualify as bad debts will be migrated along with the regular A/R open items. However, to enable a clear identification of the receivables qualified as bad debt, a clear link must be provided for between the bad debt provision and the actual receivable. The following actions need to be performed:

  - Write off all bad debts that can be written off before end date

  - Prepare bad debt provision account details about the receivables

  - Prepare detailed list with bad debt per customer/item

  - Post-bad debt on customer/item level via special ledger posting

  - Sign off takeover bad debt provisions.

- Other provisions and accruals—No other provisions and accruals are within scope of this wave.

- Other general ledger open items—Other items can include unallocated cash and checks in transit. Unallocated cash must be cleared before go live against a receivable. No unallocated cash may exist anymore within the legacy system at the moment of cut over. See also A/R open items and misrouted payments. Ensure that all unallocated cash is allocated by end date. Checks in transit from customers will be treated the same way as unallocated cash. Checks in transit for payables are not relevant.

- General ledger balances—All general ledger balances are taken over into the SAP system. Transferable items are stock, A/P open items, A/R open items, sales- and purchase accruals. Possible other balances such as some bad debt provisions and stock obsolescence provision can be under discussion.

The following actions need to be performed, before cut over:

- Ensure all relevant SCOA accounts have been created Prepare upload file, decision to use UDS A/R or G/L upload tool pending of balances per SCOA account, as per the layout defined in the A/R open item upload template (after definite balances after month-end are known),

- Check total of the file and subsequently the total of the offset account and signoff. Load the B/S totals as line items, offset against cut over account. Check total values per account, total value per file and balance on cut over account(s). Signoff upload G/L balances.

- Year-to-date P&L results—For the year-to-date P&L results, a detailed posting of period-by-period total per type of costs per cost center / internal order can be needed management reporting purposes and to ensure correct reconciliation between the legacy system and project.

- Fixed assets legacy data—Fixed asset subledger data is taken over as master data and asset values in one go The fixed assets legacy data will be taken over into SAP in period. The takeover posting on G/L level will be done using OASV, after which a check is run.

- Open sales orders and future stock transport orders—Sales orders for which the delivery is to be expected to take place after date will have to manually re-created in the Project system. This can be done starting date. All sales orders with a delivery date before date must be handled and fully invoiced within legacy systems prior to the stock take over End Date. The following actions need to be performed before cut over:

Ensure all costing of materials have been correctly set up prior to sales order entry, Ensure that all condition types, that is, WIA, MWST, and so on, have been correctly set up in the new system for the sales, Enter sales orders with expected delivery dates after date, which can be started as of date.

Process orders/process order planning—Process orders that are to be executed after date can be created in SAP before date as scheduled orders. This way, a big rush of typing production orders into the system can be avoided. The following actions need to be performed before cut over, but after date, Create process order (status CRTD, make sure not to release). Ensure contingency plan is understood and confirmed. Release production orders as of date. Implement contingency plan for production batch numbering in case of automatic batch number generation problems in SAP after go live.

Managing Issues During Cut Over

The problems arising during the cut over period, are primarily encountered during the automatic data rework during the cut over entry, it should first be attempted to analyze and solve these on the spot by one of the global team BPC's. Most problems can be solved manually. The critical data and configuration related problems/issues will be logged. I have observed authorization issues during cut over phase, based on their criticality, be communicated via phone or email for immediate resolution. If the problem cannot be solved on the spot, then the criticality both in terms of time constraints and business impact needs to be analyzed. Based on this, the decision might be to continue or to abort the cut over phase.

Typically, these problems arising in first week after the cut over period will be resolved with the support of BPSs will be available to help identify and solve problems when they arise or for any system usage question. Any specific issue related to data and configuration related problems/issues will always be logged. After go live support—During the first month-end procedure, support will be provided by the by local and global project team.

Concluding Remarks

The cut over phase can be complex, or simple with proper planning. When there are a lot of dependencies, integration with multiple systems, it is better to assign a full-time cut over manager to manage the stake owner communication, plan every task with precise date and time. If you're taking it up as part of project management activity, ensure the technical and functional trial runs are completed as planned and keep track of HW, Technical Basis activities to precision. When you turn the productive environment, ensure functional checks are done before you open the system for productive system users. You must plan required number of dry (trial) runs to ensure the final cut over plan with every single task is identified and covered as part of the plan. A final word of caution, a DR plan is critical; you must ensure a disaster recovery (DR) plan is available in case of an existing migration of the production environment. Last but not least, set up a war room as discussed to ensure availability of resources 24-7 to avoid any eventualities.

If your solution is a Greenfield implementation, upgrade, and/or rollout, ensure respective business users have done quick functional checks and technical architecture is robust, scalable in the production environment post all data migration tasks are done. The best practices discussed in this chapter will help you avoid a common pitfall of failed implementations, due to lack of planning the cut over. Now, you're an expert in planning and executing a robust cut over plan with an end to end view of required infrastructure, functional and technical focus areas with minute to minute precision. Now, you're ready to go ahead with the successful rocket launch, as the countdown starts now.

CHAPTER 7

■ ■ ■

Approach to End User Training and Support Best Practices

What is the point in implementing a robust system without adequate training provided to the end users? Now, one of the common pitfalls is the lack of training, support and transition will lead to a disaster. Let us see how we can leverage best practices to implement robust end user training, support, and transition plan. You'd concur that training is key to the success of an ERP implementation and should meet the following objectives:

- Enable end users to do their daily work with the ERP system

- Robust organizational change management to support the changes of the working dynamics by enabling the new way of working;

- Gain acceptance of the project solution through high-quality end user training, with optimal collaboration between central and local teams;

In order to achieve those objectives, your training approach should be based on the fact that local key users should always be the primary support for the local implementation of the system in their location and should function as trainers for the local end Users. The system owners are responsible for preparing, training and enabling local Key Users in their role of trainer for end users. Let us focus on how to prepare SAP user manuals:

■ **Note** The key objectives of training, support and transition is to ensure system manual, training manuals are provided by the partner team to enable the support team to understand the implementation parameters, to continue the support.

Key Tenets

You should prepare a training document that explains the following tenets of end user training:

- Highlight all necessary buttons and Screens, with screen flow in SAP and its importance to the end user.

- Explain key transaction codes used by end user.

- The functionality and use of key tcodes with navigation flow, screen shots and explanatory footnotes for each code.

- Prepare a detailed cookbook with key information such as:
    - Transaction Codes
    - Navigation Path
    - User of the Code
    - Desired Result
    - Actual Result
    - Remarks/Additional Comments

- You must highlight the common problems identified during the usage of SAP, explain the solution. You should explain the remedial steps and how to avoid such issues, in case of issue, how to register issues in the log with details.

- Explain the entire organizational management to the HCM end users. It indicates end users trained in entire organizational management activities.

- End users must be aware of SAP info types for HCM users.

- Also, educate the HCM users about the international info types with the fields of info types which have been configured for their company.

- Conduct a scenario walk-through session with exercises and solutions, provided in the manual.

- Glossary of terms and expansion of Acronyms, Abbreviations should be given. Each consultant should focus on end user training and prepare the documents.

Before we get into the training approach, let us understand the different modes of training tools and techniques:

Modes of Training:

- Study Material—Training packages for the End user must contain best-practices for business processes and advanced technology. The study material should have information on topics such as specific job roles in SAP with detailed steps involved in performing transactions in ECC.

- Computer-Based Tools—SAP Tutor is a good example of computer based tool for end user training. It is used for simulating transactions.

- Online Training—Primarily used for multiple site users to help them with remote login to access the training content either recorded sessions or it helps them to record the transactions, and re-play it when required.

- Classroom Training - This is the basic approach and helps end users to practice during the sessions in the lab. It is effective and interactive to make it more interesting.

- On-Job Training—These are on-job scenarios, where the end users will be actually working in the system with the support of instructors in the scenarios such as 'Sales Order creation'

Now, let us understand how to plan training in detail with key activities.

Training Approach

One of the common training practices is to train-the-trainer approach, without spending months in training the end users in a large organization. The End user training is the responsibility of the client, but the deployment project team supports with the coordination of the end user training program. This approach is based on the Train-the-Trainer program and consists of six steps as illustrated in Figure 7-1.

Figure 7-1. Training Approach

Training Scope and Training Plan

As the preliminary step, a training manager will assess no. of training sessions required, super users and the no. of required sessions. In addition, he would assess required training content as per standards, and knowledge of the business users. Once the guidelines are provided, a training manager works together in close cooperation with the client training coordinator to establish the training scope and to develop the Training Plan. The Project Team members are trained in required skills by the trainer, to prepare them for their role as trainers for the key users. A pre-requisite is that all client team members should have sufficient ERP System skills and knowledge to be able to train the key end users with the functionality ERP System skills.

Training Content Development

The system owner develops the global training materials using the training templates as per organization standards. The existing documentation and training materials can be used as a starting point. The local end users are responsible for localizing the materials as required. The training coordinators facilitate and manage the development process and set the standard for deliverables. There are tools available to build content using the screens with recordings. SAP SolMan provides as a good repository for training material with transaction recording with required documentation. We would see a case study, usage of automated content development tools integrated with SolMan to help you build the training content quickly with high quality content.

Train the Trainer Approach

In this step, the trainer teams are trained, which indicates the local Key users are prepared, for conducting the end user training, in their units. The system owners are responsible for training the local trainer teams in the system skills and the training coordinator arranges the required skills training. Execute training and floor walk through. In each unit, the local Key Users are then ready to execute the End user training to conduct the floor walking process, which is supported by the system owners.

End User Training and Documentation Approach

In order to ensure a seamless knowledge transfer to your team, you should assign training material to all relevant process steps with end user roles are maintained. Figure 7-2 illustrates the end user training approach.

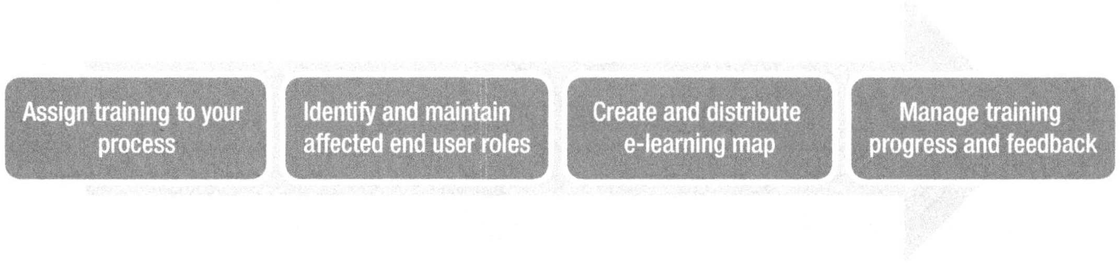

| Assign training to your process | Identify and maintain affected end user roles | Create and distribute e-learning map | Manage training progress and feedback |

Figure 7-2. *End User Training and Documentation Approach*

The learning maps can be created based on several sources. All available projects and solutions can be used according to the user authorizations. The attached training document will be assigned to the learning map as a link There are three critical parts in training, one aspect is training the end users, those who're going to use the system day in and day out for the critical business operations. Second is the functional configuration manual with details of how you've configured the system and third is the technical document with details of customization, landscape, and so on. These documents serve as the traceability for any subsequent changes. Every time, there is an enhancement request; each of these documents should be corrected as per the changes induced. The respective implementation partner should provide required trainings, manuals to help the in-house team take it forward to maintenance.

The Consulting partner provides support and training services that can help. Figure 7-3 illustrates user training in end-to-end sales and distribution.

Figure 7-3. *End-to-End Sales and Distribution Training*

End users should learn the usage of the simple navigational flow and analyze the issues, discuss with the technical team by raising a ticket in the tool for immediate resolution. The core objectives of the process training are to educate the end users on how each process integrates within SAP. They should also be aware of the navigation path, with ability to refer to the 'SAP Help' references. This would ease pressure on the technical teams, to avoid going back and forth on analyzing the issue occurred.

Now, let us assess required roles of the respective teams involved in supporting the application post-go-live. The end users should have the ability to reach out to the respective groups for required technical and/or functional support by raising ticket in the tool, such as remedy and/or any other ticketing tool used by the organization.

We have used a combination of classroom, online, and recorded training sessions to support the end users. The number of classroom sessions was agreed upon to ensure respective UAT users are available; also, the web-ex sessions were planned for remote users. It was an interactive session to train users across the Globe in different time zones. Also, as requested by the client, we had recorded few sessions for the new users joining in to train them as part of the induction program. Typically, the Implementation team will provide hypercare support post-go-live for a period of 60 days, which is required to ensure smooth post-go-live operations. During this period, the partner would plan a transition to the in-house technical and functional support teams. The functional and technical configuration manuals will help in providing adequate references to the respective teams, however in case of product related issues, PM will be responsible for raising "OSS" in SAP service portal as per the license agreement. For implementing any subsequent software upgrade or functional enhancements, client can reach out to the SAP services or partner services to implement these changes. As SAP is enhancing features in every support pack, hot packs, functional support team will be responsible to understand these changes to leverage the up-to-date and current features by implementing these changes. Hence, there will be a release plan to implementing these features as tiny projects with required testing. The technical Basis team will be responsible for upgrading the system, health checks of OS/DB, and supporting enhancements. The SAP landscape will include additional interfaces to non-SAP software, which will need to be checked for compatibility with SAP. As and when you upgrade SAP software, the respective interfaces will be tested. In each of these enhancements cycle, SAP recommended approach should be followed to ensure smooth upgrade, changes implemented as per the release cycle. For major projects, it should follow standard ASAP/AGILE approach to ensure flawless delivery.

Maximize Value from End User Training

The key question is to deliver an effective training and how do you maximize value by reducing any possible errors during transaction operations. The real challenge in developing client specific content customized for personal user experience with a comprehensive evaluation of business objectives. Now the following points are essential for end user training:

- Courseware with personalized experience for users
- Recorded sessions
- Reference guide
- Hands-on labs and exercises

As we discussed, there are few modes of training, online and classroom or recorded training sessions for experienced users. Each of these delivery methods of training is suitable for specific needs, such as a recorded session for the new users coming in at a later stage or a combination of online and classroom for a set of users in USA for example with distributed delivery for other site specific remote users in other regions such as APAC users. PM will be responsible for planning the training sessions with a training calendar booked for the respective users. Even some of the organizations have utilized the e-learning content within the portal to ensure the users understand the basics during the induction program. All business critical users must ensure hands-on training with lab facility to ensure good understanding, to avoid frequent issues raised due to lack of knowledge of SAP.

CASE STUDY: SAP END USER TRAINING

This is a case study implementing SAP ProductivityPak by RWD for support solution. SAP ProductivityPak helps you design, develop end user training content using SAP Solution Manager.

- We configured the SAP ProductivityPak as part of the SAP Solution Manager. Once the configuration is done, it is ready to use for the training. We started recording the sessions while the instructor was demonstrating various transactions in the classroom training. These documents were stored as recorded sessions, which remote users can play back as and when required. Further, end user training content document was stored as e-learning content available in html, MS Word, flash, or PDF.

- RWD provides options to create a recorded session, document, courseware, e-learning and/or a document for reference.

CASE STUDY: TRAINING PLATFORM

Background (Total number of end users = 5000)

One of the largest consulting divisions was engaged by a leading consumer goods company to transform its vision of building a sustainable SAP training into a reality with the following objectives:

- Delivery of an SAP training COE that provides a reliable SAP training platform for selected entities as they seek to improve knowledge and capability of the end users.

- Drive a consistent understanding of SAP system usage and equip the end users, maximize effective utilization. The SAP Training COE was rolled out to reach the large population of SAP end users across the globe. The SAP Training portal acts as the main point of call for SAP learning resources going forward and also a central hub for the blended training solution.

What are the main drivers for investing in SAP Training/Academy?

- End users enabled with SAP fundamentals

- Provide SAP flexible, modular training focused on improving utilization metrics in selected entities

- Establish SAP end user training capabilities

- Develop approach for a sustainable SAP training

- A self-help culture in which users take responsibility for their own learning

What has the client achieved/currently delivered?

- Developed and delivered SAP online portal that provided a reliable SAP training and learning platform for end users across the globe

- Increased SAP awareness, proficiency and personal capability across the group assisting end markets to enhance the value they derive out of the SAP system

Concluding Remarks

Now, you're an expert in conducting end user training and support by clearly defining objectives. You're also familiar with a large service delivery management concept. Refer to the SAP Best practices for the preconfigured scenarios (`http://service.sap.com/bestpractices`).

■ ■ ■

CHAPTER 8

Release Management in SAP Using a Structured Approach

Managing changes in a large SAP landscape can become complex, when you have many project deployments in parallel in a large customer landscape. It is essential to manage projects, deployment, and software patch releases in an automated way, by using a structured approach for SAP release management. Before we get into release management best practices, you should understand the importance of release management in the SAP landscape.

In one of my projects, I had the challenge of managing releases across more than 100 production instances with more than 20 interfaces, across 17 SAP landscapes. Now, you'd agree that this requires robust release management practices, to ensure that the software is up-to-date with newer patches, hot packs, and custom enhancements. The release plan should synchronize the entire landscape without major anomalies. If you don't manage releases, a host of things can go wrong—custom code that is not compliant in terms of integration, patches detrimental to the integration software, or a custom change with misaligned transport requests (SAP TRs) that could jeopardize the latest changes.

Release Management Overview

There are quite a few pitfalls to avoid, such as lack of change control, no proper planning, and poor communication, which can jeopardize a successful implementation. Each potential pitfall can lead to a failed SAP implementation, if it is not mitigated at an early stage. The solutions to these impending problems in projects are to implement a structured approach to deployments. In this chapter, you'll learn SAP release management best practices, using a structured approach for a successful implementation.

One of the complex tasks in projects is to manage software releases in sync with other products in the heterogeneous landscape during deployments and change requests (CRs). Say you're part of a large organization that requires you to manage releases to enable all requests for changes, emergency fixes, or enhancements on a daily, weekly, monthly, and/or quarterly basis. However, the real risk is the ability to conduct end-to-end integration within SAP systems, along with non-SAP systems in the landscape, seamlessly as one unit prior to releasing the software to the production system. Now, the challenge increases with number of production systems, and different change requests that are bundled into releases every week, month, and/or quarter. You may want to check the interfaces affected due to the application changes, and conduct end-to-end integration tests to avoid any issues. On one side, you'll need to manage change requests, and on the other side, there are a lot of business-as-usual (BAU) emergency fixes, which are critical to the business.

Furthermore, you'll need to be aware of the non-SAP project's impact during deployment in the SAP landscape. You'll need to resolve conflicts within projects, between projects, and with integrated systems to avoid anomalies in the software releases during deployment. Now, let's investigate a robust framework for streamlining releases in your organization by planning releases, testing every release as a work package, and scheduling the release as per the release calendar without affecting your project or any other projects in the landscape. This framework will help you avoid pitfalls such as the lack of change-control procedures.

By the end of this chapter, you'll understand the importance of planning releases through a structured release framework, with the use of tools such as Remedy, RevTrak, and the SAP Solution Manager (SolMan) ALM suite to support managing the releases. *Release and deployment management* is defined in ITIL practices as follows: "To deploy releases into production and establish effective use of the service in order to deliver value to the customer and hand over software maintenance to service operations." Because we are talking about agile methods, which indicate more and more upcoming releases in every software product, there is a compelling need to set up a robust framework to manage releases as a practice.

The SAP SolMan provides integration across phases as a centralized repository for managing the release process. This helps you to implement your IT solutions faster and operate them at a lower cost. The need for release management as a practice has grown with increasing IT landscape complexities and demanding business requirements including frequent change requests and emergency fixes. Today, business requirements and implementations are agile, meaning they aim to quickly implement changes in less time. The paradigm shift to rapid deployment necessitates a robust release management framework with greater system control, traceability, and production stability.

In most large enterprises, several teams are involved, such as the deployment team, change management team, landscape team, and release management team. These teams struggle to make the releases on time and to meet the business requirements. One of my colleagues described it as "never time to do it right, always time to do it over." You'll be able to meet business requirements, but only if you implement robust change-control software with the flexibility of tighter controls in deployment. In every organization, there's a *multitrack* approach that reflects the varying priorities assigned to different types of changes in IT development, QA, review, and approval policies.

Now, let's take a look at the release demand routes, and how each of these requests for change is classified into high (emergency), medium, or low (minor), as illustrated in Figure 8-1.

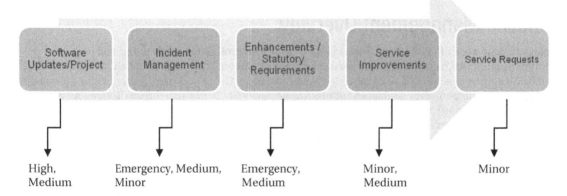

Figure 8-1. Release demand routes

For example, say a critical business requirement is absolutely mandated to move into the production system as early as possible, because it causes a high impact to the business. This might be a statutory requirement or an enhancement request from the business. Other change requests arise, such as software updates, which aren't critical but are necessary to keep your environment up-to-date as recommended by the product team. These incidents can be classified as emergency, medium, or minor, depending on the business impact. Service improvements indicate an additional feature, an innovation to be included as requested by business users. After you classify the request for change, you can assign it to the appropriate release demand routes, as illustrated in Figure 8-1. Now, let's drill down a bit on the release lanes and how they are handled.

Table 8-1 shows an example of one release strategy, which categorizes the releases into lanes indicating emergency fixes, and major, minor, and medium releases. Each organization will classify the releases based on the business urgency and impact. *Emergency fixes* are the most critical, and should be moved to production quickly; examples are exceptional statutory or financial requirements resolving a critical issue that has significant business impact. A *major release* indicates a large project. A *minor release* is a weekly release, including incidents, problem fixes, and configuration changes. A *medium release* is a monthly release, such as an enhancement project. Again, each release is categorized based on the impact to the business. Therefore, analyzing each change request is absolutely necessary to ensure correct classification during the demanding planning stages.

Table 8-1. *Change Request Controls*

Release Lane	Priority	Imp	Comments
1. Emergency fixes	Very high	High	These are critical to the business and should be quickly moved to production
2. Minor releases	Medium	Low	Enhancements, minor fixes
3. Medium releases	High	Med	Change requests, scheduled releases
4. Major releases	Medium	Med	SAP software upgrades, major SAP projects such as consolidation

The main challenge for the delivery team is to manage concurrent changes across all four release lanes efficiently. As you can see, each lane presents an opportunity to move the change request into production. As the delivery team reviews the complexity of the change, the business likely wants to push it as an emergency change request. Hence, you should be able to control the process by using change-control procedures with SLAs that define the type of request and the lane it should go through for implementing these changes.

Figure 8-2 illustrates the major release lanes.

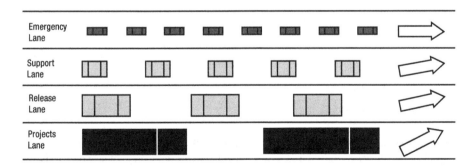

Figure 8-2. *Major release lanes*

Because of the increasing number of projects and volume of change requests coming in, there is a need to manage releases more effectively by using tools and accelerators. Before exploring these tools, let's analyze the key tenets of release management.

Key Tenets of Release Management

You'll need to understand the key tenets of release management described in this section. The main step of a release management practice is to qualify releases, classify them, and establish a change approval board (CAB) to go through the change requests and approvals. The following tasks are crucial for a successful release management practice:

- Establish a release demand route qualification process for every change, based on the business requirements. Conduct frequent gate reviews as part of the framework.

- Adhere to the release and change management policies.

- Enable CAB to make approvals.

- Capture demand requests and identify the demand release route by using an integrated demand plan (IDP).

- Identify tools for managing changes and the release process—for example, RevTrak, SolMan (ChaRM), Remedy

Now, let's look at the release framework's process controls. Your release strategy depends on the BAU and/or release changes being defined based on the criticality and impact to the business. Once you define the change as a BAU or a release change, the next step is to define the process of implementing the change to production, a.k.a. promoting to production. I am referring to controlling the process through steps to plan, schedule, control, and approve releases in order to ensure that quality releases are in tune with business requirements, as illustrated in Figure 8-3.

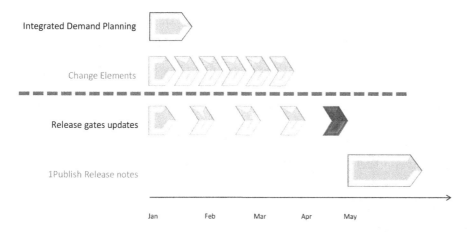

Figure 8-3. *Overview of release process steps*

Typically, the stakeholders, such as the service delivery manager, application deployment manager, change manager, CAB, application release manager, and landscape owner will agree on a release date as part of planning the application release process.

The following release preparation tasks are completed by the release management team:

- Create the change request in tools such as Remedy

- Create the SAP Solution Manager (ChaRM) implementation projects and maintenance projects

- Prepare regression test folders

- Update test plans and prepare result files

These tasks are performed by the release team to ensure that the release change request is created in a tool, and that the workflow is triggered to the respective change management and/or deployment teams. The deployment team is responsible for implementing change requests, by developing, testing, and implementing the changes. As discussed earlier, a CR can be classified into Very High, Medium, or Minor depending on the impact to the business. In any case, the deployment team is responsible for development, testing, and implementation. The Remedy tool can be used to monitor the workflow throughout the project for check-in/checkout, as soon as the respective teams complete their tasks assigned by the release manager.

Finally, the release manager conducts audits in the form of gate reviews at the end of every phase such as Design, Build, and Deploy. If found satisfactory, the release manager will sign off with brief release notes published to the entire forum. The release bundle is deployed based on the release calendar, as per the organization's release policies.

SAP Release Management Process

Typically, clients maintain a development landscape for projects and manage a support landscape for production users in case of emergency fixes. Now, the challenge is to introduce changes as requested by the business without affecting business users, thus migrating the changes from the support landscape to the production landscape. In a complex landscape with multiple systems and non-SAP interfaces, each software change relevant to the individual system must be released in cohesion with the core processes, by analyzing the impact from the end-to-end process perspective. The release plan should encompass the deployment plan with required unit and integration testing by considering changes in the relevant software.

In one project, clients had a tough time managing changes. A simple change in SAP would misalign the integration scenarios. The client managed to upgrade the release from R/3 4.6C to ECC 6.0 EHP 6.0, but the integration scenarios—such as Vertex, a bolt-on application to SAP, supporting tax details—failed due to software incompatibility. SAP recommended to revalidate the SAP RFC connectivity and requested Vertex to send out relevant patches for ECC 6.0, so we managed to resolve the conflicts caused by the software upgrade. Any change to the environment would then need to be validated; a release calendar was discussed by various parties. During that time, if a change were made to the Vertex bolt-on application, the support team would end up retesting these changes to the bolt-on application. Hence, it became imperative to manage software version changes and patches in terms of their compatibility with the interface systems holistically, to avoid any major disruption to the business. The release plan encompassed integration testing as well as a sequence of changes with a defined freeze period to ensure that the interface changes weren't allowed during this period; in addition, the end-to-end processes were tested for regression. Thus, it helps to resolve conflicts in the landscape. A simple change and release management process flow is illustrated in Figure 8-4.

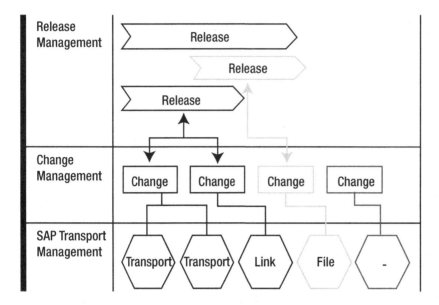

Figure 8-4. *Change and release management process flow*

The release build rolls out all the changes included in the release, and the transport phase implements these changes to the respective systems in the landscape. TRs can be managed with tools such as SolMan ChaRM or external tools such as RevTrak.

CASE STUDY 1

In one project, clients had to roll back during the Go Live, due to a data dictionary (DDIC) table. The material master table did not restore properly during the upgrade from R/3 4.6C to ECC 6.0 because one of the developers had changed the DDIC configuration. In an SPDD transaction, which is a SAP-provided transaction to modify DDIC object changes, the developer inadvertently changed a data element, resulting in a format that was incorrect, and causing more than 100,000 rows to be rejected. In addition, issues arose due to lack of sequencing the transport requests. As an end result, the system didn't boot up in ECC, causing an apparent failure during the Go Live. We rolled back the entire system to the previous version, contacted SAP to remediate the DDIC corrections, and restored the data.

This case study illustrates the lack of a release management plan: the developer changed the DDIC to restore without analyzing the impact and the integration scenarios. If the impact is not analyzed across the landscape for any change introduced, a disaster can occur. Best practices in release management call for deploying changes in a synchronized fashion by analyzing the impact to the landscape, and testing the changes in the development landscape prior to implementing them, which is called *invasive assessment*. Release management is not just the use of tools to manage your transports. It is a set of guidelines that you should comply with while managing production systems in a landscape with multiple integration scenarios. A simple DDIC object change could malign the whole project, and an activation of business processes in SAP could trigger a host of changes in the system; a minor functional enhancement such as Exit for a specific order type, could impact custom screens and users' familiarity with them. Hence, invasive assessment is conducted in every phase of the release process, prior to introducing these changes to production. In large project deployments, teams should work cohesively toward building the release deployment plan. If there are several interface systems, multiple production instances in the SAP landscape could be a challenge. Hence, through planning releases meticulously, you should be able to avert a disaster.

CASE STUDY 2

Typically, clone programs are copies of standard production code in SAP, which are altered for custom specific changes. In one project, we had challenges in BDC and clone programs, which had changed after a software release upgrade. As a result, users couldn't perform transactions in the same way as they are familiar with. These are the possible invasive changes that a team should be aware of and test prior to release changes introduced to production. A good release plan will encompass minor release bundles to implement changes in production, because major release bundles could impact multiple functionalities and testing could be challenging. If the client had developed a regression suite, that could help up front to test all critical business processes.

CASE STUDY 3

Moving incorrect transports could malign a major release. For example, changes to custom code need to managed with exact versions and transports. In one customer situation, the team had migrated old noncompliant code that worked in the system but didn't deliver the required functional changes. This resulted in a screen that held large orders, but users were unable to create specific orders. An earlier change that had been implemented didn't work because of the recent change introduced. This situation occurred primarily because of a lack of managing versions, correct transport requests, and sequencing of transports, causing the damage in production. The team salvaged the situation through emergency fixes, but it could have been averted by following robust release management practices.

Now, let's analyze the release process in a SAP implementation, upgrade, or enhancement project. There are two types of changes: BAU changes and enhancements (for example, new requirements or software updates). Though several tools are available for implementing SAP projects, Solution Manager is the latest. SolMan provides required accelerators to implement a project successfully. The ASAP roadmap is a methodology that release and deployment management uses to support the stability of the production environment by ensuring that all key controls have been adhered to during development and that all implementation procedures are fully planned, built, and tested prior to the planned rollout window. Release and deployment management includes the plans, systems, and processes to package, build, test, and deploy a release into production before handing it over to service operations, as highlighted in Figure 8-5. The release and deployment management process has three phases:

1. Plan & Design

2. Build & Test

3. Deploy & Support

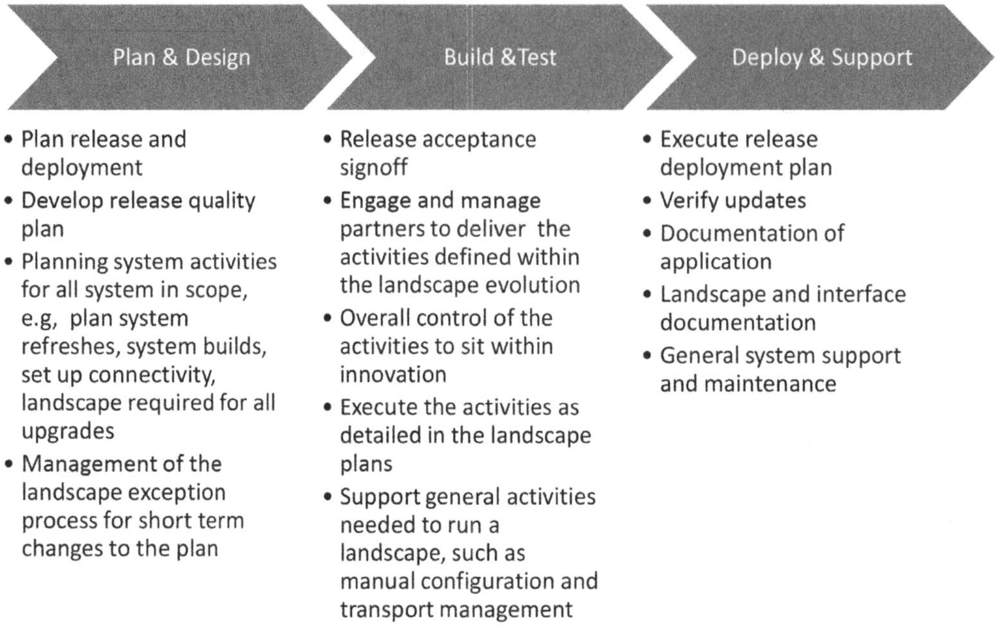

Plan & Design	Build &Test	Deploy & Support
• Plan release and deployment • Develop release quality plan • Planning system activities for all system in scope, e.g, plan system refreshes, system builds, set up connectivity, landscape required for all upgrades • Management of the landscape exception process for short term changes to the plan	• Release acceptance signoff • Engage and manage partners to deliver the activities defined within the landscape evolution • Overall control of the activities to sit within innovation • Execute the activities as detailed in the landscape plans • Support general activities needed to run a landscape, such as manual configuration and transport management	• Execute release deployment plan • Verify updates • Documentation of application • Landscape and interface documentation • General system support and maintenance

Figure 8-5. Release and deployment management process

Each phase has a set of activities for the respective teams involved. The Plan & Design phase encompasses developing a quality plan, managing a release calendar, planning systems activities such as a refresh, and building and then managing the landscape so that it's up-to-date and current. Each of these phases includes a relevant gate review conducted by the release manager. We will discuss each of the gate review audit procedures in the subsequent sections.

The Build & Test phase consists of developing the solution and performing unit and integration testing as per the test plan. This phase also includes functional configuration and transport management.

Finally, the Deploy & Support phase is the final promote-to-production effort, as you validate the deployment plan with relevant updates, and complete documentation of the landscape and interfaces. The release manager is responsible for publishing release notes.

Often release management plays the role of auditing the software, managing the release process, and so forth. For example, deployment teams are responsible for coding, testing, and integration. The audit is accomplished by a release manager prior to the promote-to-production path being approved. A release manager is responsible for promoting to production with the change manager. When situated in the support organization, the role can become adversarial in nature and may cause delays and issues, rather than being seen as integral to deployment. Now, let's explore the release management tools used, and how to plan the releases, deployments, and usage of tools and accelerators to achieve success. The release management process consists of these key activities:

- Plan the application release

- Deliver the application release

The release management process is supported by the following tools:

- SAP ChaRM (change management tool)

- RevTrak (manages transport requests)

- Remedy (manages incident resolutions to be included in weekly releases)

You can use tools such as SharePoint to manage the project scope to be included in medium releases, and the ChaRM module of SAP Solution Manager for transport management of all releases. You can use the Livelink tool for storing support documents (for example, regression test results) and the SharePoint Library to store designs.

The application release plan includes devising the minor and medium release schedule and performing the preparation tasks for the releases, such as creating release change requests. The medium release schedule is aligned to the level 1 plan, which is defined and published by the RM in SharePoint. Once a release date has been agreed upon, as part of the plan for the application release process, the following release preparation tasks are completed by the release management team:

1. Create the release change request in Remedy (all releases)

2. Create the ChaRM implementation projects and maintenance projects

3. Create the freeze change requests in Remedy

4. Prepare regression test folders

5. Update test plans, and prepare result files (all releases)

A set of regression test files (created by the RM team) are available in SharePoint, to be updated by the AM team, which is tracking the regression testing done for changes in scope of both medium and minor releases.

Figure 8-6 illustrates a change request created in the Remedy tool. This is a release RFC for a medium release in week 03. You can see that the Change Type is set to Release.

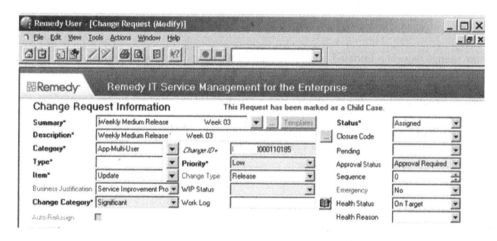

Figure 8-6. *Change request created in the Remedy tool*

In this worksheet, you can see who created the release RFC and to which group the RFC is currently assigned. Each project RFC (logical unit of work) consists of one or more change elements (building blocks) that are recorded in SharePoint, as well as the status of each change element (CE). At each gate, the CEs of each project are reviewed, and must be the correct status to pass the gate (for example, 60-Acceptance Tested to pass Gate 2B). Figure 8-7 illustrates the release management process step-by-step, with gate reviews conducted by the respective release manager.

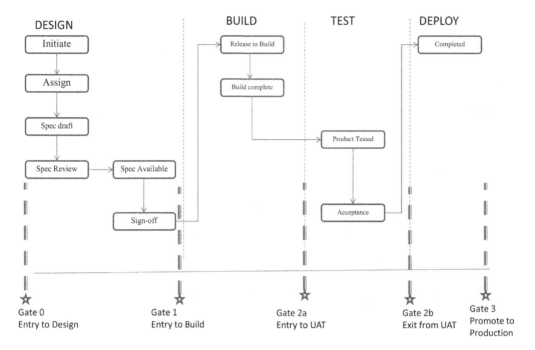

Figure 8-7. *Release management process step-by-step*

As soon as the change request is initiated, it goes through a validation (approval by the respective change approval manager). The specifications of the CR are reviewed, and approved based on the impact the change creates in the production line. In the Build phase, the application deployment team completes the code, performs unit testing, and passes the change request to the final round of product testing and acceptance by the users for a sign-off Now, the release manager is responsible for conducting gate review meetings during Plan & Design, Build, Test, Deploy & Support phases to ensure adherence to the release process, procedures, and policies. Now, let's explore how the release landscape looks in a client environment.

Release Management System Architectures

Typically, large organizations consider using an N+1 landscape, which indicates an additional landscape exclusively for managing releases outside the day-to-day BAU (N) landscape. If an N+1 landscape is not to be deployed, you might consider an alternate change process for BAU changes vs. long-term project changes (releases). In deciding whether to deploy an N+1 landscape, you need to consider the following key questions:

- How many changes will each release contain (size of release)?

- What types of changes will be included per release (impact of release)?

- How often will releases be applied to production (release frequency)?

- How many and what types of changes will make up the steady volume of BAU changes?

Now, let's take a closer look at the considerations of a release strategy for the SAP landscape. See Table 8-2.

Table 8-2. *Release Strategy SAP Landscape Considerations*

Considerations	DEV-QAS-PRD	N+1
Size of releases	Low to medium	Medium to high
Impact of releases	Low to medium	Medium to high
Frequency of release	Quarterly to biannually	Fortnightly to quarterly
Steady state BAU volume	Low to medium	Medium to high

Figure 8-8 illustrates release gate reviews conducted in project phases. A release manager is responsible for conducting the pre-gate meetings as well as gate reviews to ensure compliance.

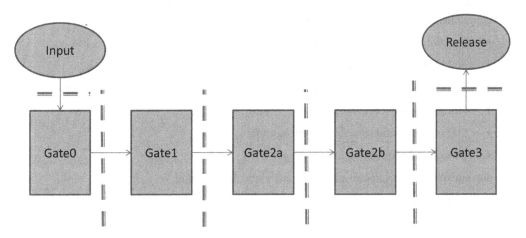

Figure 8-8. *IRelease gate reviews, conducted in project phases*

The primary objectives of the gates are as follows:

- *Gate 0—entry to design*: Ensure that preliminary design requirements are read, for a software design that adheres to software design principles with a succinctly defined scope.

- *Gate 1—entry to build*: Identify that the design is complete and that team is ready to develop the software.

- *Gate 2a—entry to UAT*: Ensure that the development is complete prior to user acceptance testing; for example, defects are resolved, and unit test and integration test requirements are met.

- *Gate 2b—exit from UAT*: Ensure that the UAT is complete and sign-off is done with the business, prior to deployment. Once a release is frozen and in progress, the release manager is responsible for ensuring that the checkpoint criteria is met prior to releasing transports for minor and emergency releases into the next environment. For major releases, the current project managers are responsible for approving the release into the next environment, up to preproduction. The release manager is responsible for approving the movement of transports into preproduction and production for all releases—major, minor, and emergency. Major and minor releases must pass the release checkpoint criteria before they will be accepted for migration into the preproduction and production environments. The preproduction environment is owned by AMS and will be used for regression testing. The preproduction environment will be refreshed from the production environment prior to every full regression run.

- *Gate 3—Final promote to production*: As stated earlier, each phase includes a set of activities, or deliverables, to complete. It is the responsibility of the release manager to ensure adherence to the standards, and any nonconformance would impact the entire product ecosystem. The following is an example list of deliverables/tasks to completed prior to the preproduction environment as entry criteria:

  - Functional specs complete and signed off

  - Build and unit test complete

  - Technical specs complete and signed off

  - String test complete and signed off

  - EUT complete and signed off by the business

  - KT to AMS complete

Production environment checkpoint entry criteria include the following:

- Regression test complete and signed off

- Operational readiness complete

- Go/No checklist complete

Release Deployment Management Process

Now, let's see each of these activities at every stage of the release management process. As you know, release management includes three main phases: Plan & Design, Build & Test, and Deploy & Support. In this section, you'll explore the activities in detail through process flowcharts, which explain the subtasks performed by various teams supporting the release management process, with the core gate reviews conducted by the release management team.

Stage: Plan & Design

The content of the release needs to be planned in liaison with change management. Depending on the criticality of functionality, the impact on the existing system, and operations and allowable downtime for the systems, the release has to be planned and scheduled. The rollout script and rollout test plans have to be prepared. To enable preparation and planning of a release, interfaces are needed for the availability management and configuration management processes.

Activity: Plan Release and Deployment

Figure 8-9 depicts how to plan change requests as part of the release management process.

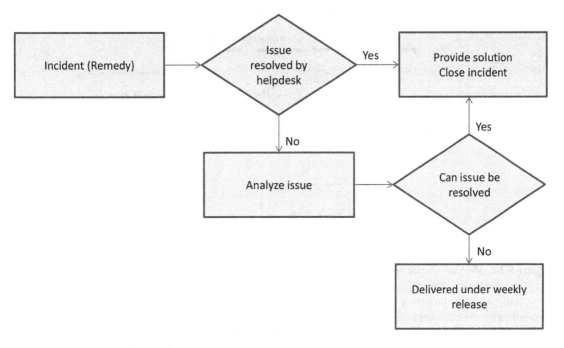

Figure 8-9. *Medium release policy*

Task: Classify Release and Align to Policy

An incident triggers the change management requirements to be deployed. Once the preliminary assessment is done, with the impact to the business analyzed, the change request is classified as very high, high, or medium and rolled up into a weekly or monthly release. Now, let's observe the process of creating a change request prior to Gate 0, which is the entry to design. Once the change request is created, it goes through a review and approval process for medium releases, as illustrated in Figure 8-10. The release manager audits the scope of changes, and determines whether the impact caused by the change is invasive or noninvasive to the business. Once the CR is created, it's linked to the release change request ID and goes for the change approval by the board (CAB). Once approved, the next steps of deployment follow.

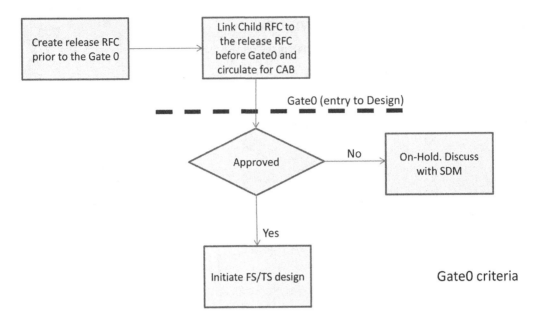

Figure 8-10. *Medium release approval*

As discussed in the earlier sections, a change request (CR) is classified into high, medium, or minor, depending on the business impact. Once the priority is assigned, and approved by the change manager, the service delivery will own the change implementation and testing. If there is an emergency BAU change, it will follow the fast track, without having to await the next weekly schedule.

Once the release planning stage is successfully achieved and the change manager's approval is received, the release implementation and deployment activities will follow:

- Finalize the frequency of the release based on the impact to the business

- Finalize the implementation approach (for example, phased or big bang)

- Integration with change and configuration management activities to ensure the integrity of the baseline

The release and deployment management intervention is to be applied for major software releases and hardware upgrades, but may be required for any size of change relating to business-critical applications or services. The release units also need to be defined specific to the implementation. These align to elements of the infrastructure that are normally released together; a specific application may be a unit, which may be broken down into subunits of code modules. The release units should be defined in a method that supports the plan, or in a schema-defined release policy or plan.

Stage: Build & Test

Now, let's look at release planning for project deployments such as enhancements.

Task: Plan Release and Deployment

Based on the classification of the release and the rules laid down in the release policy, each release must be planned as a separate entity (even when it's ultimately part of a package release). See Figure 8-11.

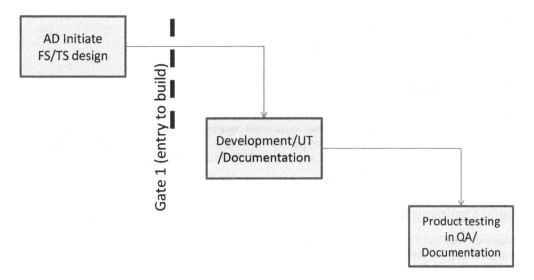

Figure 8-11. *Deployment policy*

Such planning needs to ascertain the scope and content of the release in liaison with change management, including the following:

- Identify risk assessment and profile for the release logistics and delivery planning
- Define stakeholders and affected parties
- Outline responsible teams in executing the plan
- List changes necessary and the number that can be absorbed
- Document the delivery and deployment strategy, including pilot considerations
- Produce a release schedule based on a rollout strategy responsive to geographical locations, business units, customers, and business calendars
- Define a release quality plan
- Include details on a complete back-out of the release
- Conduct readiness assessment for deployment and early support activities
- Define the authorization points through the release and deployment stages (for example, pass/fail criteria and build/test criteria)

Task: Plan Acceptance

You need to consider how a release will be accepted into production; this is normally via a test environment, where the accuracy and stability of the release is tested prior to rolling it out to production. High-level test plans and acceptance should be completed in line with the release policy and the release plan.

Activity: Configure Release

Now, let's look at configuration activities as part of the release plan.

Task: Compile Release

Building a release requires the release components to be extracted from the Definitive Media Library (DML) and compiled into a new entity (the release) and loaded back into the DML. Standard procedures must be implemented or referenced from the configuration management process for such activity within applications development. Release components may be application modules, externally sourced software, databases, data feeds, hardware, and so forth.

Task: Build Deployment Script

Whether manually deployed or via the use of a remote distribution tool, the deployment needs to be scripted, including any data changes or amendments and database initializations or hardware configurations.

Task: Produce Deployment Test Plans

Specific test data and test cases need to be built that, upon successful execution, ratify that the release deployment (or rollout) script and compilation work as expected. The test data and cases should be as representative as possible. Depending on the content of the policy, this testing expertise may be extended to fully test the impact of the new release on the production environment; within this policy, this is called operational acceptance testing (OAT).

Activity: Release Acceptance

Now, let's look at acceptance procedures in release management. See Figure 8-12.

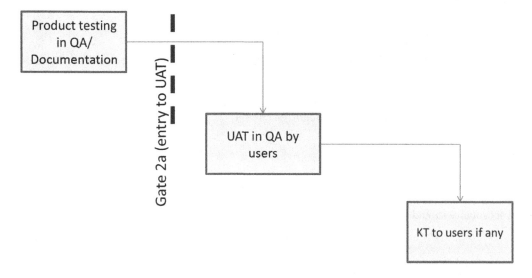

Figure 8-12. *Release acceptance*

Task: Operations Acceptance Testing

The first item to be tested is the rollout script, which must be executed as a means of introducing the release into the test environment. This ensures that if executed as planned, the end result is a fully installed release. OAT should be undertaken initially in a test environment that represents the production environment as closely as possible. The sole purpose of OAT is to test the extent of any negative impact on the production environment as a result of implementing the new release.

Task: User Acceptance Testing

Upon clear verification that the deployment script has not caused any errors or erroneous actions, the released components can be tested to ensure that they function as planned; user acceptance testing at this stage not only ensures this but also provides confidence to the client/business in the planned release. The final element of release acceptance is the execution of the back-out plan to ascertain whether all components of the release can be removed from the environment should they be deemed to have failed. Tests should not only verify that the back-out scripts are error free, but also that the resulting environment is truly returned to its previous state.

Task: Release Acceptance Sign-Off

The deployment, testing, OAT, UAT, and back-out testing should be formally signed off, and complete visibility of test data/results should be assured. See Figure 8-13.

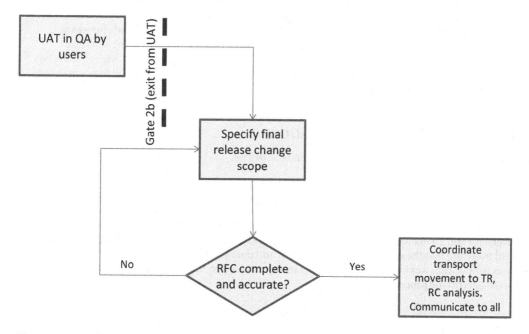

Figure 8-13. *Release acceptance sign-off*

Stage: Deploy & Support

Now, let's look at the final deployment activities of major releases.

Activity: Deployment Preparation

This section describes deployment preparation.

Task: Produce Detailed Deployment Timetable

A step-by-step timetable must be produced, detailing all events involved in the deployment or rollout of the release, including roles, responsibilities, and site-specific considerations. It is expected that meetings will be held with key personnel involved in the rollout to walk through the timetable and amend it as necessary.

Task: Produce Release Notes

Release notes are to be completed that detail versioning, all affected CIs, any known errors with the release components that will not be resolved prior to going live, and contents of the release.

Task: Training

It is the responsibility of release and deployment management to ensure that all relevant support material has been compiled and distributed to the relevant support functions prior to rollout. It may also be necessary to facilitate meetings/training sessions to communicate the key differences and changes to support operations. It is not the responsibility of release and deployment management to undertake end-user training in functionality of the released components; however, verification that such training has been completed should form part of the release acceptance. Release and deployment management should keep all stakeholders informed of rollout plans.

Activity: Distribution and Installation

Now, let's look at the distribution and installation phase activities.

Task: Execute Release and Deployment Plan

The plan is to be executed as documented and agreed upon, while release and deployment management provide oversight and escalation/communication throughout. If the release fails, the back-out plan should be executed to ensure that the earlier version is installed and operations continue. In case of failure, it will be necessary to review what went wrong and adapt the release; the script, tests, or plan is accordingly returned to the relevant step in the process.

Release Governance

In this section, you'll learn about release management governance principles. At the start of each release cycle, the release scope is confirmed and frozen. All key stakeholders involved in a release are informed of the detailed release plan, appropriate checkpoints, and sign-off points at the beginning of a release lifecycle. (The timing of release phases may vary, depending on the content of the release.) All release approvers are required to sign off within the appropriate time frame. Failure to so do will move the relevant object to the next available scheduled release. Failure to pass a checkpoint in the release lifecycle will automatically move the relevant object to a future release.

Where appropriate, business sign-off of regression testing is required before migration to production. The release manager is responsible for approving the movement of transports into preproduction and production for all releases—major, minor, and emergency. The release manager has the final approval prior to any migration to production. The following subsections provide an overview of the release management governance forums.

Approvals

You need secure approvals from the CAB, AMS SDM, and the release manager.

Communication

A release manager must be diligent in discussing the release plan with stakeholders. The manager is responsible for setting and re-setting expectations, and for communicating with users, approvers, and development groups. This includes communications to other process areas (for example, change management, configuration management, and so forth).

The RM must work closely with the team and the business/client to ensure that requirements, plans, strategy, tests, and progress reports are communicated. Communication of release content to the team, wider stakeholders, and the business end users is essential. The content of a release might change from the point at which the release scope is frozen to the point at which the release is transported into production. Therefore, the final communication of the content of the release is critical to business operations.

Principles

The following general release communication principles apply:

- Publish the release schedule to the business in order that the business may plan for complete system outages during the release windows.

- Ensure that the final scope of all releases transported into the production environment will be published to an agreed-upon central point.

- Operations is responsible for translating the release scope into business language and for communicating with all global template users as appropriate.

- Emergency release notifications will be communicated to users as appropriate by service operations. Operations will be responsible for ensuring that all appropriate training, portal content, process updates, work instruction updates, and so forth, are complete within the communicated release plan time frames as defined by the release manager.

Ownership and Monitoring

Ensure end-to-end ownership of all releases from the plan to deployment that meets high-quality standards throughout the lifecycle.

Escalation

Adopt a policy to escalate to the respective stakeholders in case of any nonconformity during the gate reviews to address issues early and resolve them prior to deployment.

Tracking

Ensure that agreed-upon plans are checked in/out with stringent documentary policies and close workflow-based tracking.

Security

Ensure that security considerations at all stages of the change/release lifecycle are met as per the security policies.

Review and Reporting

Ensure the accurate status reporting of the elements moved to production, with the ability to track every stage of an element until promoted to production.

RELEASE MANAGEMENT RACI

You will be able to succeed in managing complex releases by using the tools and accelerators previously discussed. As a collaboration platform for the project, members can work directly with the organized roadmap work packages, using the accelerators, and upload their work back into the structured packages in Solution Manager. Table 8-3 illustrates the RACI matrix for release and deployment management with various stakeholders.

Table 8-3. *High-Level Release and Deployment RACI Matrix*

Tasks	Release Manager	Change Manager	Build Manager	Client	Service Delivery Team	Configuration team	Outputs
Plan & Design	A,R	C	C	I			Release and deployment plan Back-out plan
Build & Test	A		R		C		Rollout or deployment scripts
Deploy & Support	A,R		C	I	C		Release deployed as planned Back-out executed, if required

Roles & Responsibilities

A release manager is the key person who participates in plan discussions to understand the demand. The RM also is responsible for conducting gate reviews at every phase of the project to ensure compliance. The following tasks are part of an RM's scope of work:

- Liaison with direct and indirect stakeholders

- Freeze the release scope (enhancements from CAB and incidents from AMS)

- Define, maintain, and communicate the detailed plan for each release

- Coordinate integration where necessary

- Owner of release management checkpoint sign-offs

- Approve the release into preproduction and production environments.

- Communicate the final release content to the appropriate parties and post it to an agreed-upon central location

Service Delivery Manager

The AMS service delivery manager (SDM) is a critical stakeholder in the release process, as this role manages and provides status updates on a significant portion of the release process. The AMS SDM is responsible for the following areas as part of the release management process:

- Input of incidents and prioritization of incidents into release schedule and detailed planning

- Input of enhancement estimates into the change management process

Concluding Remarks

In this chapter, you learned the best practices of the SAP release management framework. These best practices will enable you to avoid the common pitfalls that arise from a lack of framework for managing changes, as well as the risks related to those pitfalls. You've also learned the importance of a release management framework, and the roles and responsibilities of a release manager in each stage of Plan & Design, Build & Test, and Deploy & Support.

CHAPTER 9

■ ■ ■

Effectively Managing SAP Upgrades

A common challenge is the ability to adapt to changing business conditions that lead to changing IT solutions; every evolving organization needs to adapt its IT environment accordingly. This drives the need to upgrade or enhance your SAP software on a regular basis. An IT HW/SW/OS upgrade can be a systematic task accomplished on a regular basis, depending of the frequency of the software release cycle. The upgrade can be simple or complex, depending on the magnitude of the changes. Especially with SAP's continuous innovation strategy, I admit, performing upgrades wasn't easy until the advent of ECC, with its enhanced switch frameworks.

Today, SAP upgrade projects have moved from release upgrades to the concept of enhancement packages known as EHPs. The EHP updates in ECC are relatively simpler than the earlier R/3 upgrades. However, the technical, functional, and testing areas need adequate planning and coordination to ensure successful implementation of the upgrade. The objectives of an upgrade are to ensure that an up-to-date release benefits from the latest available functionality, to leverage new technologies that foster innovation, and to guarantee long-term protection of IT investments. The challenges of accomplishing an upgrade remain, in terms of avoiding scope creep, budgetary overruns, and schedule delays.

Roadmap of SAP Upgrade

Today, SAP solutions have evolved into the next generation, such as HANA or on-cloud solutions. Your SAP landscape is evolving faster than ever into mobility and cloud computing to help you run an agile business. At the same time, all activities related to the change need to be performed as efficiently as possible in order to save resources and budget. It is imperative to plan your deployments as large upgrades in a sequence for the year, aligned to the SAP releases, and it is essential to break down those deployments into simple, manageable processes to ensure incremental implementation in the business.

SAP updates are delivered via enhancement packs (known as EHPs since the ECC release). If the updates are performed as per the standard process, the updates will be efficient. However, if you deviate from the process, it will impact the schedule and deliverables. With the available accelerators and external remediation tools for ABAP, upgrades are not complex, if managed correctly.

SAP provides tools and services supporting all stages of upgrade projects. The central platform for these tools and services is the SAP Solution Manager. Knowing these tools and services is crucial for an efficient, fast, and safe transition to the new release. Therefore, we outline the most important ones in this chapter. Having the right focus helps in directing resources and attention where they are needed most at the right time. And no relevant points will be missed.

■ **Note**   The suggested upgrade implementation is based on the SAP Upgrade Roadmap. The SAP Upgrade Roadmap is derived from the more general Accelerated SAP (ASAP) principles that cover the most important aspects and phases of any type of SAP business configuration project. This detailed guideline enables project leads to control all relevant activities of a standard SAP upgrade. It is available in SAP Solution Manager (in the Implementation / Upgrade work center and via the transaction RMMAIN) and in the SAP Service Marketplace (http://service.sap.com/upgraderoadmap).

Upgrade Overview

The life of any IT solution, from the first implementation concept to the final phase-out, can be described as a series of business configuration states connected by permitting transitions. While the business scope and scale of each configuration change can vary widely, the management of these changes can best be described as a repetitive lifecycle. SAP uses the application management lifecycle described in ITIL (V3) as a commonly agreed-upon model to guide you through this sequence of business configuration processes. Figure 9-1 outlines the most important change events in the lifecycle of SAP solutions.

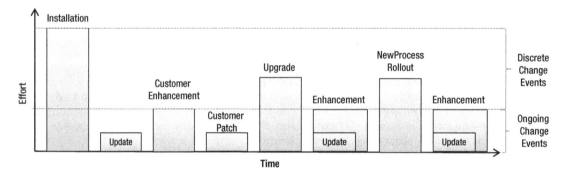

Figure 9-1. *The most important change events in the lifecycle of your solution*

These change events along the application lifecycle with frequency of the changes in the software and, hence, the impact to your solution varies depending on the underlying business customization requirements. Now, let's look at the following main life-cycle change categories.

Installation

Installation is the complete new setup of a system, mostly on new hardware. Migration might be necessary from former legacy systems. Besides the initial implementation of an SAP product, the installation of new add-ons or other software components falls under this category.

Update

An *update* is a set of corrections for software errors and severe performance problems in the SAP system. The media for this are hot fixes, support packages (SPs), or SAP Notes. Support packages are compiled periodically and made available via the SAP Solution Manager. This maintenance process aims to correct known errors in applications by minimizing the impact to any existing landscape elements and running processes. Regression tests are needed and will be nondisruptive in user interfaces. New functionality or different behavior of existing processes is not expected.

Enhancement

An *enhancement* contains a larger number of objects, and the majority do not have the aim of correcting errors but of enhancing features and functions. The media for this are enhancement packages (EHPs). New functionality is expected (enabled by switches in EHPs), but different behavior of existing processes is clearly not. Also, migration efforts won't occur. An enhancement changes the version of a software component, but not the release. Enhancement packages and switches are also the recommended technology for customer enhancements in the future.

Upgrade

An *upgrade* contains all objects of a software release. The media for this are software releases. In this case, the shipment of additional functions and features and redesigned processes is the main focus. However, in most cases, the same functionality of the previous software is also available within the higher release, which allows a technical upgrade as a first step. With an upgrade, customers switch from an older software release to a newer one. Typically, both the server component of a system landscape and components on top of this are upgraded.

Business Improvements

During a *business improvement*, new business processes are implemented in an existing system. This may include developing or updating custom programs, and customizing or activating business functions. However, the SAP software release, software component versions, and patch levels are not changed. To properly manage the planning and realization of these changes, an upgrade and release management have to be implemented in your company as part of the overall application life-cycle management. Now, let's look at the critical success factors of an SAP upgrade project.

Critical Success Factors

You should be aware of the following points for a successful upgrade, to avoid pitfalls such as a delayed implementation timeline and lack of change control.

- Impact analysis during the blueprint phase. Understand the technical and functional configuration impact, and the complexity of customization complexities.

- System availability for a POC study to finalize downtime in a similar production-like environment, which is typically a sandbox environment.

- Analyzing Impact on the custom development analysis to support analyzing the remediation efforts, timeline, and testing.

- Test analysis, test planning, and execution plan to ensure that end-to-end scenarios are tested in the sandbox system.

- Robust change and release management to ensure that a promote-to-production path is clearly specified during the upgrade, with a freeze period strategy.

- Communication plan to ensure that all stakeholders are aware of the integration risks.

- Technical landscape analysis to ensure that systems are in sync with correct patch levels and to ensure a successful upgrade.

- Integration testing must be carried out twice to ensure a successful upgrade, with non-SAP interfaces tested during the sandbox phase.

- Dry run to ensure that all sanity checks are done prior to the final prep and Go Live.

- Detailed cutover plan to ensure that hourly tasks are planned during production cutover.

- A detailed task-level project plan with a RACI matrix to ensure that all parties are involved during the upgrade.

The following are common pitfalls to avoid:

- Lack of integration testing

- Lack of communication between interface teams

- Lack of change controls

- Unrealistic resource levels

- Lack of specific skills to support the impact to the functional areas

- Lack of regression

- Lack of downtime analysis

Indeed, some of these challenges pose risks to implementing the project upgrade. Upgrade projects can be simple, if you follow a sequence of activities, plan it, and execute it. If not, an upgrade implementation project can be a major disaster, faltering your production line, with undue consequences to the business. What if you are not able to go live on time? Without a disaster recovery plan, this could be a disaster.

The only way to avoid these issues is to understand each of these phases with enough due diligence to mitigate risks along the way. I have observed that most projects start with unrealistic goals, such as a quick upgrade plan without enough due diligence in terms of analyzing real resource requirements, custom code, and integration complexities. The planning exercise must encompass a detailed proof-of-concept study to ensure that the hidden risks due to patch-level or release-level changes are analyzed. To maximize your ROI, you should also leverage options such as enhancement points to improve your custom code, or perhaps try to standardize custom code into SAP standards. There are options to activate business functions to maximize benefits derived from an upgrade project. Thus, an upgrade implementation project need not be a technical activity; it could help you maximize the value of the software by analyzing the delta business functions available in the latest release or the support-pack level.

If you're able to plan it right, the realization phase is easy to implement. Solution Manager offers roadmaps, which are project-planning capabilities that can be utilized to effectively manage upgrade projects. The next big wave of changes will be migration to HANA and cloud platforms. Hence, you should conduct due diligence in your POC activity prior to stepping into the realization phase of the project.

One of the critical projects for a large beverage company involved migrating the entire landscape from SAP on-premise to cloud with platform migrated to Linux from AIX, with over 100 SIDs. There were significant challenges in terms of migrating the interface bolt-on applications such as Vertex, and custom developed applications. Hence, the team conducted several rounds of integration testing post migration. The POC phased involved the sample execution of critical business scenarios post the migration with a plan of eight weeks.

Implementation Methodology

SAP upgrade projects follow a standard SAP ASAP methodology. Figure 9-2 illustrates an overview of upgrade project phases.

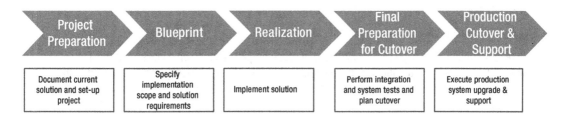

Figure 9-2. *Overview of upgrade project phases*

In the Discovery phase, you identify the critical business requirements of project setup. During the Evaluation/Blueprint phase, you look into the impacted business scenarios by leveraging tools and accelerators. Further, you build a high-risk test plan to test critical scenarios. The Realization phase encompasses remediation of ABAP custom code, SPDD for dictionary object corrections, and SPAU for modified object corrections. Once this is done, you transport these changes from Dev to QAS for detailed functional and integration testing. Mostly, I've used QTP for managing test cases. A few external tools are available for accelerating remediation of custom code, such as smartShift and Panaya, which provide automatic remediation of noncompliant functional modules in ECC. SAP provides the CDMC add-on as part of Solution Manager to analyze the impact to the custom code. Now, the SAP landscape has changed with EHP updates, which are far less complex; however, you'll need to analyze the specific scenario impacted by the EHP update and retest from an end-to-end perspective. Hence, upgrades are no longer time-consuming efforts, since you have EHP updates on ECC. The preceding ASAP methodology will remain the same, with a reduced timeline and effort, which can be part of the application maintenance cycle with periodic updates to EHP. The next wave is going to be HANA migration or migration to the cloud. In order to complete this migration, you should have a regression suite to accelerate the entire test phase. The SAP HANA Cloud Platform (HCP) is the platform provided by SAP, with minimal migration efforts. It helps in simplifying overall upgrade efforts by migrating to the cloud environment. I believe a hybrid on-premise/cloud approach would help you reduce overall operating expenses as you can take up IaaS, without having to worry about the infrastructure changes (OS/DB). You have a host of options available, to host SAP on a private cloud through partner services or even use a hybrid approach with on-premise for payroll and other solutions on the cloud. The SAP landscape has changed with the challenging business requirements; SAP delivers agile solutions to help customers benefit from the product innovation.

CASE STUDY

Now, let's examine a real-time case study of an upgrade project. One of the large utility customers planned an SAP upgrade from R/3 4.6C to ECC 6.0 EHP 6.0. This is just a snapshot of one instance upgrade; however, the client had about 19 productive instances to upgrade as a big bang upgrade approach. The following points are crucial for a successful upgrade project:

- Estimating upgrade projects depend on the customization complexities

- Infrastructure build activities

- Test planning, prep, and execution

- Usage analysis of critical transactions and custom code

- Integration tasks with focus on critical interfaces

The recommended landscape for this standard upgrade project is based on a classical three-tier transport landscape for a production environment. All systems in the landscape are connected to the productive SAP Solution Manager. We distinguished three lines of systems during the project, as shown in the following illustration.

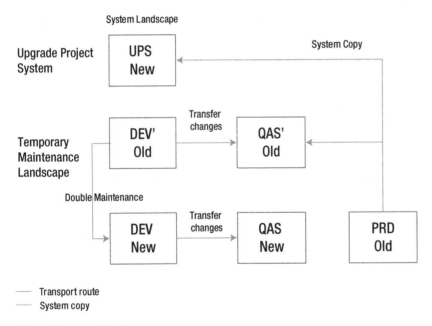

Upgrade system landscape

This figure illustrates upgrading your SAP landscape. First, a stand-alone sandbox, referred to as *UPS* in this example, is created as a copy of a productive system. This will be your POC system for analyzing the impact to the critical business process. To keep it simple, watch out for the modifications, custom developments, and scenarios impacted. After you've determined the inventory of the business processes impacted, prioritize every critical process for remediation, testing activities, and integration. Another point is to be aware of the upgrade's impact to bolt-on applications. Often integration testing might prove to be costly, with the defects identified at a later stage. Hence, you should diligently test crucial transactions in the sandbox and vet critical processes with core business SMEs. If there are changes to the modifications, document these core modifications, and train the required end users to avoid defects in UAT due to lack of knowledge about the changes. Further, clones would likely be impacted, so take necessary action to restore clone objects to standards. Knowing SAP's strategy to maximize your IT investment, you must strive to standardize as much as possible by studying the customizations and checking for ways to restore customizations to standards. In an SPAU transaction, you have an option to restore modifications to standards; you must take extreme care to blueprint necessary processes, which are planned to be standardized. Furthermore, an SAP upgrade could provide you opportunities to improve system performance, by studying the custom development usage and deactivating inactive objects.

In my view, upgrades are simpler if done correctly. They can be complex if you don't have the required skills, such as funds management, to resolve conflicts due to upgrades. The objectives of SAP are clear: to standardize the business process with a robust ECC platform. You should analyze bolt-ons for any incompatibility, check satellite systems within SAP for version compatibility, and so forth. You must plan a step-by-step approach during downtime to analyze the sequence of systems to upgrade if the landscape is complex with ERP, SCM, SRM, and CRM. If you plan for a big-bang approach, realize the challenges of longer downtime. Above all, study the artifacts of previous projects of similar size in terms of complexity and skill availability in order to embark on a successful upgrade project.

SAP Near Zero Downtime (NZDT) is an approach to support ERP upgrades with zero downtime. However, it comes with the additional expenses of a staging environment and an additional timeline required prior to Go Live. I recommend SAP Functional Go Live checks prior to the Go Live, and at least 2 x Dry Run to optimize downtime parameters and risks. Test, test, and test, if you have regression testing, it would help, or use this opportunity to build a regression suite for subsequent enhancement pack updates. Your SAP upgrade is also an opportunity to build a business process hierarchy, leverage Solution Manager for change management (ChaRM), clean up functional test cases, and build an automated regression suite.

Concluding Remarks

Finally, you know how to upgrade SAP and the pitfalls to avoid up front. This knowledge will help you avert a major disaster during downtime that could cause production issues. One of the key aspects is planning the upgrade project by analyzing its impact to the critical functionality and core business processes by using a risk-based testing approach. If the planning is done diligently with a required POC and impact analysis, you likely can avert any issues due to the upgrade. By using accelerators, remediation can be done faster and efficiently. SAP publishes its product availability matrix (PAM) in the Service Marketplace (http://service.sap.com/pam).

CHAPTER 10

■ ■ ■

Managing Projects Using SAP Solution Manager

Often projects in an organization are managed by delivery teams with little knowledge about all the artifacts related to pre-sales or proposals. This is one of the common pitfalls in failing to meet customer expectations after the sale is over; consulting organizations are no longer interested in keeping communication with the customer intact. This can result in a failed implementation caused by a lack of communication, dedication, or effort to excel in project delivery. I have seen many organizations succeed in winning a project because of excellent sales capabilities, but then fail to deliver their promises because of a lack of communication between sales and the delivery teams, thus resulting in losing customers in the long run. Sales and delivery teams need to work hand in hand as one global team with seamless communication.

But how can you achieve traceability from pre-sales to delivery? Don't you need a robust platform to support managing portfolios from an end-to-end perspective? SAP engineered a tool called Solution Manager, which initially was used for implementing support packs and landscape integration. Today it has evolved into a robust application lifecycle management (ALM) tool, supporting the implementation of SAP projects from concept, to initiation, to closure. The majority of ERP projects fail due to lack of change control or project management methodology. In this chapter, you'll see how to manage projects effectively by using SAP SolMan as well as SAP SolMan ChaRM for change requests and project management tools for the entire implementation cycle of the project, from initiation to closure.

Solution Manager Overview

The KPIs of managing portfolio projects are cost, time, and scope, which need to be monitored and controlled throughout concept, design, initiation, and closure. Any slippage of these three aspects can cause significant issues in project execution. By using an ALM tool, you can control each of these KPIs in project implementations. One of the real challenges in the industry is to manage portfolios/projects from an end-to-end perspective, from initiation through closure; project managers need a comprehensive tool to monitor and control risks, with traceability of the requirements, as illustrated in Figure 10-1.

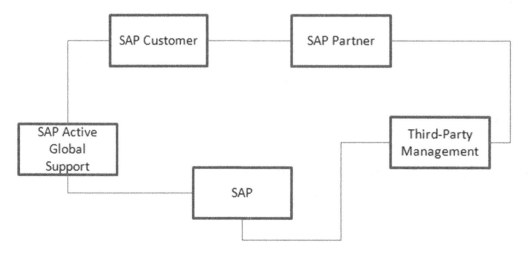

Figure 10-1. *Application management and administration*

SAP SolMan supports all phases across operations, implementation, and optimization of the processes. This central system monitoring functions as a centralized repository for detecting critical situations with alerts, and it can be extended to third-party systems. SolMan can be used as a tool for recurring tasks with drill-down capabilities and for documentation, with central access to system administration and reporting of the entire system architecture. SolMan uses work centers, displayed as tabs in a web browser, which provide easy navigation with role-based access. Let's take a look at the SAP SolMan architecture.

SolMan Architecture

SAP SolMan architecture is illustrated in Figure 10-2.

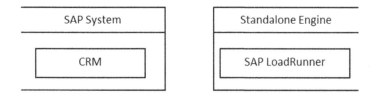

Figure 10-2. *SAP SolMan architecture*

SAP SolMan is based on CRM on ABAP, using concepts of work centers with a stand-alone engine that is not integrated with managed systems. SolMan runs on NW 7.0. It collects and aggregates data, which runs on systems. These agents send data periodically. SAP BW is integrated within SolMan, which provides analytical capabilities. These stand-alone engines are additional software installation units, such as TREX, LoadRunner for testing, and the SAP RWD productivity pack. SolMan is connected via remote function call (RFC) to the managed services with read-only access. HTTP is the communication protocol.

You'll be able to set up the basic settings, folder structure, and project templates with basic configuration settings from system prep to the realization. SAP SolMan also offers integrated test management capabilities via ChaRM for managing change requests; now let's look at the benefits of ChaRM functionality.

The SAP Solution Manager ChaRM offers the following benefits:

- Increased efficiency through the use of change management workflows and approvals

- Reduced costs, as activities such as integration/regression testing are planned and consolidated

- Reduced risk of errors due to differences in environments or transport sequences

Now, let's see how Solution Manager ChaRM can be utilized effectively for managing projects and change requests, as shown in Figure 10-3. You can track a project from the requirements phase, to the proposal, to the operational project management, through the project closure.

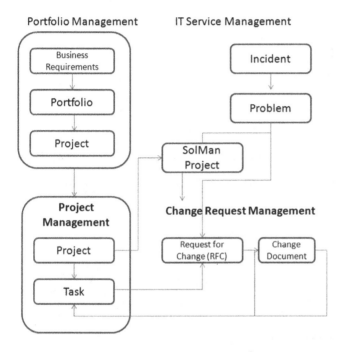

Figure 10-3. *IT project management in SAP Solution Manager*

A project is created in the Solution Manager and tracked throughout the implementation, with traceability to the requirements. The change requests, a.k.a. RFCs, are managed via Solution Manager to ensure effective tracking and monitoring throughout the project.

Solution Manager as a Project Platform

SAP Solution Manager has been used to manage software administrative activities, such as generating an installation and upgrade key, downloading support packages, or monitoring. Today, SAP Solution Manager has extended its capabilities as a proven platform for managing a solution throughout its entire life cycle—including project management, designing blueprints, implementation, and operational support for the complex system landscape. Solution Manager projects are a set of workflows and reports used to manage deployments.

A Solution Manager project can be used from blueprint to Go Live, and has methods to implement a project successfully. The following are the core functions of implementation projects using SAP SolMan:

- Project management methodology

- Project blueprint repository using standard template-based business scenarios

- Managing and executing configuration, development, and testing

- Planning and executing training with an e-learning platform

- End-to-end solution operation

- QA integration, which indicates QM stage gates established

Let's explore each of these functions in detail.

Project Management Methodology

SAP SolMan helps you track projects via a roadmap that includes solution implementation, team charter, project initiation, Go Live, and transition to the support phase, as shown in Figure 10-4. This roadmap contains a host of PMO activities such as creating a project baseline, staffing, establishing a team, and organizing the document repository.

Figure 10-4. *IT project management using Solution Manager roadmap*

Project Blueprint Repository

SolMan provides a folder structure for storing business process documents. You can create and store organizational units, master data, and business scenarios under the project folder using a standard business process structure.

One of the critical aspects of a blueprint exercise is to define a business process structure with organizational units. You create a blueprint structure with scenarios, process steps, master data, organizational objects, and interfaces. You can create a process hierarchy in various ways. You can select a scenario from a SAP business process repository, which has a standard configuration available. This is an accelerator. You can also take a scenario structure from the database, by transferring information from the project to the directory. It helps to organize documents by the respective phases (blueprint, realization, testing, and so forth). During the POC phase of the project, you can create a mock-up solution for validation.

If you select the processes from the standard repository, you'll see some documents. Other documents such as blueprints, process documents, and functional descriptions can be attached to the correct folder level.

Once you create the folder structure from the template project, and customize it to your global template requirements, rolling it out for sites becomes even simpler. All you have to do is copy the master folder structure and make it specific to the sites.

Managing and Executing Configuration, Development, and Testing

This is one of the most crucial phases of the project. After the blueprint is finished, you can manage the working documents and execute the configuration, development, and testing.

What is really interesting here is the traceability from the blueprint phase. Now you're in the realization phase, with business process/steps stored in tabs for configuration, development, and testing, as you can see in the preceding figure. All FRICE objects (for example, programs, includes, and function modules) are recorded in the development tab. For testing, recorded test scenarios can be stored in the testing tab. Most important, for testing, SolMan allows a business process structure with test cases, a recorded process available for testers to execute and report defects. These defects can be managed as *tickets* (problem messages) for resolution of errors, since SolMan is integrated with a service desk engine. These tickets can be assigned to the processor, solved, and sent back to retest. This integrated test environment is a single source for storage of test cases, execution, and defects management in the landscape. Now, you get the point: PMs can identify the business process, and crack the status of configuration, development, and/or testing. Developers can easily record objects, and jump directly to the objects in development to customize recorded IMG, develop programs, and access eCATT. SolMan provides access to the SAP standard workbench tool for testing. This tool helps you manage test plans, and build test cases with step-level details. You can assign a test list to the respective testers, execute it, and send it back if there is a retest requirement. We discussed defects management; testers can raise tickets for defects and track to completion through resolution.

Planning and Executing Training with the e-Learning Platform

With the integrated SAP RWD productivity pack, you can record training sessions as e-learning content developed for training end users. These sessions can be launched from the e-learning portal via the e-learning platform. The e-learning module is part of SolMan, which is role based and helps end users take up training. The embedded feedback functionality in the SAP SolMan e-learning modules helps users communicate to the content developer, who can update the training material or add content as required.

End-to-End Solution Operation

Now, let's analyze the critical end-to-end operations of a project, which include the following:

- *Incident management*: Managing defects.

- *Solution monitoring*: Real-time monitoring of the solution using business process management (BPM) and interface monitor tools. It triggers alert messages for immediate response without impacting the business.

- *Change-control management*: Managing changes (CRs).

- *Root-cause analysis*: Analyzing the root cause of a failure in the process.

SolMan provides real-time monitoring, to resolve issues prior to any business impact, via the BPM tool. You'll need to configure the business process for monitoring. Then, for every error in the system, it triggers automatic notification to expedite resolution of errors before they impact the business. Here are the steps involved in building the business blueprint in SAP Solution Manager:

1. Start Project Administration drop-down menu in the SAP Solution Manager work center. Enter the title and project name to create the project, as shown in Figure 10-5. To set up the business blueprint structure, choose System Landscape ➤ Systems.

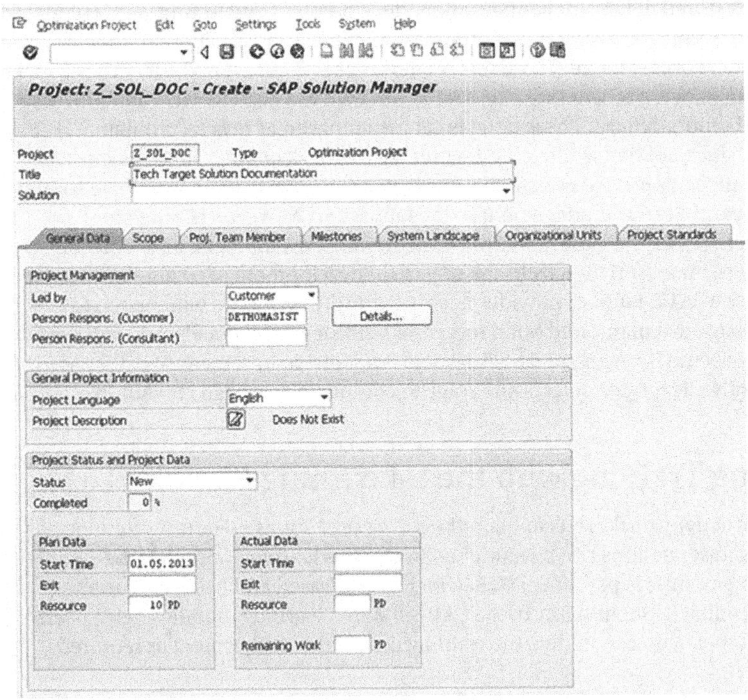

Figure 10-5. *Create a project in SAP SolMan*

2. Select the SAP SolMan Roadmap Accelerator. After you save the project, attach the SolMan roadmap to help guide you through the best practices, including use of accelerators with the /ESRV_ALM_01_CORE t-code, as shown in Figure 10-6. Now navigate to the ESRV ALM roadmap and select the solution documentation.

Figure 10-6. *SolMan Roadmap Accelerator*

3. Choose the process steps from the Business Process Repository (BPR); include all process steps to deploy SAP SolMan. You can build the business process repository (BPR) by using reference content to build your business blueprint that matches the module that you want to deploy. Now, you'll select the scenarios, as shown in Figure 10-7.

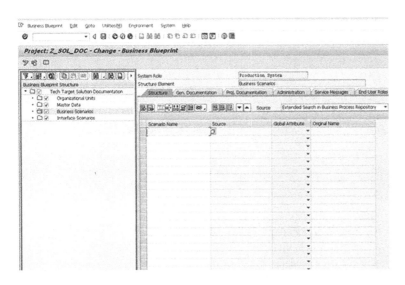

Figure 10-7. *SolMan scenarios*

4. Use the t-code /solar01 and select the structure table as shown in Figure 10-8. From the Source drop-down menu, select the Extended Search in BPR option.

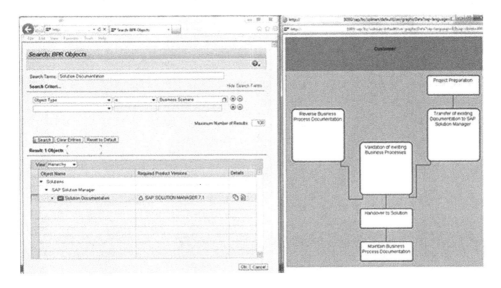

Figure 10-8. *Searching the BPR*

Enter the function you want to deploy and search.

Change the view from List to Hierarchy. Click the Show Graphic icon in the Details column to display a swim-lane diagram of the blueprint you want to create. Highlight the Solution Documentation line in the View box, and then click the OK button to drag the BPR reference content back to the business blueprint, as shown in Figure 10-9.

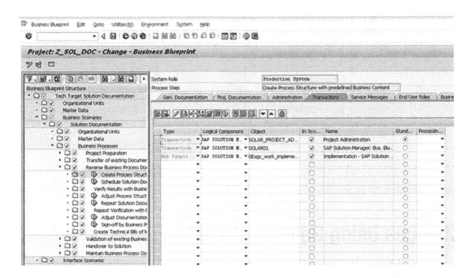

Figure 10-9. *Check the BPR content in the business blueprint*

You'll find methodology, transaction codes, documentation, and accelerators to support you during each step of the Solution Documentation module deployment. The best part is that the update of the BPR content is continuously updated via support packages. One of the important points is to use the latest release and service pack to ensure that you're using the latest BPR version.

QA Integration

SAP SolMan provides a standard quality management practice across all operational units. You can integrate test management software such as Worksoft automation, LoadRunner for performance, and HP Quality Center/QuickTest Professional (QC/QTP). Business Process Change Analyzer (BPCA) configuration will help in analyzing the impact due to the software upgrade. The SAP Solution Manager QM module does the following:

- Defines, monitors, and controls quality gates

- Provides a central repository for quality tasks

- Provides an interface for all types of transports and system landscapes

- Integrates the various development workbenches into a central transport and change-control system

One of the critical challenges addressed by Solution Manager is managing releases for deployments, as illustrated in Figure 10-10. We have addressed these challenges in Chapter 8. Release management process, which effectively integrates structured approach using SAP Solution Manager for major and minor deployments into production.

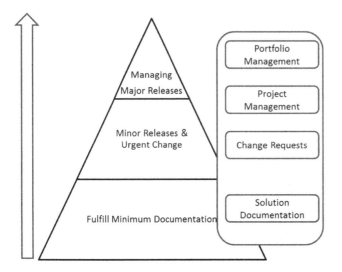

Figure 10-10. *IT project management in Solution Manager—detailed view*

Managing Changes Using SolMan ChaRM

SAP SolMan ChaRM is used to manage the transports, sequencing, and change request approval. It helps in improving transparency in a system with a required workflow for an approval process. A typical SAP landscape has a number of change requests for enhancements, critical production fixes, and support pack activities. The change manager reviews the requests, prioritizes them, and approves them by using ChaRM functionality. Each CR is created in the ChaRM request by the respective user for implementing these changes. It helps to manage incidents from assignment to closure of a ticket-based resolution. Here are the types of changes required to move into production:

- Software change, system upgrade change implementation, enhancements or non-SAP changes

- Request for change category according to severity such as normal, urgent, general change, and/or admin change

The ChaRM workflow is shown in Figure 10-11.

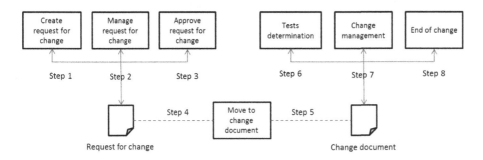

Figure 10-11. *SAP SolMan (ChaRM) workflow*

This workflow highlights the sequence of activities performed during the change management process, such as creating a change request, managing a request for change (RFC), and approving or rejecting changes. Let's review the activities performed by various roles during the RFC process, as illustrated in Figure 10-12.

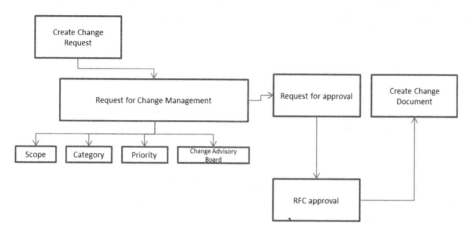

Figure 10-12. *Change request workflow*

RFCs are created, and then they're approved by the RFC manager, who analyzes scope, category, and priority. The CAB (advisory board) does the final approval. After the RFC is released by the change manager, it is approved with necessary documents.

The user creates RFCs with a change ID and priority in SAP SolMan IT service management. Now, let's review a typical RFC process flow, as highlighted in Figure 10-13.

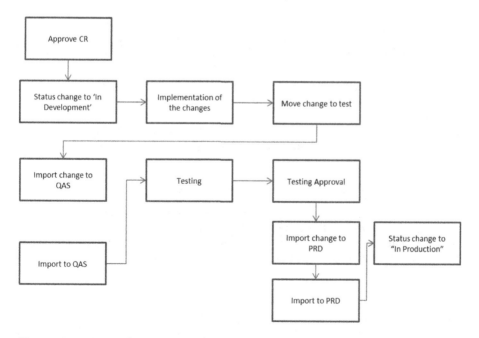

Figure 10-13. *SAP SolMan RFC approval workflow*

After the RFC is approved, the developer changes the status to In-Development until he completes the changes and tests them; then he changes the status to Development Complete and imports the changes to QAS, where they're further tested in the QA environment with the status In QAS with testing approval. When the RFC status passes the test in the QAS environment, it's ready to import to PRD, where the status changes to In Production as soon as it's imported to PRD. You can view the status of the RFC in the ChaRM RFC transaction, shown previously in Figure 10-13.

Roles in the ChaRM

Table 10-1 highlights the roles used in ChaRM.

Table 10-1. *Mapping ChaRM Cycles to ASAP Methodology*

Role	Description
Requestor	Creates requests for change
Change manager	Responsible for processing RFCs, approving or rejecting them
Change advisory board	Team responsible for approvals
Developer	Implements changes in the development system
Tester	Tests implemented corrections in QA system
IT operator	Responsible for implementing changes to test and production systems

Now, let's look at a common pitfall in managing changes in a typical SAP landscape. Figure 10-14 illustrates a three-system landscape:

Figure 10-14. *SAP three-system landscape*

Most of you have observed these challenges while managing changes to your ongoing development, and managing production changes. SAP ChaRM can help you address these challenges. Your correction transports can be bundled using ChaRM with traceability, approval workflow, and more. For example. If you're trying to move a particular transport to production, ChaRM triggers alerts to the respective landscape owner, to identify the impact and determine any conflicts prior to moving the changes to PRD.

Planning and Controlling Projects by Using ChaRM

Let's look at a few project challenges in a real-time environment, shown in Figure 10-15 This plan for multiple projects has three different project Go Lives, respectively, for projects A, B, and C.

Project A is the implementation of a new business process. Project B is an implementation to add new applications. Project C is enhancements. Project D is maintenance, which is ongoing.

Project A	Month 1	Month 2	Month 3	Month 4	Month 5	Month 6
			Blueprint	Realization	UAT	Go Live
Project B	Blueprint	Realization	Go Live			
Project C		Blueprint	Realization	Go Live		
Project D	Develop	Test	Go Live	Develop, Test	Go Live	

Figure 10-15. *Planning multiple projects*

The challenge is managing changes across projects and knowing how to synchronize transports in the landscape. Typically, you'd have a development landscape specific to projects, including enhancements and synchronizing these changes to production in a controlled manner known as release cycles. You'd have a QAS environment for integration testing prior to releasing changes to production. You can define multiple projects in SolMan. These project phases are mapped in the SolMan project cycle. Table 10-2 maps the ChaRM cycles to ASAP.

Table 10-2. *Mapping ChaRM Cycles to ASAP Methodology*

ASAP Phase	SolMan ChaRM Phase
Blueprint	Create ChaRM cycle in SolMan
Realization	Define release cycle for development
Final Prep	Define test cycle
Go Live	Go Live

Concluding Remarks

You've observed the importance of leveraging SAP Solution Manager as part of SAP projects to avoid major pitfalls in the ERP implementation. SAP SolMan is not just a transport tool; it helps you effectively manage changes. It helps in managing projects effectively with extensions to the manual and automation test suite as a central repository for the business blueprint.

■ ■ ■

CHAPTER 11

Leveraging SAP Enterprise Portal

Organizations fail mainly due to a lack of transparency among employees, suppliers, and partners. In today's competitive business landscape, you need quick access to information relevant to you. SAP Enterprise Portal (EP) allows employees, suppliers, and partners to get required information in one centralized repository with easy and quick access. There are many other portals in the market; however, SAP EP provides ready-to-use templates and role-specific SSO integration with authorization. SAP EP is a browser-based application, which means that users can access it through the browser to perform tasks anytime, anywhere. SAP EP can integrate with any landscape SAP or non-SAP to consolidate data into one repository. Also, features such as SSO can help users to access multiple systems including ERP, SRM, CRM, and non-SAP with one user ID to access information across systems.

This chapter will include:

- An overview of SAP Enterprise Portal

- Implementation methodology

What Is an Enterprise Portal?

Companies use portals for efficient. Employees connect for services such as outbound delivery. Normally, user interfaces are required to process business transactions.

It is really easy to develop EP from scratch. You can import required business packages. All you need to do is to deploy business packages with little or no configuration. However, if you want to develop a new portal, WebDyn Pro can be used to build a customized portal using NW Developer studio with predefined scenarios. For example, SAP NW Portal should be able to fetch business process details, data sources, and information about numerous companies.

The SAP Portal core functions are illustrated in Figure 11-1.

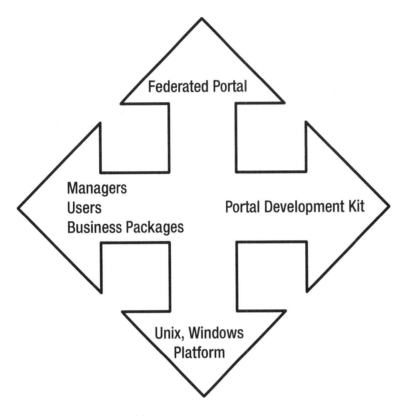

Figure 11-1. *SAP Portal functions*

The concept of a federated portal indicates scenarios where content is exchanged between portals using various de centralized portals with standard third party integration. Portal Development Kit (PDK) helps us to modify the requirements of the Implementation in addition to the portal content. SAP offers PDK's portal development kits; using NW Developer studio, you can write Java development or MSFT development, which can be integrated into the portal.

Let's log into SAP Portal: enter the URL for NW Portal. You'll see the login page. Enter `http://servername.domain.portalno` to enter into the Portal.

The navigation area is on the left. The content is in the main area, with history and personalization options. The header area contains the masthead and tool area with top-level navigation. Portal iView provides options to group lists of links to create favorites, with quick access to information. For example. Purchase Order reports can be created in iView with authorizations including manager's reviews or employee's reviews. There are several iView templates provided in the Portal Content Studio.

To display data in the portal:

- SAP Transaction iView: Used to display transactions in the portal.

- IAC iView: Internet Application Component iView to display transactions, functions, and report in the Web browser. Create IAC in the backend ERP system and then create iView in the portal.

- WDNPro ABAP iView: WebDynPro ABAP iView is used to display WebDynPro ABAP allocations, developed in the backend. You can select one of the iView templates for a specific need, including BW (Bex) report iView, BO iView, JDBC (non-SAP) iView, KM iView, and so on.

An overview of the Enterprise Information Portal is shown in Figure 11-2.

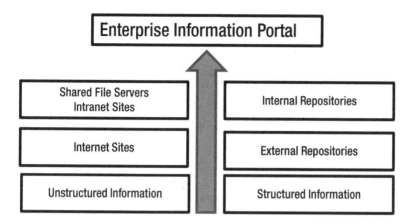

Figure 11-2. *EIP*

Common pitfalls in portal implementation include:

- Lack of defined roles

- Lack of solid business case with quantifiable benefits

- Lack of process, guidelines and authorization

- Lack of common goals across various stakeholders in respective business units

- Lack of centralized governance

In one of the projects that we implemented, there were significant challenges:

- Lack of managing information, despite spending in technology

- Rapid growth of internal and external systems

- Lack of single source of truth in terms of information, as often information was fragmented by respective business units

Hence, the mandate for us was to implement a Portal as a single source of truth for all business units with following goals achieved by the portal implementation:

- Provided single source of truth for all BUs

- Enhanced effective collaboration between employees and managers to achieve the organization goals and strategy, thus improving staff productivity

- Overall decision-making capabilities improved across the departments

- Personalized content for managers on dashboards were very useful for the business to drive quick decision points

- Internal information locked

This project used a staggered approach, as illustrated in Figure 11-3, with defined product backlogs (requirements) in stages based on the business criticality.

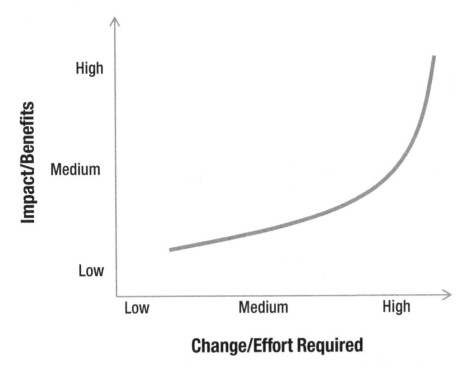

Figure 11-3. *Staggered Approach*

The Unifiers create a unified object model contextually tying the underlying applications. Data is "tied" to one or more objects in the model. The system "walks the path" from one object to another. As a result, users can surf from one application to another, without dealing with the complexity of each one. Figure 11-4 illustrates the high-level architecture of a Portal Unifier.

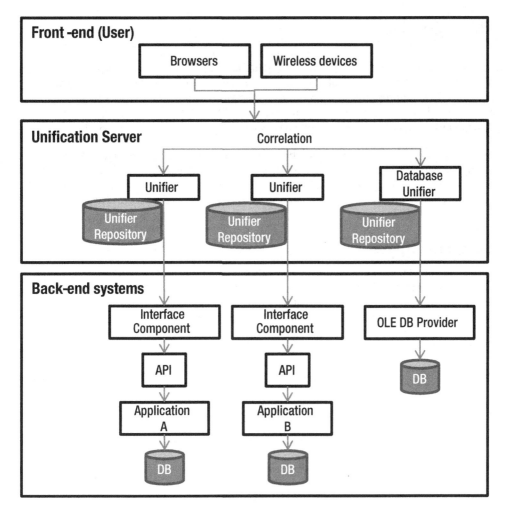

Figure 11-4. *SAP Enterprise Portal User Session Issues*

User Session–Related Issues

User X logs out and User Y is presented with User X's session upon logging in; this is one of the most common issues in Enterprise Portal. This is primarily due to lack of terminating the RFC sessions in the backend, even after the user logs off the portal, because the browser doesn't get terminated when the user clicks 'logoff' in the portal.

The problem is that EP application does not invalidate authenticated session on the server, as soon as the user logs-out. Indeed, cookies may appear to get "cleaned" but when the user returns to the logon page, the previous application session is still active.

Multiuser Logon Issues

Often times you might have noticed a user session is not terminated properly, when you open multiple sessions but returned to the pool and kept open as defined in the 'Connection Lifetime property'. Try to replicate the error, and see if it happens for all other users with different roles in different web browsers. You can check the roles with appropriate authorizations in the SME05 transaction to check sessions. Whenever portal is closed a reference is stored. From using the SM04 transaction it may appear that the sessions remain open but in fact they will only be references. But you are seeing the transaction field remaining filled?

You can select appropriate SAP Notes to resolve these errors mentioned. When a user logs off from your company portal by choosing the Log Off button, a logoff action should be triggered on the SAP portal 'SID'. When the user closes the browser or navigates out of the SAP iFrame, the mechanism does not handle logoff. Instead, your company portal must raise the terminating event when logging off from the SAP portal.

Concluding Remarks

This chapter discussed implementation pitfalls to avoid while implementing SAP Enterprise Portal. It is all about ease of accessing information for employees, suppliers, and partners, to avoid pitfalls due to lack of organized information. With proper planning and configuration using simple iViews, you should be able to design a simple transparent portal for users to fetch information as required by the business.

CHAPTER 12

■ ■ ■

Industrialized Software Implementation

One of the common SAP pitfalls is a lack of skills needed to achieve project success. As SAP's product suite has rapidly changed from enterprise to mobility, consulting organizations have failed to increase the skills or retrain its talent pool. If organizations spend time and money in hiring new people for projects from the market, there is always a learning curve to align with the industry. Therefore, the best practice is to industrialize your approach to project delivery. This approach reminds me of the Ford assembly-line technique, which laid the foundation for manufacturing across the globe and set automotive standards par excellence.

■ **Note**   The industrialized best practices use tools, methods, and accelerators along with a standardized approach to leverage experts across the globe. The focus is not just on global delivery, but on global subject matter experts who can meet the growing demand for skills and use standardized tools, accelerators, and methods to support your clients anywhere in the world.

Industrialized Software Overview

An industrialized software implementation can help consulting organizations implement projects successfully. These industrialized services, combined with high operational standards, can deliver projects by seamlessly integrating subject matter experts (SMEs), tools, accelerators, and methods. The organizations are truly global, with clients in the United States or Europe, and serviced from India, Indonesia, China, the Philippines, or anywhere in the world, without any time constraints. The challenge is to operate under uniform standards that achieve high-quality output.

The following are key tenets of the industrialized approach:

- Consistency of service through asset-based delivery across the entire pool of practitioners

- Reduced cost of development by delivering projects consistently

- Right focus and priority service

- Leveraging of expertise and continuous learning

- Flexibility and scalability of resources to achieve economy of scale

- Long-term improvements in productivity and cost efficiency

- Growth prospect and aspiration of practitioners on a broad basis

Now, let's see how to build an operational industry-based solution, organized within a standard delivery framework. The robust industry best practices will help you achieve a governance model and project metrics to succeed in implementing large and complex projects successfully with common tools, methods, and accelerators. This strategy mitigates risks due to pitfalls such as lack of skills, lack of competency, or increased demand for niche skill areas.

Industrialized Approach

The industrialized approach is a robust delivery framework using standard tools, methods, and accelerators along with an expert SME pool that delivers projects seamlessly as one global unit. As I said earlier, this approach reminds me of Ford's assembly-line management techniques, which set the standard for the entire automotive industry. Since then, the further advent of six sigma principles has improved productivity.

The characteristics of this approach are as follows:

- Robust delivery framework with standard tools, methods, and accelerators.

- Overall cost of development is reduced by delivering projects by using a shared services model, thus increasing productivity.

- Increased quality and reduced delivery defects.

This framework requires two actions:

- Use standard processes, methods, and tools for implementations

- Define a robust governance framework

The following is a model framework for industrialized operations. The framework can be expanded based on your requirements to support worldwide clientele.

- Uniform process, methods, and tools

- Central asset library

- Well-defined roles with automation

- End-to-end status and measurement

The industrialized solution framework provides a platform for real-time and easy access to SMEs for different areas of SAP expertise. Table 12-1 provides a sample list of knowledge management and collaboration platforms for this industrialized approach.

Table 12-1. *Knowledge Management and Collaboration Tools*

Tool	Description	Benefits
Collaboration tool	Real-time access to SMEs.	Reach SMEs anytime, anywhere
Dynamic learning	Create on-demand learning content based on SAP Help training material. Can be used as a search engine to search any technical topic or for creating a mini-course for in-depth study.	Update your learning as a continuous process
Reusable asset library	Develop assets that will help enhance practitioner knowledge. Delivery method will institutionalize submitting as well as reusing these assets.	Accelerate development with the asset library

Operational Framework

Building an operational framework for the industrialized approach takes time, requiring well-defined processes, established standards, and agreed-upon metrics. Let's look at the basic constitution of the framework, as illustrated in Figure 12-1.

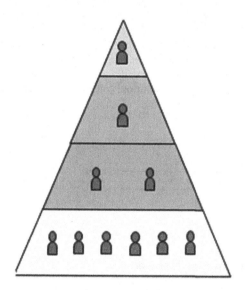

Figure 12-1. *Industrialized operational framework*

This industrial operational framework has the following characteristics:

- An atom is the basic service delivery of the industry framework; it is the smallest microcosm.

- An atom is internally structured like a pyramid that is made of functions performed by skill-based resource groups.

- Functions provide increased value, which are added as you move upward from the base of the pyramid. These functions include development, subject matter expertise, and management.

- Typical practitioner roles are developer, senior developer, subject matter expert, and atom leader.

You have the flexibility as a project manager to include practitioners as part of the core resource pool or as a flexible resource pool to the atom. Resources can be tagged as *Flex* resources based on the project complexity and requirements. The core resources specialization group (SG) is established with multiple atoms that have functionally aligned groups such as Functional and Development (FRICE). Each functional group encompasses subatoms such as the following:

Finance & controlling (FI/CO), supply chain management (SCM), supplier relationship management (SRM) and customer relationship management (CRM), enterprise mobility (Fiori), SAP tools team (testing, accelerators), analytics (BI/BO), and HANA and Enterprise Portal (EP) with SMEs tagged from across the globe.

One interesting approach is well-defined governance with exact hours of SME utilization to help projects succeed on time and on budget. I've observed that most projects fail because of a lack of skill or availability of SMEs required during a specific phase of a project. It is not feasible to bill SMEs at the same cost as full time equivalent (FTE), because of budgetary constraints and the largely diversified expertise required in any SAP implementation project implemented as work packages. For example, you cannot hire a person for environment, health and safety (EHS) implementation for a short-term billable activity..

If you're able to mitigate these risks in implementation projects, you're well on your way to building another successful case study. Further, pooling SMEs into this shared services unit known as the atom model will help you optimize your use resources, instead of using an FTE-based approach. Because most projects are fixed bids, it is imperative to follow a shared services model, where you'd get the SMEs to support for the billable hours, instead of full-time resources, as in a time and materials model. In essence, the atom model provides a productive use of resources, and further keeps employees interested with multiple assignments. If you're able to consider a price reduction during the proposal stage of the solution, you have a good chance of winning the proposal. This will help you remain competitive and truly global.

Table 12-2 outlines the roles within the industrialized approach.

Table 12-2. *Roles and Functions*

SNO	Industry Functions	Roles
1	Development	Developer
2	SME	SME
3	Atom management	Atom lead
4	Service management	Project lead / atom delivery manager
5	Location management	Integration manager
6	Services request management	Services delivery manager
7	Delivery management	Services delivery manager
8	Quality assurance	Quality assurance lead
9	Program operations	Project management assistant
10	Management	Industry program lead

Typically, some of these roles (such as service delivery manager) may reside outside industry management, as industry alignment is primarily skill based. Now, let's look at an example of an industrialized services delivery organization.

Work Allocation

Figure 12-2 shows how to allocate work in an industrialized service delivery organization.

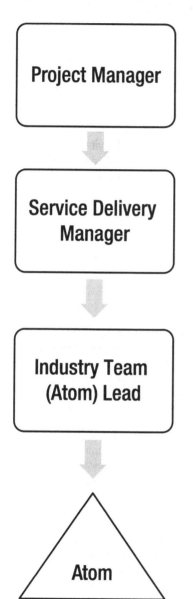

Figure 12-2. *Industry work allocation*

The unit of work is defined by the respective project manager, and assigned to the respective service delivery manager, who will own the delivery. The service delivery manager is responsible for allocating a unit of work based on the service capabilities of the atom, which is further subdivided into respective atom pyramids, which are activated based on the skill requirements to deliver the project as one global team.

Industry Project Organization

Now, let's look at what an industry-based project organization looks like, as highlighted in Figure 12-3.

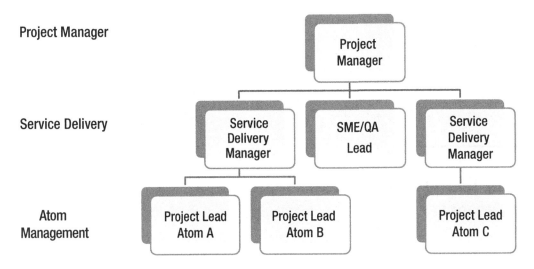

Figure 12-3. *Industry project organization*

Typically, the industry lead and the integration manager are co-located in the same region as that of the client, in a delivery center or even the client location, to understand the requirements. Once the scope is defined, with the specific atom's responsibilities, atom will go through the atom organization for the service delivery. Each atom lead/project lead reports to the service delivery manager, who in turn reports to the on-site integration manager. The QA lead is responsible for setting up the metrics, implementing a quality framework, and measuring defects. The SME lead is responsible for bringing in the respective SMEs across the globe, to fit the niche skill requirements in SAP. Each of these advisory SMEs provides support to ensure project success. Project meetings are conducted on a daily, weekly, monthly, and quarterly basis. The meeting participants vary, depending on the frequency and the subject point. Usually, management reporting is monthly, with detailed metrics such as cost, scope, and schedule variance discussed among all key stakeholders (on-site lead, service delivery managers, integration manager, and respective atom lead).

Governance

The challenge is to build a robust governance model to adapt to complex projects. These projects should be aligned with the industrialized program governance, as highlighted in Figure 12-4.

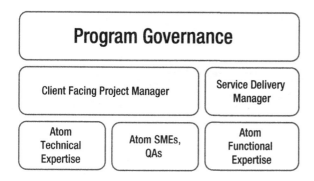

Figure 12-4. *Industrialized solution program governance*

There is a global central program governance, as highlighted in the figure. Client-facing teams are on-site, and an offshore team executes projects in this industrialized approach as offshore delivery units, which may be in one or multiple locations. The work plan is defined based on the project complexity. The following key characteristics set the basic ground rules for a successful implementation of projects using the industrialized approach:

- The service delivery manager (SDM) is part of the on-site program governance.

- The atom shared services team has required remote service delivery and is measured by KPIs.

- Global HR is responsible for talent acquisition, work allocation, and delivery.

- The atom program lead is responsible for managing quality and SLAs.

Table 12-3 indicates the benefits and challenges of the industrialized approach.

Table 12-3. *Benefits and Challenges of the Industrialized Approach*

Approach	Benefits	Challenges
Using industrialized solution	Improved productivity High quality Shared KPIs High employee retention Global standards	Need trust on both sides High quality management Well-defined services model Geographical and cultural sensitivity Well-defined processes, roles, and responsibilities to avoid conflicts

Figure 12-5 illustrates the benefits in a nutshell of leveraging an industrialized software implementation approach. These benefits are summarized in terms of the following:

- Cost savings

- Productivity gains

- Defects free

This approach uses unified project management, common governance, tools, accelerators, methods, metrics, and KPIs. Overall, it reduces risks to delivery, and implementation has a high success rate.

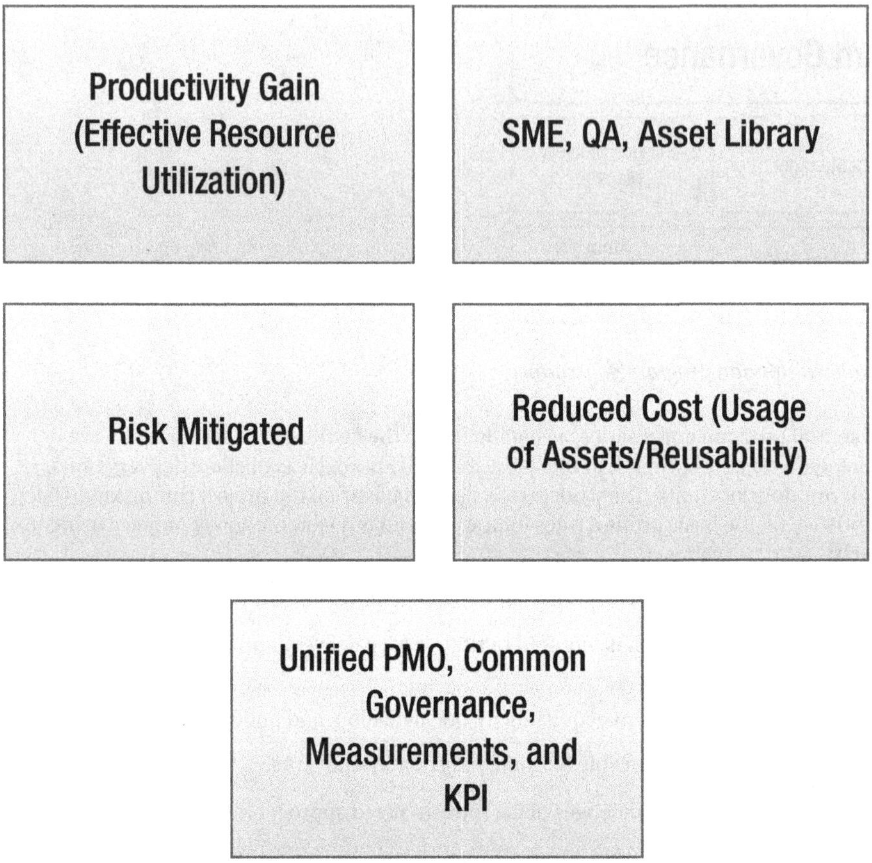

Figure 12-5. *Benefits of industrialized software implementation*

Key Performance Indicators

The core objective is to deliver projects with reduced cost and effort, on schedule, and with quality. Now, let's see what metrics are required as part of the industrialized solution approach, including the frequency of measurement and goals to achieve. Table 12-4 illustrates the key performance indicators and project metrics.

Table 12-4. *Knowledge Management and Collaboration Tools*

Category	Metrics	Definition	Frequency
Cost and Effort	Effort variation	Actual vs. planned	Monthly
	Effort savings due to reuse	Ratio of effort savings due to reuse asset library vs. actual development	Monthly
	% budget on delivery	% deliverables achieved within budget	
	Size variation	No. of deliverables different from the estimated size	Monthly
Schedule	Schedule delay	Indicates the schedule slippage	Monthly
	% on-time delivery	% delivered on time as compared to the estimated	Monthly
Quality	Defects injection rate	Ratio of in-process defects	Monthly
	Delivered defect rate	Ratio of defects / dev hours	
	Cost of quality	Ratio of rework / actual dev hours	Monthly
	Cost of poor quality		

Key solution considerations utilizing the industrialized global delivery framework:

- Consideration of the governance model.

- Choosing the right service delivery model as opposed to the extended team model.

- Agreed-upon delivery with KPIs/SLAs, and with defined performance targets with clients.

- Flexibility to align with the operational model.

- The service request manager will adopt standard industry ways of working (processes, tools, templates).

Key considerations of team requirements:

- Differentiate between the Core and Flex team requirements.

- IT infrastructure & IT security.

- IT infrastructure, security, and access-control mechanisms determine how systems are accessed from remote locations. The nature of infrastructure across multiple clients determines whetx`her common service delivery units can be shared for them.

- Agreement with clients need to deliver using an industry-based approach.

The following is a sample engagement model for a client, utilizing an industry-based implementation approach. However, this can vary, depending on organizational vision and strategy.

Key Engagement Rules

Let's look at the key engagement rules below:

- The service request manager (SRM) adopts standard industry standard ways of working.

- The service delivery manager (SDM) is responsible for activating the respective atom units, with the industry organization based on skill and requirements.

- Services delivered by each atom should be modularized with delivery standards and expectations met as per SLAs.

- Every industry engagement is characterized by a service requesting manager who channelizes work to industry atoms.

- The industry lead is the single point for each engagement that is identified. This person works closely with the service requesting manager.

- The industry has standardized templates/standards/checklists/assets and accelerators.

There are basic requirements that need to be fulfilled, such as the network requirements and remote connectivity. The client may have additional security needs, such as physical isolation/client-imaged machines/dedicated network. There are substantial benefits to the client in projects such as managed services, as you can optimize delivery to the pay-per-ticket type of model, rather than T&M model, which is gaining prominence.`

Concluding Remarks

The industrialized software implementation approach and delivery is a best practice followed by most Fortune 100 companies to achieve projects that are completed on time, on target, and on budget. Indeed, this should be the way to mitigate most of the risks in SAP implementation projects. SAP is ever expanding, and the skill requirements are rapidly changing from enterprise back-end software to enterprise mobility. Therefore, there is a compelling need for consulting organizations to provide expert SMEs across the globe, as one team that's extremely skill based, to support the growing demands of clients. You cannot bill SMEs for five hours per week or plan to hire a consultant for a few months for expert solution advice. The industrialized approach will help you pool SMEs as one global team to support any challenges faced during implementation projects. Today, ERP mobility is increasingly modular; because you'd approach project implementations using ASAP-Agile, the skill requirements cannot be linear throughout the project phases. I am sure you should approach planning and implementation by using an industrialized approach, as discussed in this chapter.

CHAPTER 13

∎ ∎ ∎

Accelerate SAP Implementation Using RDS

Typically, ERP solutions are perceived to be complex with too many unknown risks that you might discover along the way. The irony is that most issues escalate during the integration and UAT phases, thus plaguing the ERP implementation project due to pitfalls such as scope creep, and lack of end user or business SME support. You need options such as an agile methodology for faster implementations using a rapid build approach, instead of a big-bang approach, where users have the visibility to test the solution. SAP RDS is a rapid prototype method, where preconfigured scenarios are easy to deploy in less than eight weeks.

In this chapter, you'll explore the benefits of Rapid Deployment Solutions (RDS) and how it helps you avoid major pitfalls in ERP implementation projects such as lack of scope control, to be able to achieve a successful implementation of Go Live on time, on budget, and on schedule. The RDS solution is available for almost every industry to adapt to specific business scenarios.

Why do customers go for RDS implementation? Customers are delighted to realize that implementation with a baseline configuration in 12 weeks is a phenomenal turnaround in the history of ERP implementations. It's really agile, with release bundles in accelerated Go Lives to the business, which means measured outcomes in less time. Typically, it takes months to complete a business blueprint, which no longer exists in the RDS methodology that uses a real, accelerated ERP implementation approach with over 100 preconfigured scenarios including rapid data migration services for industry solutions. More and more customers are migrating to the cloud to optimize service delivery with accelerated SAP HANA cloud services.

RDS Overview

SAP provides RDS for implementing business solutions faster, in weeks with a baseline package, instead of spending years customizing it. RDS provides a quick return on ERP investments, with ready-to-use scenarios that businesses can benefit from. A traditional ERP implementation will take 6–12 months with a blueprint which normally takes eight weeks. In my view, customers don't know what they want, unless they see what they want! RDS provides a rapid prototype to showcase the end-to-end solution.

Especially in a complex landscape where you interact with various departments to consolidate requirements, blueprinting business processes takes a lot of time. Furthermore, analyzing solutions in SAP with configuration and customization requirements can go beyond a few months. When you hit the actual realization, development phase is already delayed, and developing custom programs, testing, and integration takes more time. Instead of all these uncertainties, with RDS the scope is almost frozen as you realize the end-to-end business process. Above all, RDS data migration is really simple when using RDS DM tools. Often failed implementations are due to the pitfalls of lack of a data migration plan, lack of control, and lack of end-product vision. All of that has been mitigated in the RDS methodology by leveraging software best practices and RDS expertise. In a traditional approach, the duration is longer than 12 months and sometimes even longer, and the implementation till may not be done due to scope creep or integration issues.

It's staggering to realize phenomenal savings in the blueprint phase, as no blueprint workshops are required in an RDS implementation. The preconfigured scenarios write off all blueprint requirements and testing efforts, and these scenarios can be used for analyzing the business process instead of being bogged down by customer development, testing, and integration. In the kickoff of RDS, you'll hear best practices, and instead of asking questions, you'll play back the scenarios to the business SMEs and user groups to support the implementation team. Overall, risks of deployment are mitigated up front with an end-product vision using RDS. It's a lot easier to implement RDS compared to the traditional approach.

Now, let's take a look at what RDS contains. Each phase (Start-Run-Deploy) has a bunch of relevant documents, with required accelerators such as a standard scoping questionnaire.

You have started discovery, decided to go for RDS, and collected a bunch of questions in the scope as part of the RDS Start phase. Now, let's move on to the RDS deployment details. The Deploy phase includes ready-to-use reports such as the following:

- Financial reporting
- Sales reporting
- Shipping
- Purchasing
- Master data reporting

In a nutshell, RDS provides the following:

- Preconfigured software for standard scenarios such as order-to-cash
- Content developed in RDS for quick start-up pack
- End-user enablement with training pack available in RDS
- Implementation services

You can deploy solutions using RDS as an on-premise, cloud, or enterprise mobility option.

AP Finance and Controlling on HANA

SAP provides accelerated finance and controlling using HANA. HANA helps in reporting of CO-PA, overhead, material ledger, and production costs. RDS replicates CO tables in the HANA database with minimal changes to accelerate its function. SAP net-margin analysis by SAP HANA helps to improve net margins by eliminating hidden costs, with drill-down capabilities and product-level detail. You can use the CO-PA accelerator built in HANA along with the power of BW for quick, analytical capabilities.

In addition, the ISAP Rapid Migration tool helps in quick migration to SAP HANA from SAP NetWeaver BW, and it enables faster decision making by leveraging HANA capabilities.

Operational Reporting

Let's review enhanced reporting capabilities in HANA.

- Deliver real-time analytical capabilities
- Deliver powerful end-user reporting with slicing and dicing capabilities
- Enable more business transparency across the organization by utilizing all data

- Rapidly respond to the business needs and to react more quickly to change with SAP HANA

- Get quick time to value with predefined data models

Now, let's have a look at the RDS implementation methodology.

Implementation Methodology

With SAP rapid deployment solutions, you know the cost and scope of your implementation up front—including rigorous timelines for the delivery of a completed implementation. See Figure 13-1.

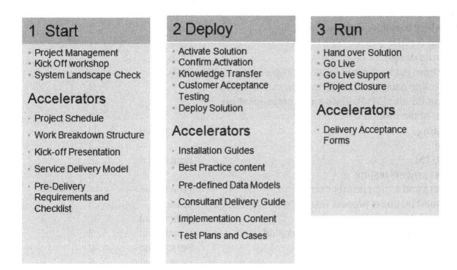

Figure 13-1. *RDS implementation phases*

Table 13-1 shows a summary of the rapid deployment phases.

Table 13-1. *Rapid Deployment Phase with Activites and Deliverables*

Phase	Activities	Deliverables
Start	Project management, kickoff workshop, & system landscape check	Delivery guide Project schedule WBS, service delivery model, roles & responsibilities Templates, process-flow documents, kickoff presentation, consumption guide, pre-delivery requirements and checklist
Deploy	Solution realization, master data load, refinement workshop & refinement realization, KT to key users	Install guide, solution documentation, SolMan content, best practice content (preconfigured), configuration activities, and implementation content
Run	Performance tests, end-user training, sign-off solution, Go Live prep & Go Live, post Go Live support and activities Improvements & roadmap workshop	Test cases, delivery acceptable forms, training materials, & Go-Live checklist

Now, let's look at the key tasks in a typical RDS implementation project, with the roles and responsibilities of the Basis and Functional teams, as shown in Table 13-2.

Table 13-2. RDS Project Plan

Phase	Task	Responsible	Duration (Person Days)
Start	Install hardware prerequisites	Basis	1
	Kickoff & solution vision		1
	Perform SAP installation ECC 6.0 EHP 7.0		1
	Install RDS add-ons as required	Basis	1
	Implement RDS ERP baseline package	Basis	1
	Configure SolMan for RDS	Basis	1
	Implement security design	Basis	1
	Implement ERP base package for FI (create company code, etc.)	Basis	2
	Activate ERP baseline package of configuration in SAP best practices Solution Builder (MM). Plant and storage location		3
	SD, PP activation of the module		3
	Perform unit testing	Functional	2
	Activate PM/QM		2
	Activate HR.OM/TM	Functional	2
	Perform business process testing		2
	Create master data and assign number range	Functional	2
	Perform end-to-end business process testing	Testing/ Functional	2
	Use RDS data upload tool suite for master data load	Functional	2
	Perform end-to-end cycle I & II testing	Functional	2
	Perform user acceptance testing	Functional	5
	Complete final prep & Go Live		2
	Provide support	Functional	2
		Functional	5
			10
		Functional	5
		Functional	10

RDS Baseline Packages

You can select the RDS appropriate to your business by navigating through the list and searching for the right RDS baseline package. The lists are divided by relevant industry, product category, and line of business.

Now, let's explore one of the RDS baseline packages by selecting your LOB. You can also search for an RDS baseline package in the SAP Store. For example, you can search for "Finance" to find solutions, including specific RDS partner solutions with reviews. SCN can provide details about a specific RDS solution.

Technical Data

Let's explore the technical RDS package details available in SAP SolMan as an add-on release. Table 13-3 lists the technical details.

Table 13-3. *Basline Package*

Technical Name of Template	RDS_BL_ERP607_US_V3 SAP RDS for ERP 607 Baseline Package_US_V3
Available as of SAP Solution Manager Content Add-On Release	ST-RDS 100 (latest support package)
Industry	Baselines (country specific)
Business Variant	None
Line of Business	FIN/Trade/Manufacturing/Service industry
Country or Region	United States
Product Releases	SAP enhancement package 7 for SAP ERP 6.0, version for SAP HANA

Features

With the following SAP Solution Manager template, you can perform implementation of the RDS ERP baseline solution packages, for these entry levels: Services, Financials, Manufacturing, and Trade.

In Solution Manager, you select a solution package attribute value and then the entry level value, as shown here:

- SAP ERP607 for Baseline BAiO_<Country Abbreviation>_V3 ➤ All Entry Levels

- SAP ERP607 for Service_<Country Abbreviation>_V3 ➤ Services

- SAP ERP607 for Finance & Controlling_<Country Abbreviation>_V3 ➤ Financials

- SAP ERP607 for Manufacturing_<Country Abbreviation>_V3 ➤ Manufacturing

- SAP ERP607 for Trading _<Country Abbreviation>_V3 ➤ Trade

CASE STUDY: SAP RDS SOLUTION FOR DEMAND PLANNING

A customer wants to use an RDS solution for a supply-chain demand plan for a fixed project with defined scope. In the area of sales and operational planning, the customer sales lead is responsible for analyzing the sales forecast after the local plan. The lead checks the plan as a last step, and the sales rep uploads the plan data to ERP. Once the new demand plan is uploaded, the regional lead validates the promotions. Let's review the RDS capabilities in enhancing planning. The workflow of the demand plan process steps are highlighted in the following flow chart.

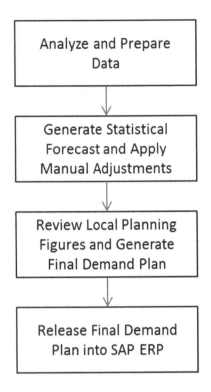

The following is an example of a planning book used by the customer for planning details. You can review the forecast. Furthermore, the manual forecast can be changed by the local planner. The key figure can be made editable. You can review the local plan, and the marketing planner can adjust the statistical forecasts. The aggregated statistical data can be realized. Some sales can be 30% higher than the actual. The customer was able to review the planning book by using the standard scenarios to test how it works. RDS had significantly reduced efforts to build the processes and additional time in regression. It was easy to use, with four to six weeks of effort for activation of the RDS solution for demand planning.

Concluding Remarks

RDS methodology is the way to implement SAP solutions faster and smarter, in weeks rather than months, to reap the benefits of ROI and to implement projects successfully. You can implement projects faster and smarter because you can use preconfigured scenarios. As more and more customers embrace RDS methodology and cloud migration, SAP has increased its out-of-the-box solutions to support this growing need for faster implementation on budget.

CHAPTER 14

■ ■ ■

Transforming to SAP Enterprise Cloud

Most often, implementation projects fail due to one of these major pitfalls: cost, schedule issues, or complexity of the business process. What if your business could run without worrying about network hassles, infrastructure needs, and software change requirements? It's possible—the cloud is literally changing the way enterprises manage their businesses. Instead of running your enterprise applications on-premises in the traditional way, you can access information globally with a cloud-based enterprise solution.

Using the cloud is less expensive, which is important for executives who are concerned about their IT spending. But there's more to it than the cost factor. A hybrid model that combines the power of on-premises solutions with cloud-based solutions can mitigate risk. You can avoid failed ERP implementations with the cloud, because its service-delivery model has the inherent ability to run quickly by virtue of being an integrated package. For example, you don't have to worry about lost productivity due to server downtime if you choose infrastructure as a service (IaaS), which is governed by SLAs as part of the service subscription model.

Cloud-based implementations avoid issues such as scope creep, budget overruns, and schedule problems, because most projects are driven by a defined scope, and your budget is based on a subscription. Less turnaround time is required to deliver applications, because you aren't using the entire ASAP/agile process; you just use the activated services, which come as part of the SAP Business One package. Implementation costs are significantly lower, because there are no up-front expenses, and infrastructure investments are literally zero. You can stay focused on deliverables.

A platform is offered for development with the platform as a service (PaaS) model. If you have many integrated applications and plan to use IaaS and PaaS services but want to develop custom applications as well, then you need to explore beyond the standard software as a service (SaaS) or perhaps take it up all by yourself, in which case the risks applicable to implementing critical applications remain. However, you don't have to worry about risks related to infrastructure, platform, and so on. You can focus on custom development—and even these risks can be mitigated if you adopt best practices from SAP and use agile with comprehensive testing solutions offered by SAP.

You can have disaster recovery (DR) solutions in the cloud to support your critical business operations. Today, more and more businesses are going agile, with no time to spare on IT or waiting years for ROI. Shareholders expect returns every quarter! Hence, there is a constant need to improve your business processes, with scalability for continuous improvements. Enterprise mobility—for example, planning sales meetings with customers using a CRM sales solution, or doing on-demand planning using SAP RDS—has turned agile in response to customer requests. However, the real challenge is to be flexible in the changing IT landscape.

Consumers' lives have also changed, with the evolution of the cloud from a simple mobile gadget application. Now home appliances use cloud-based services, and enterprise applications are turning nimble. These changes have paved the way for a new mode of communication. Future cloud-based enterprise software will include industrialized software services and ready-to-use component-based service models. Gone are the days of costly ERP implementations; and gone are the days of technology struggling to catch up with business requirements.

Today solutions are being implemented for space technology, unmanned aircraft, drones, navigation systems to support driverless cars, and refrigerators that are automatically replenished by a grocery store app. More and more apps are being developed, and for the first time in the history of technology, technology has surpassed business. This leads me to believe that technology is no longer just back-end support. It may turn out that vital, decision-making front-end software will drive business units instead of supporting business as mere enablers. These changes are apparent with the advent of analytics and Big Data over the last decade.

SAP provides HANA Enterprise Cloud to quickly deliver flexible solutions that can be implemented and supported with no up-front investment via an easy-to-use, subscription-based services model. Let's explore these options with a case study to analyze the business benefits in more depth. Cloud adoption is increasing every day; eventually, almost every organization will run applications on the cloud, similar to how we have adopted mobile applications as part of our lives. The IT landscape is changing constantly, and enterprises are adapting to increased demand that they optimize resource costs. The cloud model leads to new enterprise startups that can quickly scale up as viable competitors to large global players.

Large enterprises may struggle a little as they begin the transition to the cloud, but they will change in a way similar to how they revamped their applications for Y2K compliance or how they have adopted CRM and enterprise mobility. Amazon increasingly has cloud-based services as a forte, along with PaaS; and giants such as IBM have invested heavily in cloud data centers for IaaS solutions. The new-age enterprise with cloud-based delivery can be set up in no time with DR and high availability that let you run applications on the cloud with ease.

In a nutshell, the cloud provides the following benefits for organizations:

- Flexibility

- Enhanced DR

- Freedom from capital expenditures

- Quick software updates and enhancements

There are several types of cloud:

- Private cloud: Exclusive cloud for the customer, with hosted data centers for the client, security enabled, and SLAs

- Public cloud: Available to all, with a secured data-center model, security enabled, and SLAs

- Community cloud: Cloud sharing with others in a similar line of business, similar to a public cloud by LOB

- Hybrid cloud: Combination of the public and private models

The next section discusses the merits of these cloud deployment options.

SAP Cloud Overview

With S4 HANA Cloud Platform (HCP), you can use simplified finance, accounting, procurement, and manufacturing applications in the cloud. SAP HCP provides an abstraction layer so that without giving up your business needs, you can support your changes on a regular basis. You can move to standardized and scalable governance. SAP HANA Enterprise Cloud is the bridge to the S/4HANA private managed cloud environment or a hybrid cloud landscape, as shown in Figure 14-1.

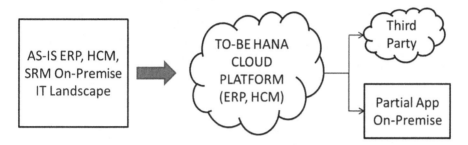

Figure 14-1. *SAP HANA Cloud Platform (HCP)*

The good news is that you can make choices regarding the hybrid landscape, in terms of governance, security, customization complexity, risk mitigation, innovation, and so on. SAP has a cloud strategy to support your cloud portfolio and help you run your entire operation in a simple, agile, on-cloud manner. SAP's investment in Success Factors, which is primarily a cloud company, shows its commitment to migrating enterprise applications to the cloud. Essentially, the partner landscape will change along with the associated delivery models: instead of global delivery, you will use cloud service delivery with a consumable partner delivery approach.

Now, let's look at the basics and benefits of cloud computing. Amazon Web Services tops the list of cloud enterprise solutions. The power of cloud computing is increasingly reaching the masses: the election campaign done using AWS services had a significant impact on cloud computing in the United States, and buzz is increasing across the globe. As businesses become more and more cost-conscious, there is constant pressure to reduce IT spending, and most enterprises are migrating to the cloud: investment is estimated to increase from USD $40 billion in 2011 to USD $240 billion in 2020 (see Table 14-1).

Table 14-1. *Cloud Services Revenue Forecast*

Cloud Type	Year 2011 $ B	Year 2020 $ B
Public Cloud	25.5	159.3
Private Cloud	7	66.4
Virtual Private Cloud	7.8	15.9

According to a Forrester report, cloud computing consists of IT-based services that are offered by service providers using Internet protocols and that scale automatically to demand. Figure 14-2 shows the key attributes of the cloud computing model.

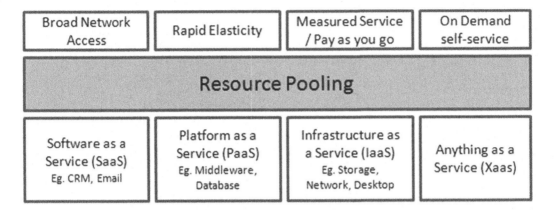

Figure 14-2. *Cloud computing attributes*

This revolution has changed the software-delivery model. Global delivery centers are investing in cloud-based solutions in terms of training resources and are providing private hybrid cloud infrastructure deployment models as part of their delivery approach. The tools, techniques, and implementation guidelines of the IT delivery landscape are changing rapidly. Essentially, solutions are made for the cloud, ready to be deployed on the cloud as consumable services. Simple, mobile apps are available for download from the Apple and Samsung cloud networks. It's exciting that businesses can download consumable services and use simple enterprise solutions for order processing, procurement, reporting, and so on.

Table 14-2 compares key attributes of the cloud versus the on-premises model.

Table 14-2. *Cloud vs. On-Premises*

Key Attributes	Cloud	On-Premises
Broad network access	High network access is available everywhere regardless of the number of users. For example: Gmail has over 1 billion users.	E-mail setup for an organization is individual and takes time, with limited network bandwidth.
Rapid elasticity/ scalability	You can rapidly extend your capabilities. For example: newsfeed channels have an increasing number of users. You can increase the number of services in no time.	Limited capabilities.
Measured services (pay as you go) subscription model	You can subscribe to the services you need to run the business, such as CRM	
On-demand self-service	You can demand specific services, like a satellite TV network.	
Resource pooling	You have easy access to SMEs across the globe.	

Now, let's look at the parts of the service-delivery model in the cloud, as shown in Figure 14-3:

- Software as a service (SaaS): The application is hosted centrally, with all business software available to the consumer as services. For example: CRM, SalesForce.com, Gmail, GoToMeeting, WebEx, and so on.

- Platform as a service (PaaS): The entire platform of services, such as the database, is available as a service. You can develop applications on the platform provided, such as a database or mobile API, with a pay-as-you-go model; for example, you can use Google API services and post applications on Google.

- Infrastructure as a service (IaaS): This is a consumption model with a virtualized desktop, where the infrastructure is provided to you: a virtual server, virtual desktop, and virtual memory. Infrastructure is available whenever you need it and is scalable. You can use a desktop as a virtual server with high bandwidth and unlimited storage services, and you can host your applications. For example: Amazon Web Services (AWS) and Tata Communications are service providers.

	Saas	Paas	Iaas
	Consume	Build	Host
Consumer	End User	Application Owner	Application Owner
Type of Services	Completed Application	Run Time Scenario	Cloud Storage Virtual Server
Covera at Service Level	Application Uptime & Performance	Environment Availability Environment Performance No Application Coverage	Virtual Server Availability Time to Provision No platform or application coverage
Examples of Services Provided	CRM, emails, ERP	Application Development Decision Support Web Streaming	Caching Security Legacy System Management

Figure 14-3. *Service-delivery models*

Now, how do you deploy applications on the Cloud? A hybrid cloud is a combination of a public and a private cloud, whereas a community cloud hosts a group of companies in a similar industry. The best part is the unlimited resources, such as high computing capabilities. You can request AWS services for a supercomputer, and they're set up and running in minutes. Table 14-3 describes the cloud deployment model and its benefits to customers.

Table 14-3. *Cloud Deployment Options*

Key Attributes	Public	Private	Hybrid
Infrastructure and services	Mega scale	Finite	Combination of two or more clouds
Publically available	Yes	Enterprise owned	Mixed usage of private and public
Multitenant applications and services	Yes	Charged back to LOBs	Yes
Access virtually unlimited applications	Yes	Cloud computing in company's data center	Yes
Mixed usage of public and private access	No	Only private access	Yes

Figure 14-4 shows a classic case study of a hybrid cloud model.

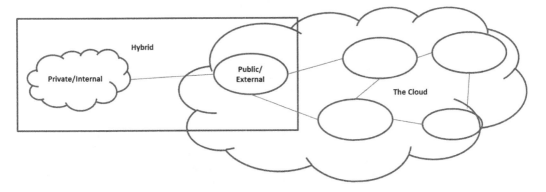

Figure 14-4. *Hybrid cloud model*

In summary, a hybrid cloud gives you the flexibility and power a private cloud with the extensibility of a public cloud. Some typical concerns that organizations have are as follows:

- Loss of control
- Integration (authorization)
- Interoperability
- Accessibility

To alleviate these issues, SAP customers can choose WFT Cloud: a certified SAP cloud computing solutions provider that has pioneered SAP private cloud and hybrid cloud offerings. WFT had transformed its own data center into a software-defined data center (SDDC) for SAP. The WFT Cloud Center of Excellence has created an offering to help customers transform their data centers, which helps reduce their total cost and improve ROI.

Enterprise-Class IT in the Cloud

Today, enterprises need a robust cloud platform to host applications securely and with high efficiency. SAP HANA is the answer: it provides a secure platform in an SAP-hosted environment, with the analytical power and transaction-processing database of HANA to support your client requirements. Figure 14-5 shows cloud-hosted services with multiple databases and applications hosted in the cloud.

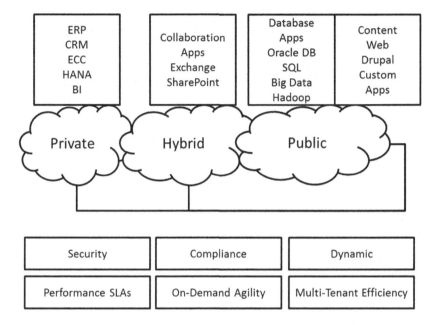

Figure 14-5. *Cloud-hosted services*

SAP Business One Cloud

SAP Business One Cloud is a browser-based ERP. With a browser on any devise, you can run SAP applications in the cloud. Figure 14-6 illustrates browser-based access to SAP.

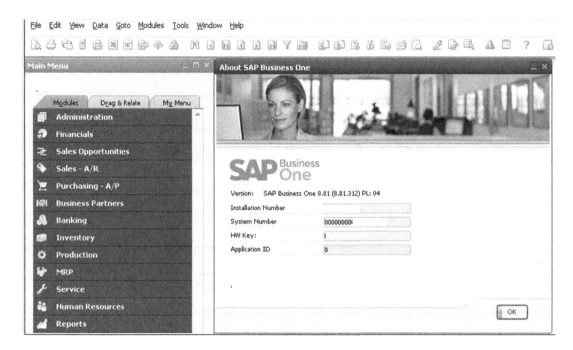

Figure 14-6. *Browser access to SAP Business One cloud*

You can make sales quotes, select products, and showcase them to customers. These standard functionalities are activated once you procure the software. You can use any browser to locate transactions: whether you use IE, Chrome, or Firefox, the system connects to SAP Business One Cloud. It's quick, simple, and easy to access SAP Business One Cloud solutions anytime, anywhere.

With SAP Business One it is easy and fast to enter and record customer orders and issue invoices. It helps you access complete inventory across multiple warehouses in one order entry. It provides options for alternate items to make the sale if you are out of stock.

Now, let's look at how to build a private cloud to run SAP enterprise software. One of the large India-based multinational provides IaaS; its services include data centers with a SaaS model using a simple application to build infrastructure service capabilities. This section explores how to set up IaaS services by building virtual machines, configuring and installing SAP Business One components, and deploying SAP in the cloud center.

End-to-End SAP HANA Cloud Platform

The example business scenario assumes you're doing claims assessment in the back-end system. You need to create a native mobile app for claims agents. Let's see what is required to expose this functionality using Fiori. First you need an API and an API management solution such as Insurance Claim to expose services for external consumption. Create the API and publish the claims process.

To manage security, you need to subscribe to the API. The interface the API exposes comes from the back-end gateway services. Create the application using Web IDE, as shown in Figure 14-7.

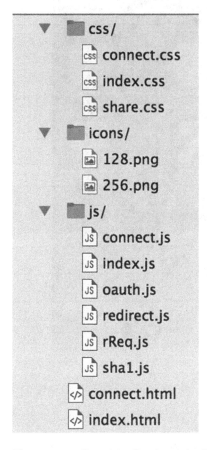

Figure 14-7. *Create Application using Web IDE*

Now you can create a new project. Use the Fiori template, and link it to the back end SAP using the API. You can preview as well. If you want to change something, you can edit the XML file using an editor. The app can also be modified using the editor. You have defined the API and created the app, and now the app is moved to the cloud. Anyone who logs in to HANA Cloud can use the app if they have the relevant authorization. You can also move the app to mobile. You've created a new application, loaded an application from the app store, used a template for iOS, and published to the company app store, as shown in Figure 14-8. It's simple to build apps in SAP HCP, as illustrated in the following case study.

Figure 14-8. Corporate app store

Case Study

Let's work through a case study of setting up IaaS using a third-party cloud infrastructure offering. Users can set up a specific configuration using a simple request online. Here are the steps:

1. Select Instance within a data center specific to location.

2. Let's set up this data center in Singapore for supporting operations in Asia Pacific. Choose Singapore in the Availability Zone list. Select a template to build the virtual machine with Windows Server 2002 R2 with a 20GB primary disk and RDP enabled.

3. Select your instance's core and RAM requirements. If you're running domain controller, the 1 Core, 1 GHz, 1 GB RAM option should be good enough. You can choose larger values if you want more cores, and so on.

4. Select a data disk. For example, you can choose 100GB Disk.

5. Let's move on to network offerings. You can connect over the Internet using a dedicated network by setting up a public IP address or using a MPLS network, which is a private network. Here, select Internet Connected Virtual Network.

6. Review your service choices. You can provide a name for the instance, in case you're planning to use multiple instances using different configuration parameters.

7. Click submit. The system will provision the environment for you. You receive a message when the instance has been created successfully. You're given a new password to log on to this particular instance.

You've successfully created the domain controller; you many want another one as a backup. Follow the previous steps to create the backup domain controller with prebuilt virtual machines. It's exciting. Now, log in to the virtual machine, using a remote desktop or partner console to connect using a web browser.

Migration to Enterprise Cloud

Let's look next at a massive global SAP ecosystem in an outsourced environment.

Background

A large client in the consumer industry was migrating to the private cloud with over 100+ SAP instances and 20+ bolt-on applications. The challenge was to migrate in waves (I, II & III), to avoid the risks of a "big bang" approach. The overall SAP Cloud migration involved 40 weeks for migration of SAP applications to the cloud including the 4 weeks of proof-of-concept (POC) execution to study the impact. There were key learnings from the POC regarding critical business processes and integration scenarios that were likely to be impacted by the OS migration from AIX to Linux.

There were two teams: one primarily focusing on the cloud migration and the other focusing on application testing. This testing was conducted during the wave migration of the applications, based on a risk-based testing approach. This included identifying key business processes, such as Order to Cash (OTC), Procure to Pay (PTP), and Ready to Report (RTR) scenarios. Each scenario's steps were reviewed carefully. The testing team conducted baseline performance tests in the as-is, on-premises infrastructure prior to the migration, and then conducted cycles I and II in the post-migration instance on the cloud using an HP QC software test solution. In addition to the manual functional testing, the team developed a regression suite for critical business processes, using the Worksoft Certify tool to automate critical scenarios. Thus, the team had a robust regression suite for testing the migration's impact.

Implementation Plan

The cloud migration (see Figure 14-9) included conducting a detailed POC study to identify the critical business scenarios to prioritize for testing. The cloud SI was responsible for migration from SAP applications on AIX to Linux. The SI conducted the migration using tools with the required infrastructure, and the testing partner was responsible for testing the solution pre- and post-migration in the environment. Risk-based testing was done in POC, DEV, and TEST instances, with checks during the Dry Run with Go Live support to ensure a successful migration. The real challenges were the bolt-ons: some of them had to be upgraded to be compatible with the cloud integration. Additionally, there were challenges in automating test cases due to data requirements, and these had to be redone in TEST environments. There were about 250+ test cases to automate; the team conducted both manual testing and automated testing, using the Worksoft Certify tool for regression testing.

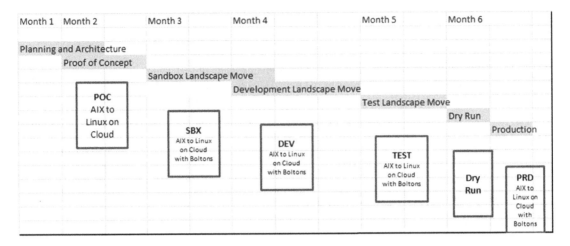

Figure 14-9. *SAP Cloud Migration plan*

The testing team was responsible for conducting the risk-based testing, as shown in Figure 14-10.

Figure 14-10. *Risk-based testing for SAP Cloud Migration*

The risk-based testing approach was used to efficiently minimize the risk and ensure fully functional coverage ("pick the right tests out of the infinite cloud of possible tests"). It involved a comprehensive risk assessment, prioritizing requirements, and a corresponding test strategy. The following steps were performed as part of the cloud migration testing project:

Risk assessment:

- Identify existing SAP test cases in scope.

- Perform a detailed risk assessment of test cases based on criticality, impact, and functional coverage, with the help of functional and business teams.

Risk prioritization:

- Prioritize the test cases based on the risk assessment.

- Sequence the test cases based on execution flow and criticality.

- Include exceptional condition coverage depending on risk.

- Have business teams review and sign off on test cases to ensure prioritization and coverage.

Risk-based testing execution planning:

- Plan the test execution, considering risk priority.

- Identify prerequisites for test execution, such as test data, stubs, and so on.

- Schedule and allocate resources.

- Test high-risk functionality thoroughly. Put minimum effort into low-risk functionality requirements.

Figure 14-11 shows the high-level architecture with AWS services connecting suppliers and customers using a VPN gateway connecting to the SAP PRD and non-PRD applications hosted in the cloud.

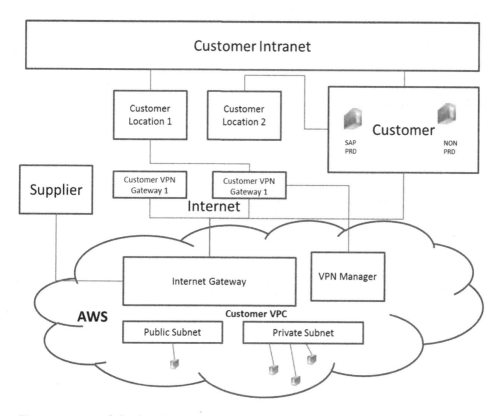

Figure 14-11. *High-level architecture*

The project plan illustrated in Figure 14-12 highlights various activities performed during a typical SAP cloud migration project. During the blueprint, the network and architecture team finalizes the design and the financial and risk review. The project involved on-premises SAP systems migrating to a private cloud running Linux. The team conducted multiple reviews, and functional and integration testing to ensure each of these migrated systems are fully operational in the cloud with bolt-ons intact.

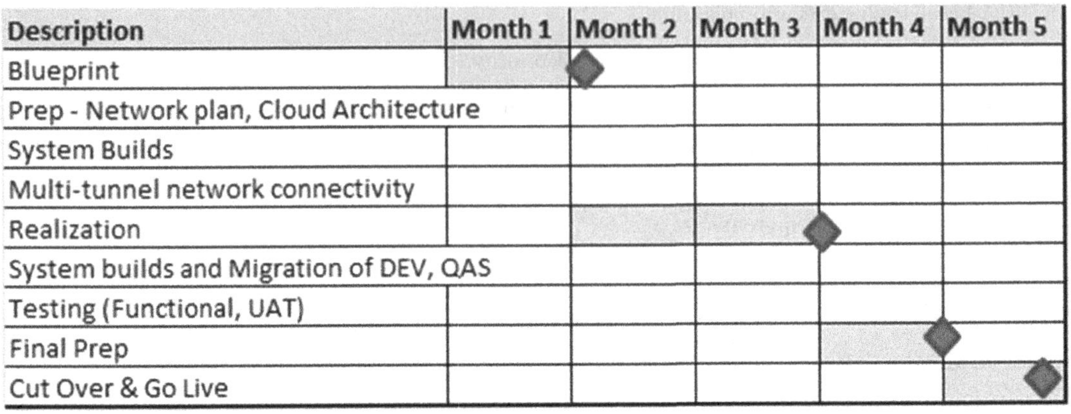

Description	Month 1	Month 2	Month 3	Month 4	Month 5
Blueprint		◆			
Prep - Network plan, Cloud Architecture					
System Builds					
Multi-tunnel network connectivity					
Realization			◆		
System builds and Migration of DEV, QAS					
Testing (Functional, UAT)					
Final Prep				◆	
Cut Over & Go Live					◆

Figure 14-12. *Cloud migration project plan*

Concluding Remarks

This chapter described the cloud and the transition of traditional software into cloud-based enterprise computing. SAP is a pioneer in ERP software implementations and has invested in the cloud to support its customers that are migrating their IT infrastructures. By moving to the cloud, you can focus on business operations rather than worrying about IT spending and ROI. A cloud-based subscription model has no up-front cost. Hence, you can avoid pitfalls such as implementing business processes from scratch with the associated infrastructure requirements. This alleviates problems that may arise when you add users, such as the need to upgrade hardware, operating systems, and databases. The risk to the business is zero when you migrate your applications to cloud-based services such as IaaS and PaaS. Therefore, you can run your business more efficiently and use a continuous improvement strategy.

As discussed in this chapter, the deployment model can use a hybrid, public, or private approach. It is up to you to choose the best option for your business. In my view, the hybrid approach is most exciting: you can use the best practices of both on-premises offerings and the cloud, thus maximizing your investment.

■ ■ ■

CHAPTER 15

SAP HCM Implementation Roadmap

There are significant challenges in implementing SAP human capital management (HCM) software, because the product is constantly evolving and includes a new bundle of features in every release. One of the major pitfalls is a lack of HCM product knowledge, which can lead to failed implementations. The HCM software has evolved as an excellent tool for HR Managers. Most of the common issues are related to planning and understanding the HCM product ecosystem. Planning appropriately to implement HCM is essential to boost productivity. SAP HCM helps integrate employees by providing a simple workflow and preconfigured scenarios to help your organization collaborate with, engage, and inspire employees to achieve organizational goals.

This chapter covers the following:

- Overview of HCM

- Implementation methodology

- Case Study

Overview of HCM

The corporate landscape has changed. It has evolved due to increasing demands from customers and internal employees. HR managers need to support employees by providing a work environment that is conducive to operational success. Thus, companies require a suitable software solution that caters to employees, handles travel, takes care of compensation, and so on; it should also be user-friendly, easily customizable, fully integrated, and flexible to implement.

SAP HCM Solution

Let's explore SAP's HCM capabilities. SAP HCM offers an enterprise structure, a personnel structure, and an organizational structure. In the system, you can set up hierarchies and store and administer employee data. Every employee is included in this structure, and the validity of their data is checked. The organizational structure is based on an organizational plan. The organizational plan provides a complete model of the personnel and enterprise structure, laid out in a hierarchy.

Figure 15-1 shows the enterprise structure.

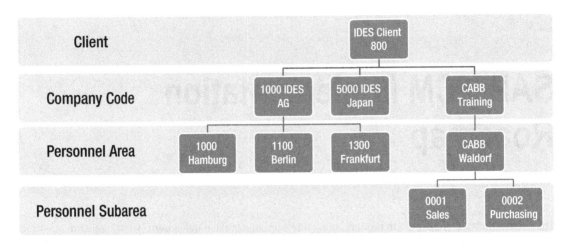

Figure 15-1. *Enterprise structure*

A *client* may be valid for a company code or for the entire corporate group. The *company code* is a legally created entity. A *personnel area* (PA) is used for personnel administration and is unique for a client. Each PA should be assigned to the company code. For administrative purposes, employees are divided into to two levels: an employee group (PA) and a subgroup (personnel subarea). You can define values for subgroups: for example, you can make Payroll the organizational unit used for managing payroll. All employees are assigned to Payroll and to payroll account areas.

Figure 15-2 shows the HR organizational structure.

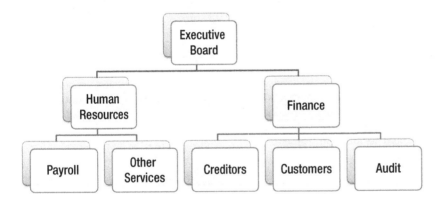

Figure 15-2. *Organizational structure*

Let's see how to create an organizational structure in the SAP system, starting with the Easy Access menu.

Select Human Resources ➤ Organization Management ➤ Plan ➤ Staffing.

You can see various departments in the enterprise structure created for POC purposes .
Click the Configuration button to check an entry's code and ID. You can find staff assignments in the respective organizational unit.

You can create accounts payable (AP) and accounts receivable (AR) under the organizational unit to create positions for them.

After you create a position, the next step is to assign a person to the position and change the position start date. You can maintain tasks and the relationship between tasks and positions.

Finally, you need to assign tasks to the respective work center. The work center is the location where the task will be carried out.

SAP Human Capital Management

As you know, HCM is a critical function of any corporation. Today's growing global organizations need help managing multiple languages, various currencies, and regulatory compliance requirements, across multiple geographies. The HCM capabilities in SAP provide HR functions such as talent management, recruitment, payroll, training, and organizational structural management.

SAP's integrated HR module supports development of employees by helping you set goals and objectives, determine evaluation criteria for appraisal, and so on. The HR module includes Personnel Administration (PA) and Personnel Development (PD) and applies SAP's unique concepts to HR functions.

You'll encounter the term *infotype* in the HR module. Let's explore what an infotype is and examine its actions technically and functionally.

Infotype and Actions

An infotypes is basically a screen. Each infotype is a screen in the HR application that stores a particular set of information about an employee: payroll data, personal data with specific attributes, time constraints, and so on. Hundreds of infotypes are offered in the ECC HR modules.

Figure 15-3 shows the Personnel Actions infotype. A series of infotypes are combined to complete a logical unit of work called an *action*. It is imperative that you understand infotypes, which must be bundled as actions to perform tasks for your company. For example, the Actions infotype controls the master data and is automatically included as the first infotype for all actions. As a first step, you configure these actions using an IMG guide to simplify complex personnel procedures such as hiring a new employee.

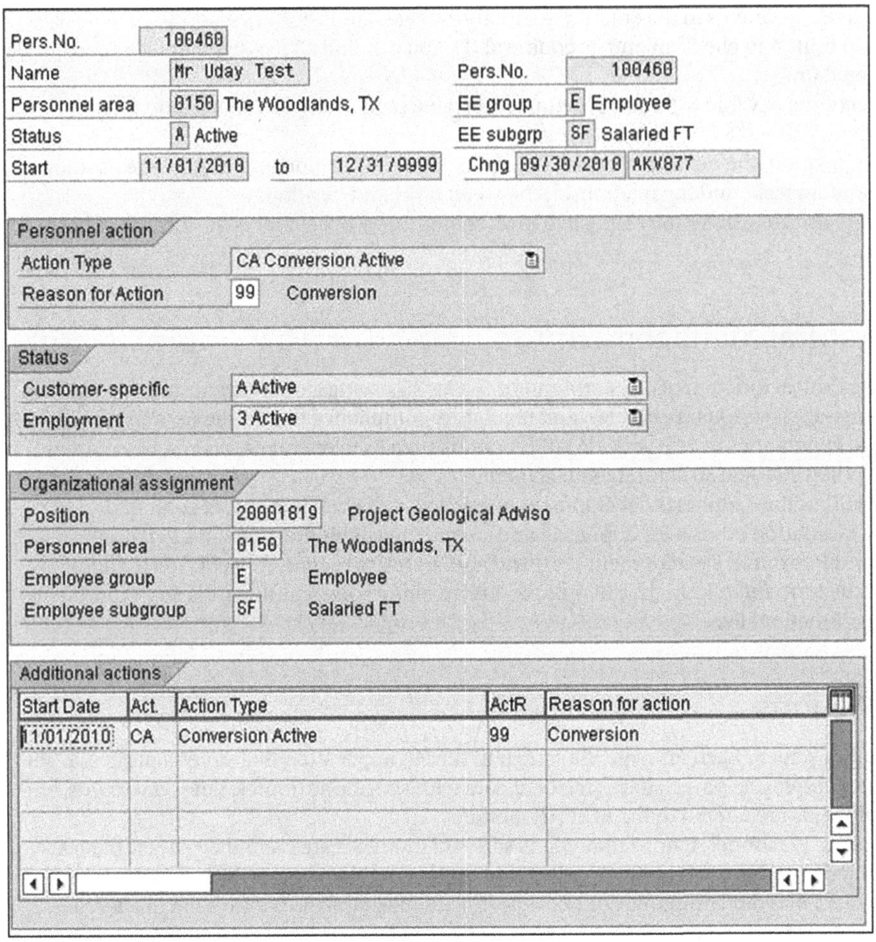

Figure 15-3. *Personnel Actions infotype*

You can use personnel actions to do the following:

- Hire an employee.

- Make or change an employee's organizational assignment

- Change an employee's pay

- Set an employee's status to early retiree or pensioner

- Document when an employee leaves or re-enters the enterprise

SAP HCM Components

Now, let's look at the core SAP HCM components:

- *Personnel Administration:* The SAP PA module runs the gamut of employee administration. It takes care of payroll, employee benefits enrollment, and compensation. *Benefits Administration:* This module provides benefit plans to employees such as eligibility requirements, evidence of insurability, cost tracking and management, flexible spending account claims processing, benefit terminations, and so on.

- *Compensation Management:* This module is used for the company's employee compensation plan. It includes salary administration, job evaluations, salary reviews, salary survey results, compensation budget planning and administration, and compensation policy administration. It helps HR managers create pay grades and salary structures by analyzing the internal value of the positions within your organization.

- *Personnel Planning and Development:* You can use this module to manage the process of employee recruitment, from creating a position vacancy, to adding and tracking applications, to notifying successful and/or unsuccessful job applicants.

- *Training and Events Management:* This module helps you coordinate, plan, and execute business events, including conventions, trainings, and seminars. It assists with allocating costs and billing for company events.

- *Human Resources Information Services (HRIS):* This module is primarily intended to provide HR report with various levels of granularity. For example, HR reports can be generated for the PA and PD components of the HR module. The Infoset Query tool is handy and easy for HR managers to use to generate employee reports.

- *Employee and Manager Self-Service (ESS/MSS) portals:* As its name implies, the ESS is an employee-friendly portal used to assign dependent information, claim, and policy details without spending too much time on HR policies. It empowers employees to retrieve and modify employee data via web-based technology. The ESS gives employees real-time access to HR data and maintains up-to-date records. The MSS is the equivalent manager portal for managing reportees. The MSS has the following components, supporting various functions that assist with managing a team effectively and retaining team members:

    - Recruiting process management

    - Employee skills, competencies, and experiences

    - Keyword searches of employee records

    - Planning, budgeting, and execution

    - Compensation planning

    - Annual compensation reviews

- *HCM Success Factors:* This module primarily deals with SAP HCM functionalities in the cloud. It offers an SAP suite in the cloud or via a hybrid solution involving on-premises and cloud-based offerings with preconfigured HCM scenarios. There are specific regulatory requirements for HCM for healthcare, and SAP offers an exclusive suite this purpose. SAP Payroll is easy to adapt, thus maximizing your HCM implementation with standard tools and templates for migrating legacy payroll data to SAP Payroll. It takes few weeks to get the simple, easy-to-use system up and running to support employee payroll.

Next, let's look at common Pitfalls in HCM implementation projects.

Common HCM Pitfalls

A common pitfall in HCM implementation is lack of planning for migrating data from the legacy application, which can cause inadvertent delays in payroll. Most global organizations have similar HR policies, governance, and so on, so it is prudent to design a global template and then roll it out to the different regions; however, in some projects it happens the other way around. There is always a lot of rework that impacts the design, and companies miss out on opportunities to have common core HCM business practices. Also, a global template helps enforce standard best practices adherence across regions, instead of region-based HCM practices: for example, talent acquisition, training, assignment, succession plans, travel plans, and workflow-based approvals are all standard HCM practices, regardless of geography. Benefits may change according to the region, such as leave policies, succession requirements, and so on. The real challenge is in the integration scenarios such as third-party systems. SAP Adobe interactive forms are user-friendly, easy-to-use forms provided with preconfigured scenarios. Listed below are the common HCM pitfalls to avoid in HCM implementation projects:

- From a design perspective, consolidate all global requirements and HCM best practices to ensure that all regions are on the same page and have a common blueprint.

- Build a communication and business readiness plan and strategy to ensure that the HCM community including managers and HR leaders is prepared and educated on the solution.

- It's always a good practice to conduct a detailed POC with tangible deliverables. Agile is the best methodology combined with SAP ASAP to ensure releases in bundles instead of a Big Bang.

- Create a detailed project plan as part of the blueprint, with time commitments from resources and dedicated business SME's.

- Test, test, and test with test data.

- Ensure that integration scenarios, and compatibility and test issues are taken care of.

- Validate the solution/configuration documentation in as much detail as possible.

- Data migration and cleanup is a critical activity that should be done prior to testing. Conduct reviews and regular quality audits to ensure top quality.

- Managing SAP software versions to avoid conflicts in configuration and development objects transport is essential.

Next, let's look at HCM implementation specifics.

Implementation Methodology

Figure 15-4 shows the HCM implementation methodology. Although the implementation framework is standard using the ASAP methodology, tasks vary depending the product suite implemented. HCM is primarily user-focused, so considerable validation is required from the business to avoid major pitfalls such as lack of support from end users and business SMEs (who are primarily the HR managers, talent acquisition leads, and policy makers). At every step of the implementation, you should use their knowledge and HR best practices to support their operations.

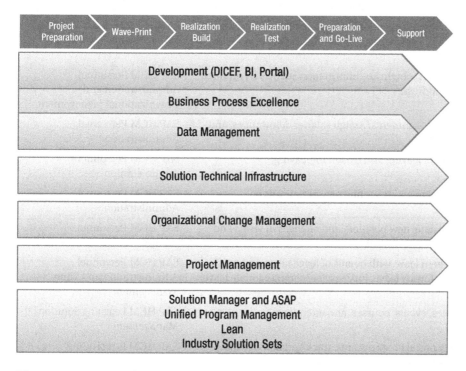

Figure 15-4. *HCM implementation methodology*

Blueprint

You begin the blueprint phase with an analysis of the existing landscape and the availability of an existing SAP HCM team; you should use them as much as possible during the project. You should make a blueprint workshop calendar that includes the modules and the required business process owners so you can capture the future-state global requirements. The HR business partners or business process owners are key to the global rollout of SAP HCM. In my experience, they are critical to providing the correct localization requirements and act as change agents as the implementation progresses.

Now, let's see how the HCM requirements phase looks with deliverables. A lot of planning is required to understand the current (as-is) landscape, to demonstrate your understanding in the current legacy HR environment so you can migrate to the to-be landscape; see the requirements mapping in Table 15-1. This table lists workshops and questions to ask relevant teams at the customer site as you gather requirements prior to planning the HCM scenarios in SAP. After sign-off on the baseline configuration document outlining the HCM as-is and to-be scenarios, the actual realization begins.

Table 15-1. Requirements Mapping Table

Requirement	Proposed Solution
Onboarding of new employees: after accepting a role, prospective employees are to be given online access to allow them to enter personal details such as date of birth, marital status, ethnicity, address, primary and secondary emergency contact, e-mail address, phone number, and bank details. In addition, functionality is to be provided that lets a check-off be recorded against policies and completion of a medical questionnaire.	SAP HCM Personnel Administration, ESS, and MSS
Establish and maintain the organizational structure of positions, titles, who reports to whom, and cost-center assignments (Finance own the cost center structure).	SAP HCM Organizational Management
Starters: for new employees, obtain key information such as NI number, position, and business address.	SAP HCM Personnel Administration and Organizational Management
Establish organizational assignments. Assign salaries, allowances, and deductions.	SAP HCM Personnel Administration
Leavers: record the date of leaving and reason for leaving.	SAP HCM Personnel Administration
Transfers: record internal moves reflecting new organizational assignments.	SAP HCM Personnel Administration
Promotions: record the date, new position, and changes in terms and conditions.	SAP HCM Personnel Administration
Absence: track entitlement leave with details of leave taken and outstanding, such as maternity leave, jury service, compassionate leave, and so on.	SAP HCM Personnel Administration and Time Management
Training: track delegates, events, courses, and attendees.	SAP HCM Learning Solution Management
Recruitment: provide a portal for applicants, track and manage the recruitment process, and maintain a talent pool.	SAP HCM E-recruiting
Key reports and interfaces: • Monthly and as required to Bluefin Orbit flexible benefits system • Annual report to Asperity regarding long service award entitlements • Quarterly statutory reports for the National Statistical Office • Monthly report for health care provider • Monthly report for The Travel Company regarding season tickets • Employee Change Report (ECR) weekly, based on last month: new starters, leavers, cost center changes; sent to Security, Facilities, IT, reception desks, and others • Monthly/Weekly flexible benefits system	SAP HCM Reports (Standard and Custom)
• Monthly administrative reports: triggers and reminders on probation dates, end of contract, long service, work permits, advances and recoupments; 3-month future horizon • Active Directory: changes to Employees (starters, leavers, moves, manager ID)	HCM interfaces

(continued)

Table 15-1. (*continued*)

Requirement	Proposed Solution
Employee interactions: leave requests, updating personal details (address, emergency contact), updating bank details.	ESS
Manager interactions: processing leave requests, viewing team member information and team calendar.	MSS
Mass-upload capability. Load annual bonus. Load annual salary increase	LSMW tool

The following benefits may be realized as part of a multiple-release strategy:

- Establishes a true global design for the core SAP HCM (PA/OM) modules.

- Provides a robust foundation on which additional modules can be successfully implemented

- Accelerates releases 2–3 through specific learning from the first release.

- Modules such as Talent Management (Compensation and Performance Management) require that the core HR processes are well understood. Consequently, it is more effective to implement them after the core HR has been designed, tested, stabilized, and adopted rather than using a single-release strategy.

- Reduces the complexity of change management and site readiness.

- Partner's approach is designed to help limit risk and complexity. The approach may help the client dedicate resources to support and own the business processes within scope without disrupting everyday business. By spreading all training and site-readiness activities across multiple rollouts, the impact on client resources may be lessened compared to a Big Bang approach. In addition, this provides an opportunity to reuse resources at the various locations and industrialize the process.

- Reduces the complexity of testing and cut-over activities.

- Deploying all functionality to the client at one time may increase risks due to change management, testing, and cut-over activities. Splitting the functional scope across two releases may reduce this risk.

- Respects regional differences.

- Drives toward global standards while addressing local needs.

Eventually, a PM is responsible for a host of activities such as finalizing the solution with the respective SMEs and planning the implementation in phases or as a Big Bang, depending on the complexities of the solution and the number of sites across the globe.

Realization

Once the blueprint phase is complete and signed off, realization begins. You work with the respective client team to jointly build the solution. This provides efficiency because concepts relating to SAP HCM are provided by the partner using accelerated SAP (ASAP) methodology and tools mapped to the ASAP methodology.

Testing

When it is time for functional integration testing and user-acceptance testing, you should propose that members of the client production support team be a key part of the integration testing. In many implementations, users are not experienced with SAP; involving them in testing provides significant ramp-up time for them to learn the new system and processes.

Go-Live

Upon go-live, the client should be able to rely on the implementation team to provide production support and the regional business partners to be the super-users in their respective regions. By using SAP's new Roadmap Composer tool, you can build accelerators and enablers based on your SAP delivery experiences to further enrich the methodology. The SAP method defines various components, phases, and work streams covering the full engagement life cycle and a single work stream encompassing important aspects of engagement management. Depending on the scope of the work, an engagement can consist of many components, phases, and work streams from the life cycle, in addition to the work stream for engagement management.

CASE STUDY OF HCM IMPLEMENTATION

Business Scenario

A client experienced challenges when implementing HCM. The company is one of the largest beverage makers in the world, headquartered in the United States. It sells about 400 brands in over 200 countries, and it has 18,000+ employees. Obviously, this was an SAP global implementation with a global template, using a rollout-based implementation approach. The client wanted to automate the following primary HR functions:

- Organization management

- Employee administration

- Workflow-enabled approvals for managers

- Compensation

- Performance management

- Time and attendance

- Learning solutions

- Enhanced analytics capabilities

I categorized the following tasks as priorities:

- Talent acquisition, including hiring, retention, and policies

- HR services such as ESS and MSS with workflow-enabled approvals

- Strategic business partners such as culture, transformation, and so on

The Organization had key constraints to consolidate business practices across geographies.

The strategic business partners aligned with business strategies, such as culture, capability, and talent and change. The COE was responsible for the design and rollout programs, which included policy, recruitment, leave, job design, tracking, and new-hire orientation. Finally, Global Business Services was responsible for routine transactions between managers and employees, such as service changes, awards, benefits, company cars, employment surveys, and address changes.

The ESS was designed based on tiers such as performance management, career and development, compensation, benefits, and policies. Employees could edit plans such as performance and/or development and career plans. Further, the enterprise university helped with cross-skilling resources by providing e-learning programs in SAP Learning Solutions (LSO); this provided options for employees to select relevant courses and book in advance.

The MSS helped with manager activities such as employee promotions, position changes, and requisitions for new hires, appraisals, and separations (typical functions of managers in the various departments). The best part of SAP HCM is that it helps set up specific rules for departments. Figure 15-5 shows a sample MSS page for performance, recruiting, and hiring.

Figure 15-5. MSS

The employee promotion process shown in Figure 15-6 gave HR a standard configuration for promotions, demotions, and lateral moves. This scenario included managers promoting an employee (initiating manager, promotion manager, and approval manager).

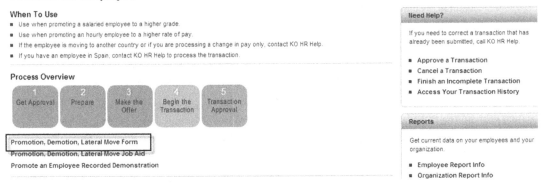

Figure 15-6. *Employee promotion process*

Typically, HCM implementations take 6 months or more, depending on the complexity of the scenarios, customization requirements, and number of regions. A typical project plan is shown in Figure 15-7; this is a wave-based rollout approach, and the figure shows Wave 1 deployment.

Project Tasks	Oct	Nov	Dec	Jan	Feb	Mar	Apr	May	June	July	Aug
Prep & Blueprint	███	███									
Usability sutdy			███	███							
Functional & Technical Design											
Realization											
Development Wave I				███	███	███	███				
Integration Testing Wave I								███			
UAT Wave I									███	███	
Deployment											
WAVE I											███

Figure 15-7. *Wave based rollout plan*

As you can see, increasing the number of waves lengthens the schedule, because you have to repeat the development, integration testing, UAT, final preparation, and go-live phases for every wave.

Concluding Remarks

Let's recap what we have discussed in Chapter 15:

- Overview of SAP HCM with common pitfalls to avoid

- Implementation methodology

- Case study

■ ■ ■

CHAPTER 16

SAP TM: Deliver Fulfillment Across Global Logistics

You may be surprised to learn that the total cost of logistics in the United States is more than $1 billion annually. That's a staggering amount. SAP customers produce 86% of the world's sport shoes, 70% of the chocolates, 50% of the branded jeans, 72% of the beer, 9 million tons of cheese, and so on—and all of these products need to be transported and stored. The transportation and logistics network plays a vital role in collaborating with shippers, customers, and carriers. The real challenge is integrating systems to optimize your business's overall logistics costs. A common pitfall is the failure of project teams to assess the complexity of this integration, which can lead to failed implementations.

This chapter examines a case study in which a customer faces significant challenges in integrating SAP Transportation Management (TM), SAP Enterprise Central Component (ECC), SAP Advanced Planning and Optimization (APO), and a third-party logistics provider ecosystem. First you need to understand the basics of SAP TM as a product and how it is implemented; the chapter discusses various facets of implementing SAP TM and its subprocesses to help reduce logistics costs.

■ **Note**   This chapter covers SAP TM basics, product implementation, and pitfalls that can occur during integration due to lack of ecosystem awareness.

Key Tenets of SAP TM

Most SAP TM project implementation failures occur due to a common pitfall: lack of an integrated system and insufficient understanding of the product configuration, while trying to customize it for a specific business process. There are many custom products for managing logistics and change, but integration remains as a significant challenge. SAP's supply-chain suite uses TM for logistics seamlessly with SAP products such as Event Management (EM), Extended Warehouse Management (EWM), and native ERP as one unit in an integrated fashion. However, there are substantial challenges involved in integrating third-party logistics service providers (LSPs).

Following are some critical business scenarios in which a TM implementation can help a business significantly by driving optimization in terms of costs and increased flexibility of services to customers. These scenarios present significant challenges in managing logistics:

- *On-time delivery*: On-time delivery to customers is a common logistical challenge, as there are receipts from vendors and bulk replenishment at the warehouse level.

- *Utilization of resources*: Consolidating goods while achieving maximum utilization of resources (such as containers) and optimizing network planning can help with cost optimization.

- *Penalties*: You may be charged penalties due to non-compliance or misuse of resources, and lack of transparency in tracking functionality can result in demurrage and detention.

- *Warehouse capacity planning*: A key concern is the availability of warehouse space, such as cross-docking availability to use the warehouse to its fullest capacity.

- *Logistics suppliers (LSPs)*: Ensuring the right capacity at the right time and at the right cost is very important when you're dealing with third-party LSPs.

■ **Note**   Companies around the world are concerned about their carbon footprint. SAP TM can help you tap carbon-related information via a robust, flexible data setup that you can use wherever required by the SAP TM platform.

- *Cross docking*—it's a challenge for the transportation world to use resources to their maximum capacity. Various ports and cross-docking warehouse can implement measures such as using radio-tracking devices to optimize alerts regarding incoming vehicles or ships, readiness to empty or repack cargo, loading for the next trip, and so on.

SAP TM can help you alleviate these concerns by using a workflow-enabled system to track every logistical process step. For example, it triggers a reminder for an analytics report to track and measure the stages in the shipment process. The following case study presents some practical considerations in implementing SAP TM.

PRACTICAL CONSIDERATIONS

A chemical processing entity produces plastic granules in megatons per month. These granules are used by various customers from automobile to pharma around the world, as a raw material to manufacture their own goods.

The products are of various grades. The prime grade is made available to customers on demand, and the secondary grade is sold in bulk on first-come, first-served basis. Demand is so huge that production capacities are constantly being increased. Due to the high cost of the material, customers normally do not carry inventory and expect just-in-time delivery. It's challenging for the distribution lines to match the increased demand with on-time delivery to customers across the globe.

Customs authorities impose many regulations, and LSPs and shipping companies expect guaranteed business in order to plan and provide timely service. So, customers proactively approached the distribution teams to trace out their orders in order to obtain on-time clearance from Customs. At the same time, the distribution teams were under constant pressure to meet the growing demand and coordinate with shipping lines. In addition, the finance team had to accurately trace the transportation charges and settle them with respect to their reference documents. Typically, the business had a contract with each shipping line (carrier) to provide a percentage space allocation or pay a penalty. If a carrier continually failed to provide the allotted space for shipments or containers in a timely manner, the business could bar the carrier line from further shipments. These are common pitfalls in the transportation industry, and they can be solved by using the SAP TM module to approach automation from an end-to-end perspective.

The main distribution structure of the business looks like this in the example scenario:

- Local distribution to Middle Eastern countries is via roadways, where a fixed vendor is appointed to distribute goods from the local warehouse. The warehouse maintains a stock of goods that is replenished from the production plant, which is situated near the sea. Goods are transported by trailer.

- Most of the Asian countries are served from Singapore as a base hub, although it is served from the base production plant as well. The Singapore hub is replenished via a sea route from the base plant in the Middle East.

- There is another model in which the Singapore hub caters to Australia and New Zealand via sea routes.

- A processing plant in China caters to the local market via sea routes and trucks. The raw product is still replenished from the Middle East.

- Due to a growing rail network in the Middle East, the company wanted a robust solution to cater to its growing transportation needs.

Current System

The client has implemented SAP and the core modules Sales and Distribution (SD), Material Management (MM), and Logistics Execution (LE-TRA) to manage distribution, sales, and procurement. Outbound distributions are currently set up as inbound for procurement; returns are not necessary, because returned products are normally scrapped to avoid quality issues. Procurement distributions are generally handled by vendors.

The VP for Distribution, along with the executive committee and CIO, have decided to appoint a third-party vendor to study the situation and come up with a solution that addresses the following key challenges:

- Increased transportation cost per containers

- Shipping-line commitment of the business in terms of container availability and timely delivery

- Business commitment to shipping lines to guarantee regular business or pay a penalty in the case of a failure per the contractual obligation

- Monitoring the cost of containers and ensuring that Finance pays in a timely manner

- Tracking and tracing shipments from the beginning until they reach either customers or ports

- Booking shipments online with carriers and monitoring events for delays, failure to book, and so on

- Liaison / approval of shipments with Customs authorities

For a multimillion-dollar business, nominal savings on distribution charges have the potential to lead to huge savings on logistics costs. Hence, you propose implementing SAP TM to support transportation planning and optimize transportation expenses.

Let's examine the key challenges in implementing SAP TM while catering to the business's requirements. The following scenarios describe how to mitigate risks by presenting proposed workarounds to potential pitfalls arising from lack of end-product vision and goals.

Overview of SAP TM

You need to understand how a transportation and logistics network operates, and the crucial players and collaboration required. The question is, how do you plan and execute the physical storage and movement of goods? Often, I have observed that there is no end-to-end integration of systems supporting logistics with heterogeneous systems, and obtaining real-time data is a challenge. Now, SAP offers an end-to-end solution for integrating logistics systems between shippers, customers, freight forwarders, and carriers. Everyone can be on the same page, with real-time analytics as part of the SAP TM solution.

One of the compelling challenges in the logistics industry is the end-to-end supply chain platform and providing accurate, real-time data for all parties involved. SAP answers this need with its supply chain (SCM) suite of products and solutions, including Extended Warehouse Management (EWM), Event Management (EM), and TM.

The SAP Supply Chain Execution platform has the following features:

- Synchronized SAP EWM/TM/EM delivery

- First EWM/TM integration via ERP

- Load appointment management

- Stock-keeping unit of measure

- Other analytics (cross-distribution center dashboard and top KPI reporting)

Solution Overview

SAP TM started with version 6.0 and has evolved over time to its current version, 9.3. Let's analyze SAP TM from a business perspective and see how it reduces overall logistics costs.

SAP TM supports all activities connected with the physical transportation of goods from one location to another. You can use SAP TM to manage end-to-end logistics operations across seven micro-verticals:

- Railways

- Third-party logistics providers (3PLs)

- Freight forwarders

- Buses, taxis, truckers, and road freight (occasionally roads and toll-ways)

- Ports (air and sea)

- Hotels, casinos, and other gaming

- Airlines

The out-of-the-box comprehensive SAP TM solution for shippers provides synchronized TM/EWM and EM delivery as indicated here, with integration to ERP transportation:

- SAP TM:

  - Order management

  - Freight planning and tendering

  - Freight execution and monitoring

  - Freight settlement

  - Dangerous goods and compliance

  - Export handling

- SAP EWM:

  - Claims and returns process

  - Synchronized SAP EWM/TM/EM delivery

  - First EWM/TM integration via ERP

  - Load appointment management

  - Stock-keeping unit of measure

  - Analytics (cross-distribution center dashboard and top KPI report)

- SAP EM:

  - Transportation execution monitoring with high-performance scenarios

Table 16-1 outlines the solutions for external communication and connectivity.

Table 16-1. *Collaborative Transportation Management*

Solution	Tool	TM Solution
1. Tendering collaboration	SAP TM tendering	Request for quotation. Carrier UI view.
2. Subcontracting	SAP TM order management	Enhancements, minor fixes.
3. Event tracking and monitoring	SAP TM planning cockpit	SAP EM: Web UI for carrier event notification.
4. Trading partner, third-party connectivity	SAP TM	Connectivity to the third-party partner systems.

Order Management

SAP TM Order Management provides end-to-end integrated order processing and management with high customer service levels and satisfaction. It can help you integrate order-to-case and procure-to-pay scenarios and integrated freight settlement with ERP-based billing and invoicing. Further, it helps with forwarding, freight, and booking (sea and air) orders with full document flow and life-cycle management; it provides centralized order data management for planning, tendering, and execution.

Table 16-2 illustrates the integration between SAP ERP and SAP TM.

Table 16-2. *Integration between SAP ERP and SAP TM*

Solution	Process	Integration
SAP ERP	Sales order	Y
	Purchase order	Y
	Stock transfer	Y
	Delivery	Y
SAP TM	Freight order, forwarding order, freight booking: a. General and item data b. Subcontracting data c. Order status d. Link documents e. Dangerous goods data	Y

SAP TM is used to create and monitor an efficient transportation plan that fulfills the relevant constraints: for example. managing transportation costs, SLAs and availability. This in turn helps you to determine optimized transport methods and resource utilization to reduce costs. Thus, it helps you with transportation planning and managing any transportation events that may occur. Furthermore, SAP's integrated solution with enterprise mobility and analytical capabilities gives you faster access to real-time data anywhere, anytime. SAP TM uses the Sybase Unwired Platform (SUP) for partner mobile solutions. It uses intra-enterprise solutions for all warehouse execution processes. Now, let's move on to the next process: managing freight planning and tenders.

Freight Planning & Tendering Overview

The SAP TM Freight Planning & Tender module helps reduce costs and improve operational performance by improving carrier collaboration and resource utilization.

This module provides advanced, interactive transportation planning with the following features:

- Flexible, configurable transportation planning cockpit

- Drag-and-drop, graphical capabilities (map integration)

- Manual or automatic transportation optimizer planning

- Constraint-based, multi-variant mode scheduling and routing, with zero-click planning from order entry to carrier settlement

- Domestic and international shipment planning, including ocean freight booking and Customs/compliance management integration

- Best-in-class, collaborative tendering

- Manual and automated tendering (direct and RFQ-based)

- Multiple tendering types: peer-to-peer and broadcast

- Flexible carrier communication (web and mobile UI, e-mail, SMS, B2B) for RFQ processing and status visibility

Freight Execution & Monitoring Overview

SAP TM Freight Execution & Monitoring helps you conduct an efficient logistics and fulfillment process, with improved visibility and responsiveness.

This module provides comprehensive transportation document management:

- Document creation, printing, status management, out-of-the-box form templates for bills of lading (road, sea, air), labels, and forwarding instructions

- Integrated logistics and fulfillment management

- SAP ERP integration for inbound and outbound processing

- SAP Environment, Health, and Safety (EHS) integration for handling dangerous goods and integrated Customs and compliance management

- SAP Global Trade Services (GTS) for export documents and Customs procedure processing with transportation execution visibility and monitoring

- Shipment visibility to customers, supplier, and carriers

- Integrated event management for event notification and handling

Freight Settlement Overview

SAP TM Freight Settlement provides accurate transportation costing, with integrated transportation management and billing details:

- Freight agreement management

- Flexible tariff and charge management

- Advanced charge calculation

- Integrated freight and forwarding settlement

- SAP ERP Financials integration for freight carrier payment and customer invoicing

- Partial invoicing and billing

- Full document flow / lifecycle management

Table 16-3 shows the integration between the SAP TM Freight Settlement and SAP ERP Financials processes.

Table 16-3. *Freight Settlement Integration with ERP Financials*

SAP TM (Freight Settlement)	SAP ERP (Financials)	Participants
Freight order: settlement document	Credit memo, carrier invoice, invoice payment and confirmation	Carrier
Forwarding order: forwarding settlement document	Customer invoice, invoice confirmation	Customer

In summary, SAP TM with EWM and EM modules supports the logistics outlined in Table 16-4. The RDS solutions result in reduced implementation time, effort, and cost.

Table 16-4. *SAP TM Processes and Scenarios with Rapid Deployment Solutions*

SAP TM Processes	SAP TM Scenarios	RDS (Rapid Deployment)
1. Managing transportation requirements 2. Managing forwarding orders 3. Managing freight and bookings 4. Planning freight and selecting carriers 5. Tendering freight 6. Executing and monitoring freight 7. Settling freight orders 8. Settling forwarding orders	Domestic inbound transportation Inbound logistics Outsourced transportation Domestic and international outbound transportation	Domestic transportation planning Domestic freight tendering

SAP TM Architecture

This section analyzes how SAP TM fits into the overall product architecture; see Figure 16-1.

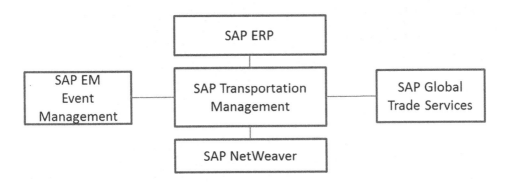

Figure 16-1. *SAP TM architecture overview*

This architecture diagram shows how SAP TM fits in the SAP ecosystem including SAP ERP, EM, GTS, and mobile devices. SAP TM compatibility with each module is assessed during a project's preliminary blueprint phase. Let's see how the master data is set up in SAP TM.

SAP Master Data

Master data is integrated via SCM, Typically in batch mode (transaction data) and integrated via web services. This is a real-time, trigger-based transfer, with hazardous configurations transferred from EHS (add-on to ERP) via ALE. Figure 16-2 shows the transport network master data setup in SAP TM, which is primarily focused on the transportation network.

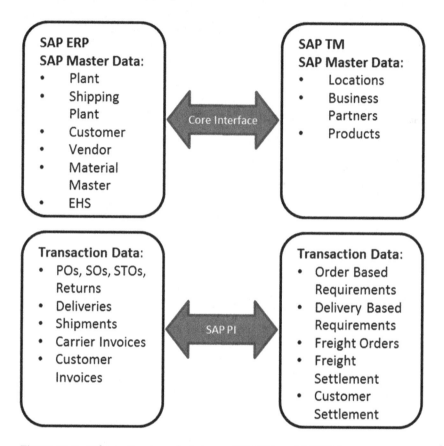

Figure 16-2. *Information transfer between SAP ERP and SAP TM*

The network includes several master data elements:

- Locations (customers, vendors, shipping points, plants)

- Transportation zones and hierarchies.

- Transportation lanes

- Schedules

- Business partners

Certain master data does not have to be maintained for LSPs, because they do not have products of their own. Transaction data, such as sales orders, stock transfer orders, deliveries, and shipments are transferred via Process Integration (SAP PI). This creates requirement objects called OBTR (for sales orders), DBTR (for deliveries), and FO (for shipments). Customers, vendors, shipping points, and plants transferred from SAP ERP to SAP TM are created as both locations and business partners. Business partners transferred from ERP assume the role of general business partners in SAP TM. Any extra roles required can be assigned to business partners in SAP TM.

SAP TM Order-Based vs. Delivery-Based Transportation

This section investigates the key differences between order-based transportation (OBTR) and delivery-based transportation (DBTR). You can push sales orders, stock transport orders (STOs), or deliveries to SAP TM. Whether to go with the sales order first or the delivery depends on how early you plan freight orders, as shown in Figure 16-3. OBTRs can be used as the basis of transportation planning. An OBTR corresponds to a single order in SAP ERP and cannot be edited in SAP TM.

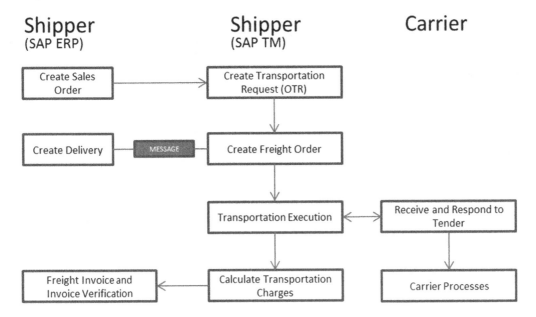

Figure 16-3. *Order-based transportation (OBTR)*

If you plan well in advance, I suggest that you go with OBTR and then DBTR. Another set of master data is maintained in SAP TM:

- Resources (mode of transport, equipment types, and so on)
- Transportation lanes
- Planning profiles
- Incompatibility definitions

Figure 16-4 shows the process flow for a delivery that is created in the SAP ERP system and sent to SAP TM, where a corresponding OBTR has *not* been created in SAP TM.

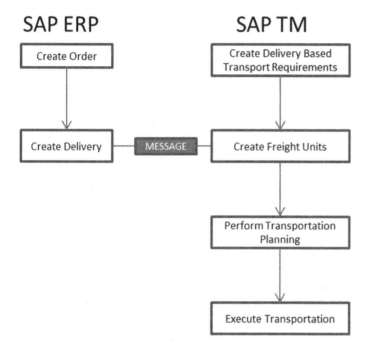

Figure 16-4. *Delivery-based transportation*

The next section examines SAP TM implementation considerations.

SAP TM 9.x Implementation Considerations

Your implementation process needs to be aligned with the standard scenarios and key elements of SAP TM. Business requirements may force movement away from these standards, but you need to consider these challenges and prerequisites:

- SAP modules should have the required version and service pack to align with the SAP TM 9.x release version.

- Integrating with a third party sometimes calls for the use of middleware that exists in the company landscape, which poses another challenge. This results in the following integration flow:

    a. SAP ECC to SAP PI to SAP TM.

    b. SAP TM to SAP PI to TIBCO (third-party middleware) to INTRA (transportation platform) to the carrier portal.

- You must ensure correct activation of the SAP TM functionality required. Some business functions are irreversible and may land you in trouble. If you are not sure, make a backup before implementing these functions.

- You may need to build roles and authorization queries and assign them to the right roles.

- SAP technical and functional skilled resources are required, because SAP TM has new architectural aspects:

    - It uses a NW Business client as the front end and not SAP GUI.

    - The core SAP TM foundation is BOPF technology.

    - The standard offering connects to ECC or any other SAM TM module via SAP PI. There are ways to connect without SAP PI, but I do not recommend this option.

Custom development depends on the requirements. If there are specific customer practices, implementing and testing a custom program will take a lot of time, due to the integrated modules impacted by the customization complexities. Hence, you should be aware of changes impacting SAP GTS, managing dangerous goods without implementing SAP EHS, because development mostly touches ECC, PI, TM, and other SAP modules.

Now, let's investigate a major case study.

REAL-TIME SAP TM CASE STUDY

One of the largest European conglomerates producing electrical equipment globally implemented SAP TM to optimize logistics costs. The strategy was based on a phased implementation at the local, regional, and global levels, with controls placed at all the levels to gain the advantage of transparency, use the existing setup, and reduce costs at all levels.

The customer was dealing with dangerous goods, courier delivery, and consolidation of goods at the plant level. The ADR - European agreement concerning international carriage of dangerous goods by road, includes provisions for the carriage, loading, unloading, and handling of dangerous goods. Classification of material is required, and a matrix determines which classes can and cannot be in the same packaging or on the same vehicle.

The classification matrix is vast, resulting in thousands of incompatibilities, and it is practically impossible to maintain. There was another peculiar requirement related to the transfer of small packages of very low weight, containing documents (referred to as *courier delivery*). These documents require little to no planning because they weigh very little, and they are required to be sent on a day-to-day basis without being consolidated. Another strategy was to build a full truckload scenario, which could mean either a large truckload (25 tons) or a small truckload (22 tons). The proper vehicle was chosen and the full load was consolidated at the plant level. In another scenario, the company could change the customer address and route shipments accordingly.

The solution was to provide SAP TM with a full-fledged transportation cockpit for a planner to plan the shipments of dangerous goods and transportation zones. A high-level personalized object work list was required to prevent unauthorized people from accessing documents.

KEY CHALLENGES

This section explores key challenges you face when implementing SAP TM.

Scenario 1: Delivery Dates and Order Scheduling

Suppose you are implementing SAP TM with ECC and APO in an integrated environment, where scheduling is done in SAP APO. The first challenge is integrating SAP TM for sales order scheduling with APO. The dates sent by SAP TM after optimizing the results with the required planning profile are overwritten by dates from SAP APO.

Figure 16-5 shows the simple process flow of a scenario related to sales order scheduling.

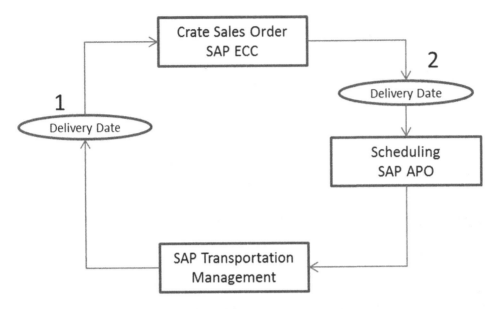

Figure 16-5. Sales order scheduling in ECC

When you schedule an order from SAP ECC to SAP TM, SAP TM proposes the most appropriate delivery date based on optimized transportation. However, the customer had implemented SAP APO, which typically handles the delivery date. When you integrate these two products, you end up with two delivery dates. The SAP APO delivery date overwrites the TM proposed delivery date, so you miss TM's optimized plan, and you can't obtain the actual delivery date from TM.

To overcome this issue, you have two options: optimize the data in SAP APO with the average time per route and carrier and then carry out the delivery-based transport route (DBTR), or use SAP's Exit method to customize the standard behavior by stopping the scheduling process in APO so dates planned by SAP TM are not overwritten. Another approach is to maintain the master data for routes in sync with APO, ECC, and TM. However; this approach can be cumbersome and involve multiple user-entry screens, plus the additional overhead of maintaining and synchronizing the master data.

The solution was implemented to optimize data in SAP APO with the average time per route and carrier and then carry out DBTR-based planning, stop the scheduling APO so the dates planned by TM are not overwritten, or maintain the master data (routes) in sync in APO, ECC, and TM.

Scenario 2: Optimized Use of Containers

The company needed to determine the best use of containers, as part of container management to optimize costs. Different containers are priced differently, and the cost is time dependent: for example, two 20-foot containers are sometimes cheaper than one 40-foot container. Hence, there is a need for a dynamic way to select the most appropriate container. At times, customers demand that their orders be delivered as per their container requirements, such as order-to-cash.

Containers can be mapped as a means of transport, but this has the heavy restriction that a freight order is created per means of transport, so there are as many combinations as there are freight orders. This makes it difficult to handle these freight orders.

Scenario 3: Freight Unit Selection

A custom solution was developed to punch in the container requirement at the delivery level and then from the freight unit, as per the requirement for appropriate products. This has a drawback: an incorrect entry results in selecting the incorrect freight unit.

The existing inventory of containers from shipping lines is maintained and monitored via third-party software known as the JADE system. The current ECC setup replaced the handling unit formed by the appropriate container from the Z table, which fetches the container data from the JADE system.

When a container reaches port or is received by a customer, the custom SAP Data Dictionary (DDIC) Z table is updated. The basic requirement is to provide containers on first-come, first-served basis, to avoid penalties related to late delivery of containers to the shipping line. Another constraint was that the proposed container may not be available immediately, because it may be stacked at the bottom of other containers or it may be damaged.

The solution designed is to replicate the Z table with container details populated from the JADE system ECC to TM and provide containers to freight orders on a first-come, first-served basis. Once deliveries are created from the freight order, the actual containers are overwritten at delivery based on availability, thus optimizing container selection. These are actual containers at the delivery level, whereas at the freight-order level they are proposed containers. To sync the data, the flow is written back to the freight order.

Scenario 4: Route Determination

The manufacturing plant and the port are connected by narrow sea route where empty containers are made available from port to the plant via feeder vessels. The cost of the feeder vessel needed to be captured, so the setup involved three leg shipments: a freight order from manufacturing plant to port, where the feeder vessel charges and other planning-related costs are captured; a freight booking, which is the main leg from port to port; and another freight order from port to destination. If you are implementing an incoterms-based scenario, SAP TM can execute the legs using incoterms mapping: for example, if DDP is implemented, then there is no the third leg. If an incoterms scenario is not implemented, then this can be mapped as a zero-distance scenario for the third leg. But the creation of a freight order should form the predecessor and successor documents as pre-carriage (first leg) and on carriage (third leg) in the main carriage (second leg) freight order. So, the single freight order contains all the details, and you can create the deliveries or shipment from it. If you have three freight orders, it is tedious to handle these orders and create the subsequent documents in ECC. Use transshipment locations as much as possible.

The existing SAP ECC setup had the process of capturing the container details in the handling unit with Z enhancement; the solution has to fit in with this, as well as the batch determination via Z logic with container details attached to it. The freight order has proposed containers, and the delivery has actual containers that are picked on the basis of availability in the stack, not necessarily as proposed in the freight order. The actual data actual is written back to the freight order level via enhancement at PI. This data about containers and their capacity is used to book orders with carriers.

One of the key requirements was Business share, to calculate whether rejecting a shipping line affects its share being fulfilled. The TM optimizer transportation proposal does not include the business share as a field you can check to decide manually whether to go with a particular carrier.

Business share is a soft constraint and does not restrict someone from manually accessing it. The standard business share cockpit can be used to manually block a carrier if it isn't required. In addition, there is no standard workflow for approval of freight orders. If the freight order exceeds a certain value, it requires an approval.

To overcome this pitfall, when the charge is calculated, if the value of the freight order exceeds the required value, the order is blocked. This block can be removed by authorized personnel.

The main flow between ERP and TM is asynchronous in nature, meaning they do not dynamically interact with each other regarding a transaction instance; this poses challenges, such as the fact that orders can be deleted even though the subsequent document in TM (such as OBTR) has been created. This can be overcome by using a custom (Z) field that displays a check mark on the order when the output is triggered to send the docs to TM. This field is checked during deletion. All blocked orders are sent to TM as soon as the output is triggered. Next, let's look at an overview of SAP TM.

Container Management

Now, let's observe few more challenges related to the containers, Different containers are priced differently and is time dependent situation where two 20 feet containers would be cheaper sometimes compared to one 40 feet container. So a dynamic proposal was required where you choices to select between the two either to go with one 40 feet or two 40 feet. Sometime customer demands their order to be delivered as per their container requirement. Basically an order to cash requirement.

In order to overcome the requirement the container could be mapped as means of transport, but this has a heavy restriction that freight order is created per means of transport and as many combination as many freight order which makes it quite difficult to handle these freight orders. The Implementation team proposed a custom solution to punch in the container requirement at delivery level and then form the freight unit as per the requirement for appropriate products. This is a drawback that a wrong requirements punch would result in to formation of wrong freight units. The existing inventory of container from shipping line as well as their own are maintained and monitored via the third-party (JADE) system. The current setup of ECC is to replace the handling unit formed by the appropriate container using the custom table (ZTABLE), which retrieves container data from the JADE system. The situation of container either reached at port or received by the customer is updated in this custom table. The basic requirement is to propose the container on the first come first serve basis, so that it will avoid the penalties related to late delivery of the container to shipping line. Another constraint to this was proposed container may not be available immediately for filling the material as it may have stacked at the bottom of other container or it could have been damaged.

The solution was designed to replicate the custom table (ZTABLE) with container details, which is populated in third-party (JADE) system. Once the deliveries are created from the freight order the actual container gets overwritten at delivery, based on the availability and damage situation discussed above. These containers which are actual container at delivery level and there is a difference at Freight order where there are proposed container. SO in order to sync the data the flow is written back to freight order. The manufacturing plant and the port are connected by a narrow sea route where the empty containers are made available from port to the plant via feeder vessels. The cost of the feeder vessel to be captured.

So the setup is three leg shipments: first is freight order from manufacturing plant to port where the feeder vessel charges and other planning related are captured, next is a freight booking which is the main leg from port to port basically a schedule and third is again freight order from port to destination. Please note if you are implementing the incoterms based scenario where, SAP TM has the capability to execute as per incoterms mapping for example if DDP is implemented then the third leg would not come into existence. If Incoterms scenario is not implemented then this can be mapped as zero distance scenarios for third leg. But the creation of freight order should form the predecessor and successor documents as pre-carriage (first leg) and on carriage (Third leg) in the Main carriage (second leg) freight order. So the single freight order has all the details and you can create either the deliveries or shipment from a single freight order. If you have three freight orders then task becomes tedious to handle these orders and create subsequent documents in ECC. Make you use of transshipment location as much as possible this would make your lanes.

The existing setup of SAP ECC had the process of capturing the container details in the handling unit with custom enhancement and the current solution has to be fit in with this, as well as the batch determination was z logic with container details attached to it. Because there are proposed container at freight order and the delivery has actual container which is picked on the basis of availability in the stack not necessarily as proposed in the freight order. The data which is written back to freight order level via enhancement using SAP middleware (PI).This data of containers and their capacity is used for booking order with shipping line carrier. Business share was another key requirement with soft lock logic and to calculate the rejection from shipping line as a part of their share being fulfilled. The SAPTM optimizer/ Transportation proposal had pitfalls of not proposing the business share as field, where one can check and decide it manually whether to go with a particular carrier or not.

As Business share is a soft constraint and does not restrict manually from someone cross it. The standard business share cockpit can be used, with the ability to block a carrier in case, it is not required. As well as there is no standard workflow for approval of freight order. In case a certain value exceeds in the freight order it requires an approval.

The workaround is charge calculation is performed and if the value in the freight order exceeds the required value the freight order goes in to block. This block can be removed by the authorized personnel with an authorization object having this block approval to be removed.

The main flows between SAP ERP and SAP TM are asynchronous in nature, meaning they do not dynamical interact with each other at a particular instance of a transaction; hence it poses some challenges like deletion of sales order can be done even though the subsequent document in TM like OBTR are created. This can be overcome by a custom field, which will have a check mark in the sales order as soon as the output is triggered to send the docs to TM. This field will be checked for during deletion.

These scenarios explained are common in most of the SAP TM Implementation projects.

Concluding Remarks

The key to a successful implementation is to analyze the integration's complexity and assess the limitations of the product ecosystem, because you cannot build an end-to-end product that matches all custom requirements. This chapter has presented best practices for the SAP TM implementation to help you achieve a reduction in your logistics costs. It gave you a good overview of SAP TM, EM, and EWM as part of the SAP SCM suite. You're now familiar with the challenges of implementing SAP TM and the critical areas to focus on, such as third-party suppliers (LSPs) and the integration between SAP ERP, TM, EM, EWM, and mobile devices.

■ ■ ■

CHAPTER 17

Implementing SAP CRM 7

Corporations most often lose clients because of failed relationships: they don't follow up with customers. Each lost customer or prospect is a lost opportunity. To avoid such problems, you need a robust platform that lets you collaborate with customers in a personalized manner. You need to satisfy your customers to sustain and grow your business, and to do so you must closely monitor the process from lead generation to the prospect stage, sales, and post-sale services.

Suppose you had a mobile app you could use to record customer likes, dislikes, and preferences; create orders; personalize customer experiences; and predict and enhance customer behavior, all based on your relationships with customer. You can do all that using SAP Customer Relationship Management (CRM); it offers predictive analysis and enterprise mobility with the ability to analyze customers individually using handheld devices. This chapter presents an overview of CRM, discusses the implementation methodology, and walks you through CRM case studies to help you understand best practices and common pitfalls.

■ **Note**   SAP CRM 7 is the latest software from SAP. It has enhanced capabilities that can help you offer personalized experiences for your customer. The mobility features enabled in CRM 7 helps salespeople generate leads, monitor and analyze sales, and follow through with customers.

CRM Overview

Every organization strives to succeed in the marketplace with quality products and solutions and, above all, customer service. Companies need to retain existing clients while also exploring avenues to build new products and to increase customer satisfaction. SAP CRM is designed to optimize customer interactions. This suite of business applications is integrated from pre-sale to post-sale, to help you personalize customers' experiences by understanding their behavior.

Customers can be confused by snippets of information from web portals, product catalogs, and sales pitches. They need a single source of information. SAP CRM is just that, providing information about products and services and acting as a single face for your company, to help you achieve your CRM strategies.

There are two types of business scenarios: business-to-consumer (B2C), where goods are delivered directly to the customer, and business-to-business (B2B). In a typical B2B scenario, purchasing is handled by Material Management (MM) / Supplier Relationship Management (SRM), and selling is handled by Customer Relationship Management (CRM) / Sales and Distribution (SD), as shown in Figure 17-1.

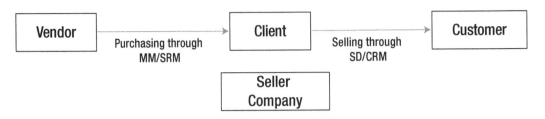

Figure 17-1. *B2B scenario*

The following SAP solutions make up the SAP Business Suite:

- SAP CRM

- SAP Product Lifecycle Management (PLM)

- SAP Supply Chain (SCM)

- SAP SRM

- SAP ERP

The SAP Business Suite is based on the SAP NetWeaver platform. NetWeaver provides the development and runtime environment for SAP applications and is used for custom development and integration with other applications and systems.

Channel Architecture

The SAP CRM channel architecture is shown in the CRM product portfolio in Figure 17-2:

- Internet app (sales, customer self-service, price configuration)

- Mobile app

- Mobile sales, service, and interaction center

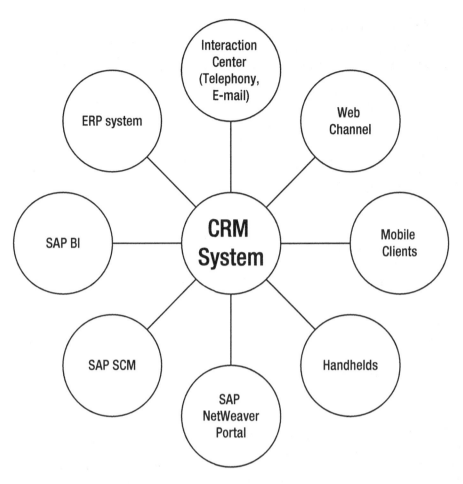

Figure 17-2. *Architecture*

SAP CRM offers sales software you can use to publish product catalogs for end users, who can then configure and purchase products. End users can request service online and use the Internet price-configuration component for product pricing.

Overview of SAP CRM Architecture

Figure 17-3 shows the SAP CRM components. Connectivity to ERP, SCM, and BW is provided via plug-ins and adapters, with access through various channels.

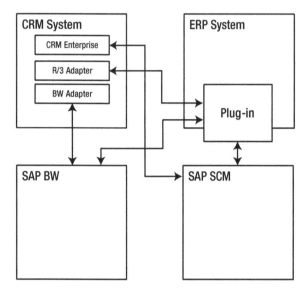

Figure 17-3. *CRM architecture*

Interaction Center

The CRM Interaction Center (IC) is used for communicating with customers via VoIP protocols, linked via the CRM web client. Salespeople can take notes, trigger emails, create activities, work on business transactions such as service orders, and so on. The IC can interface with third-party products, thus enabling multichannel options.

Mobile Applications

SAP CRM mobile sales and service components give sales reps access to customer data via their devices. These services can be enabled using CRM middleware, and Mobile Application Studio can be used to customize mobile apps.

Web Client User Interface

SAP CRM web client user interface is personalized via role-based authorization. The user works with a simple UI and can access and process only relevant tasks. For example, a sales rep, who is not concerned with marketing can only access sales-related processes, as shown in Figure 17-4.

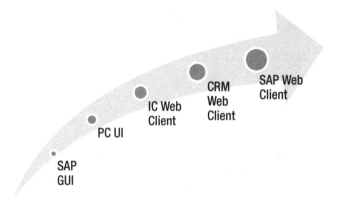

Figure 17-4. *Evolution of CRM web UI*

The CRM web client has a header at the top, a navigation bar, and a work area.

The header area contains predefined system links such as the Log Off hyperlink, saved searches, the work area title, and the user history. The header's position is fixed and cannot be changed (see Figure 17-5); it helps users navigate between pages and the work area with assignment blocks.

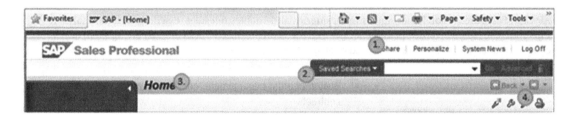

Figure 17-5. *The UI header area*

Common CRM Implementation Pitfalls

The most common pitfalls in CRM implementation projects are related to the following modules:

- CRM Sales: Sales Order Management, Account and Contract Management

- CRM Services: Service Orders

- CRM Marketing: Marketing plans

- CRM Middleware: Queue monitoring, data loads, and so on

- CRM IC: Account identification and service requests

Evolution of CRM 7

SAP CRM has evolved in marketing and sales areas, so let's see more on that subject.

SAP CRM Marketing

SAP CRM 7 includes the following marketing features, as shown in Figure 17-6:

- Marketing planning
- Campaign management
- Lead management
- E-marketing, analytics, and customer segmentation

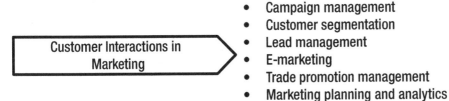

Figure 17-6. *CRM Marketing*

SAP CRM Sales

SAP CRM Sales focuses on handling customer queries and enables telesales, e-selling, and field sales. It helps your sales force be efficient and effective and focus on productive activities, by giving them access to account management, sales planning, and analytics functionality (see Figure 17-7).

Customer Interactions in Sales

- Customer order management, quotations, and contracts
- Account and contact management
- Opportunity management and pipeline analysis
- Activity management
- Commissions and incentives
- Sales planning and analytics

Figure 17-7. *CRM Sales*

SAP CRM Service

CRM Service is primarily focused on service orders, from customer inquiry to billing. It includes quotations, service orders, and assignments to field service representatives (see Figure 17-8).

Customer Interactions in Service

- Service request, service order, and contract administration
- Complaint management
- Case management
- Installed base management
- Workflow and escalation management
- Workforce management
- Service planning and analytics

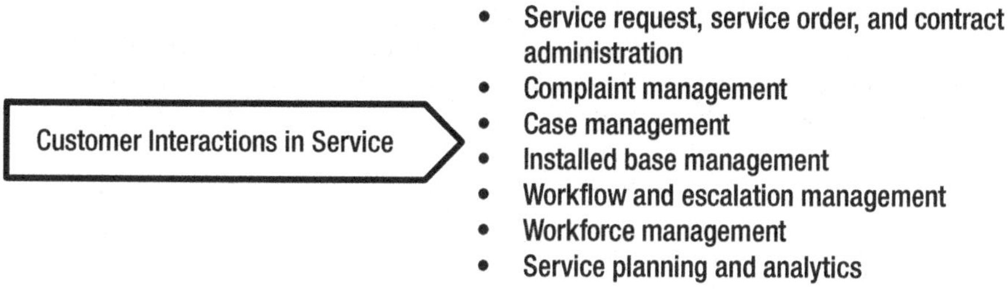

Figure 17-8. *CRM Services*

SAP CRM Channels

CRM Channels coordinates sales via the Internet, mobile devices, telephony, field sales, and partners, thus helping to optimize customer interactions (see Figure 17-9). As discussed earlier, CRM provides a UI for interacting with customers.

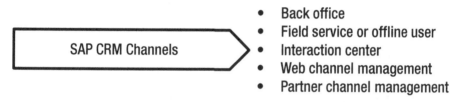

SAP CRM Channels

- Back office
- Field service or offline user
- Interaction center
- Web channel management
- Partner channel management

Figure 17-9. *CRM Channels*

Using role-based access, field reps can access CRM through mobile devices or the Internet anytime, anywhere. The IC integrates multiple communication channels and keeps track of transactions. Web channels provide a platform for e-services, e-commerce, and e-marketing and help you provide personalized and reliable customer services. The partner channel is enabled for dealers, resellers, and agents, to support partner management.

Implementation Methodology

Implementing SAP CRM 7 poses significant challenges, because the product has evolved to a large extent, and this release includes many new features. Releases until CRM 5.0 had fewer challenges; but CRM has now become a sales, services, and marketing tool for SAP customers. Most project failures are due to a lack of planning and failure to understand the CRM product ecosystem.

Let's look at the steps involved in implementing CRM, as shown in Figure 17-10. They follow the ASAP methodology. The first step is to understand the business requirements. Then you configure SAP, using setup screens to choose specific functionality that is eventually used by end users (see Figure 17-11).

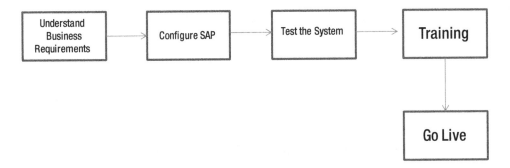

Figure 17-10. *Implementation steps*

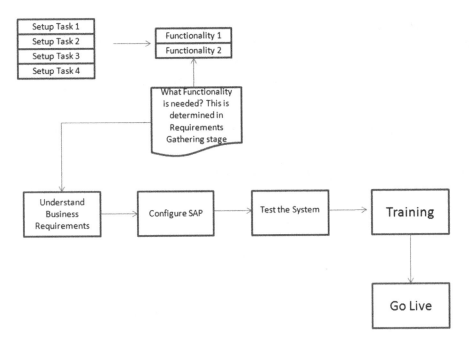

Figure 17-11. *Configuration steps*

You need to have the target functionality in mind, such as a specific screen flow or logic to implement (perhaps a specific order type, and so on). You must understand the required functionality in order to make necessary customizations and to standardize business processes per industry best practices. Once the configuration is done, you test the system and move it to production.

Let's look at a simple business server page (BSP) configuration (web client) for developing the UI for end users with the CRM application. Log on to SAP Easy Access CRM, right-click Favorites, and add a BSP application for the web client.

Select the BSP web client to connect to the SAP NetWeaver web application server in a browser.

You can use SU01 for role maintenance; a common profile is the CRM_UI_PROFILE role. Once you log in as a service professional, you can personalize the screen. Now you can adapt the web client UI by personalizing the menu on the landing page.

You can configure the layout, skin, text, performance testing, and so on, and you can synchronize with Microsoft Outlook. For example, under Account Management, you can search for corporate accounts or groups.

The bottom line is that you can personalize the UI without needing much technical expertise.

CASE STUDY OF CRM IMPLEMENTATION

The client is the largest energy company in the UK. Facing external gas/electric market and internal cost pressures, the client's British Gas Business (BGB) division embarked on a project to consolidate its legacy billing systems to reduce cost to serve and improve customer advocacy.

The partner was engaged to conduct a review of the first release (for gas customers) of the program and recommend ways to ensure its successful implementation. Following these recommendations, and with ongoing program support from the partner, release 1 successfully went live in 2007. Subsequently, the partner was engaged to perform a review of the suitability of the solution to ensure that the design supported the objectives and strategies of BGB for release 2 (electricity customers).

Project Background

Release 1 of the project implemented an SAP Utilities and CRM system (upgraded from 5.0 to 7.0) that was a billing and customer management solution for industrial and commercial gas customers. The solution helped the client realize its objectives of reducing cost to serve and improving the customer experience.

For Release 1, the partner provided direct support for the following:

- Program management and governance: Primarily managed by the client. For fixed-price projects like PSAP and Teradata, the partner was responsible for program management.

- Program office (including planning and reporting).

- Solution architecture and integration: The partner team was involved in all major architecture and design decisions in the areas of contract management, customer management, the task and exception hub, the agent dashboard, and PSAP and NETSAP programs.

For the validation of the design for Release 2, the partner was responsible for the following:

- Ensuring that the published design incorporated the latest process best practices, met the business requirements, and was "owned" by the business

- Implementing SAP CRM 7.0 Sales and Service, integrated with ISU, marketing, the IC web client with CTI integration, and loyalty management.

- Implementing a custom-built agent workbench UI framework to support BGB call center functionalities.

- CRM functionality, configured to integrate with ISU.

- Integrating the agent workbench with existing non-SAP applications such as Siebel, Banner, and so on, using SAP PI. The partner team was involved in interface design for Siebel, Banner, QAS, and SAP MRS.

CHAPTER 18

■ ■ ■

SAP Governance, Risk, and Compliance

One of the critical challenges faced by enterprises is the need to manage governance requirements and comply with regulations. It is important to manage these risks in order to prevent organizational processes from collapsing. For example, Enron, one of the largest energy companies based in the United States, failed because it didn't implement governance, risk, and compliance (GRC) control measures; it lost its value, impacting millions of shareholders.

Suppose you're driving a car. You have requirements such as holding a driver's license, adhering to the government's pollution standards, and following all traffic laws. Thus multiple parties are involved in enforcing rule-based compliance. In addition, there are safety requirements such as inspecting the car's tires, changing the oil, and driving carefully. What is the advantage of meeting all these requirements? You reach your destination safely.

Similarly, SAP GRC can help you run your business the right way by focusing on three major areas: financial GRC, IT GRC, and operational GRC. The main objective is to automate compliance with rules and regulations. Implementing SAP GRC makes compliance requirements visible, so stakeholders are aware that you are adhering to requirements. This increased transparency also improves shareholder confidence, thus resulting in better overall performance. In addition, an offline risk analysis provides a Segregation of Duties (SoD) and health check for clients that don't have a GRC installation.

SAP GRC solutions include the following:

- SAP Access Control

- SAP Process Control

- SAP Risk Management

- SAP Fraud Management

- SAP Audit Management

- SAP Global Trade Services

- SAP Electronic Invoicing for Brazil

The critical elements are as follows:

- SoD analysis across all roles, profiles, and users in the SAP landscape

- The SoD end-to-end analysis

  - Provides a report that highlights conflicts and violations in the current SoD

  - Can be repeated periodically (quarterly, every six months, or annually)

SAP GRC Overview

SAP GRC helps companies develop insights into risks and compliance initiatives—critical areas in which it is easy for organizations to lose focus. For example, implementing the Sarbanes-Oxley Act (SOX) according to US regulations is a daunting task without such a tool-based approach. SAP's unique GRC solutions have evolved based on regulatory requirements from GRC 5.3 to GRC 10. An important task for all major stakeholders is to control fraud and access; this can be achieved by implementing SAP GRC solutions, including offerings such as SAP Access Control and SAP Process Control.

SAP Risk Control

Let's look at the objectives of implementing the SoD management process, which is a key element in reducing organizations' SoD conflicts and is essential in achieving SoX compliance. Table 18-1 lists the six critical steps in this process.

Table 18-1. *SoD Management Process*

Steps	Description
1. Risk recognition	Analyze SoD conflicts, and define unacceptable risks.
2. Risk building	Based on step 1, build the rule set to analyze user or role assignments.
3. Risk analysis	Find ways to eliminate risks discovered by analyzing GRC Access Control.
4. Remediation	Evaluate the conflicting tasks in SoD with an outcome of very low risks remaining.
5. Mitigation	Remediate the SoD conflicts with an outcome of no risks.
6. Continuous compliance	Ensure that every access request is reviewed as per the SoD conflict matrix with an outcome of continuous compliance to keep the system clean.

User management in SAP GRC 10.x involves the steps shown in Figure 18-1.

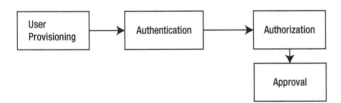

Figure 18-1. *GRC user management*

The first step, user provisioning, uses an automated process to create users in SAP GRC. The authentication step refers to implementing user credentials that can be used for authentication, and the authorization step addresses end-user access requirements by assigning roles to the users. The final step is approval, which involves re-authentication as illustrated in Figure 18-1.

The next section discusses implementing SAP GRC.

SAP GRC Implementation

A large implementation partner deployed SAP's latest version of GRC (version 10.1), which requires a base NetWeaver version of 7.4. The GRC implementation approach is illustrated in Figure 18-2.

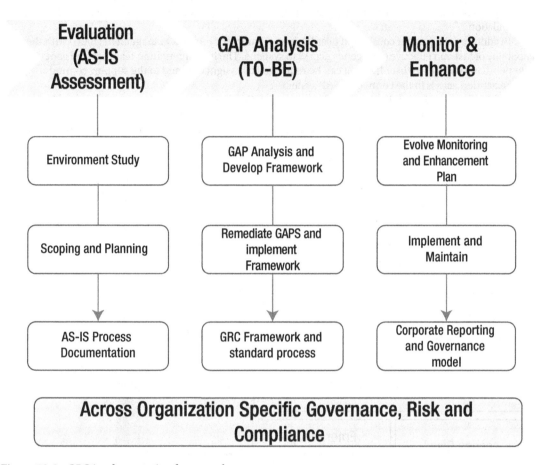

Figure 18-2. *GRC implementation framework*

By utilizing a phased approach to GRC delivery, each phase supports the next seamlessly and allows for immediate realization of benefits while continually moving the client toward achieving its compliance goals. In this case, the implementation team split the activities into three phases to enable customers to pick and choose the elements most suited to their requirements and ensure scalability for future enhancements to the solution (see Figure 18-3):

- *GRC Phase 1:* Deployment of Access Risk Analysis and Emergency Access Management

- *GRC Phase 2:* Deployment of User Access Management and (optional) Business Role Management

- *GRC Phase 3:* Deployment of Process Controls

During Phase I, the partner proposed to implement Access Risk Analysis (ARA) in order to proactively identify any potential security weaknesses in the current role design and access levels in its ABAP-based systems. Deploying the SAP standard rule set delivered with GRC v10.1 provides a "broad spectrum of identifiable risk" based on SAP best practices and its experience with a multitude of clients. The partner activated all standard dashboard reports that relate to the ARA and EAM elements of GRC. Many of these standard reports contain drilldowns that can be exported to external tools such as Excel for additional manipulation.

In addition, the partner configured user ID–based Emergency Access Management (EAM) with the capability of fast and effective emergency access to systems. The implementation team created generic function-based firefighter user IDs that can be requested or assigned by and to the support community to allow extended access in the connected SAP system.

A firefighter user is identical to a standard user, with the advantage of having vastly extended SAP access that is unsuited to an everyday user or would cause significant SoD conflicts. As such, these IDs are tightly controlled, and their assignment can be approved for specific activities and for short, targeted time frames, thereby reducing potential exposure to risks defined in the SAP standard rule set.

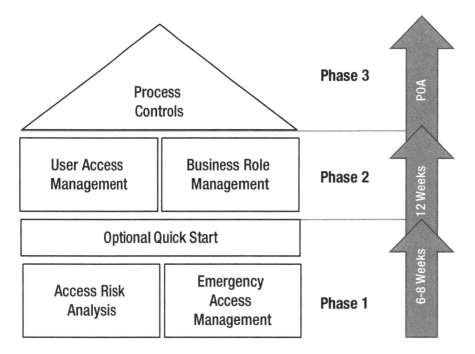

Figure 18-3. *GRC phased implementation*

The main infrastructure required for GRC phase 1 and subsequent phase 2 deployments are shown in Figure 18-4. The client defined all sizing recommendations as suggested by SAP. All infrastructure-related issues (and subsequent technical issues arising from infrastructure) were managed by the client.

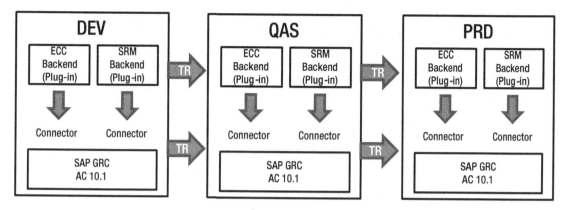

Figure 18-4. SAP GRC Landscape

Let's review the high-level implementation plan.

High-Level Project Plan

The client had a mandate of completing the project within a span of ten weeks, as shown in the project plan in Figure 18-5. The implementation team planned the project and milestones in line with these requirements, resulting in a focused engagement that allowed the client to achieve the goals of the project on time and deliver all required elements.

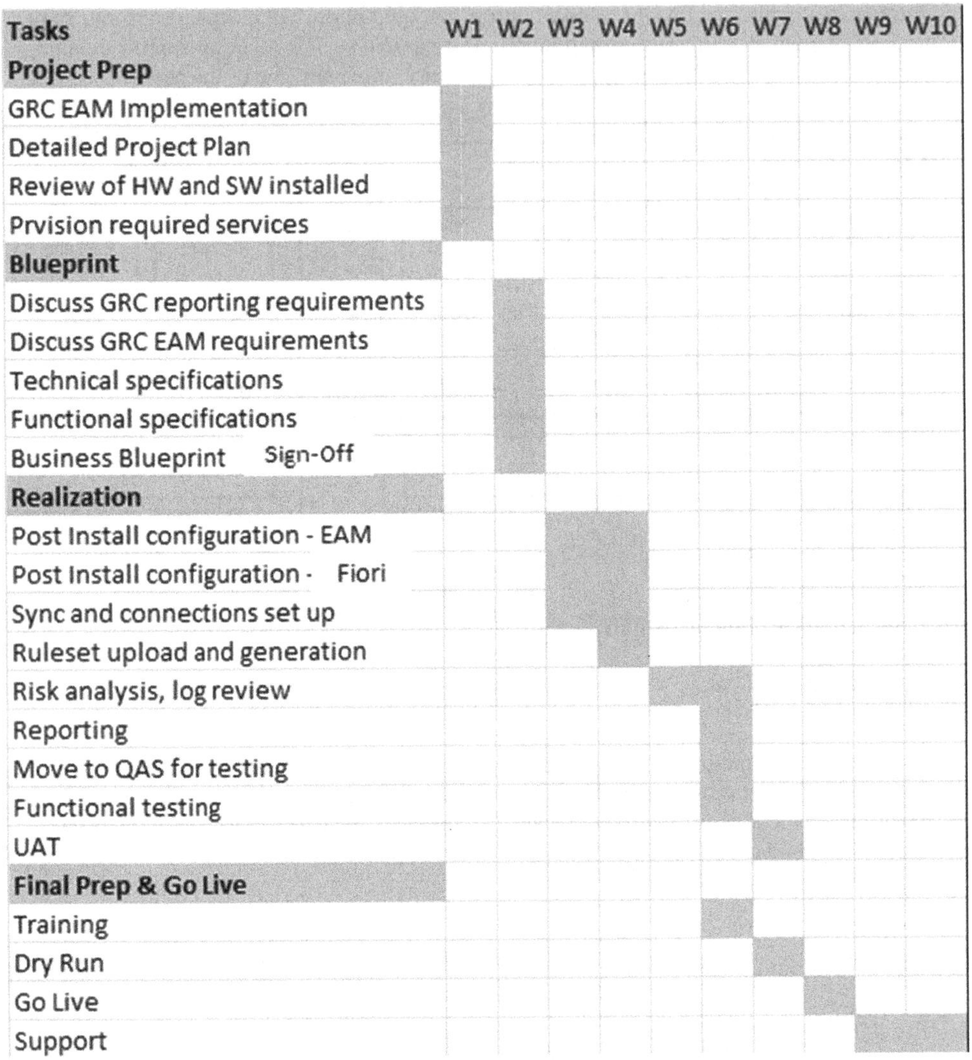

Tasks	W1	W2	W3	W4	W5	W6	W7	W8	W9	W10
Project Prep										
GRC EAM Implementation	▓									
Detailed Project Plan	▓									
Review of HW and SW installed	▓									
Prvision required services	▓									
Blueprint										
Discuss GRC reporting requirements		▓								
Discuss GRC EAM requirements		▓								
Technical specifications		▓								
Functional specifications		▓								
Business Blueprint Sign-Off		▓								
Realization										
Post Install configuration - EAM			▓	▓						
Post Install configuration - Fiori			▓	▓						
Sync and connections set up			▓							
Ruleset upload and generation			▓							
Risk analysis, log review					▓	▓				
Reporting						▓				
Move to QAS for testing						▓				
Functional testing						▓				
UAT							▓			
Final Prep & Go Live										
Training						▓				
Dry Run							▓			
Go Live								▓		
Support									▓	▓

Figure 18-5. *GRC implementation plan*

GRC Deliverables and Milestones

Table 18-2 lists the deliverables and major milestones of the GRC implementation project.

Table 18-2. *Deliverables and Milestones*

Milestone	Project Phase	Deliverables
Development installation	Design	Design Document
QA installation		
PRD installation		
Ruleset file preparation	Realization	Ruleset document
ARA configuration guide		Configuration guide
SAP GRC role conversion to customer namespace		GRC roles mapping
SAP standard SoD analysis reporting	Test	SoD report
Operational dashboard	Implement	Test scenario / Plan
Knowledge transfer		KT documents
Test plan / test cases		

CASE STUDY 1: IMPLEMENTING THE GRC CAPABILITY MODEL

How do you connect roles within an organization? Let's look at the Capability Model. Organizations struggle with regulatory and risk-compliance requirements, due to the impact of change, lack of a strong IT architecture, and lack of shared processes. GRC helps with risk governance and supports businesses so they can transform into high-performing organizations.

In a financial organization, GRC audit resources were using manual process to reconcile audit documents. There was an inability to provide risk assessment or planning with intuitive forecasting ("Which risks concern me? Which risks can be used to compare/aggregate? and so on). Even some of the GRC implementation was done at the department level, resulting in redundant data and an inability to provide risk normalization. GRC can help normalize risk across the organization.

Collaborating across departments

GRC helps consolidate information through role collaboration across different departments. In general, this refers to common technology information. GRC provides value by managing risk and compliance so the company can be agile rather than reactive in a changing business environment. Your landscape may include finance, procurement, supply chain, and EHS—GRC covers all of these business functions. *Governance* indicates how you're managing risks, by controlling and evaluating an entity, process, or resource. *Risk management* is the act of managing processes and resources to address risks, and *compliance* is the state of being able to prove fulfillment of a requirement or obligation. GRC can support your governance to define integrity risks and ensure compliance. How do you know your organization is operating within the boundaries? Risk-management practices require risk governance and compliance.

You also need to manage uncertainty. Sometimes risk managers spend a lot of time in defining performance management criteria that is not required. Risk management is already part of performance management. Every risk is an opportunity for reward.

GRC is all about the integrity of the organization; GRC addresses integrity by implementing risk and compliance. Enron had paper-based compliance programs but minimal integrity. Think about how you implement policies and corporate responsibilities with integrity. A major financial organization with unhealthy compliance and lacking ISO 31000 implementation and governance standards will have problems. Let's see how SAP GRC addresses these compliance issues.

Figure 18-6 shows the GRC capability Model, which integrates these components: Organize, Assess, Proactive, Predict, Detect, Respond, and Measure.

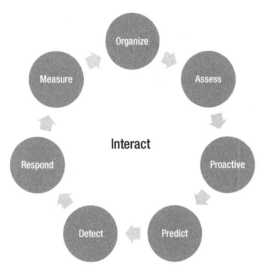

Figure 18-6. *GRC Capability Model with integrated components*

The outcomes of using this model are as follows:

- Achieve business objectives.
- Enhance the organizational culture.
- Increase stakeholder confidence.
- Prepare and protect the organization.
- Prevent, detect, and reduce adversity.
- Motivate and inspire.
- Improve responsiveness.
- Achieve overall optimization.

Figure 18-6 has Interact at the center: this refers to the tight integration necessary to achieve business objectives such as a governance culture, an ethical organizational culture, and so on. The goal is to change the external and internal culture and objectives. For example, rule-based ethics (following a set of rules) and utilitarian-based ethics (making judgements based on inputs) impact business decisions. A bad culture can ruin an organization, and building a company's reputation can take years. Context is everything.

GRC is not only about risk management and auditing; it also involves bringing in transparency across departments at all levels of the organization. Everyone plays their part in GRC. GRC helps in proactively implementing policies such as regulatory, training and preventive controls, and detective controls in various environments to curb fraudulent transactions. You need good crisis planning to measure your ability to prevent events before they happen. This includes continuous monitoring of process, improving performance of GRC and communicating to the various stakeholders. GRC helps in connecting disparate risk and audit systems in order to gain insights into the investigation of specific events with respect to policy.

To address risks, you need efficient sources of information so risk management is not scattered. You should consolidate risk, such as a COE for risks related to the technology architecture. Integrated information for all roles in the organization marries GRC with the business. The GRC strategy encompasses the following components:

- Project charter

- Mission and vision statement

- Outcomes and maturity milestones

- Metrics

- Effectiveness and agile

Revisit your values and objectives to understand how to move from as-is to to-be. Then, figure out the costs and benefits so you can make the business case for implementing GRC. For example, a large company in the United States had over 50 employees dedicated to internal audits and many more dedicated to federal audits. Multiple groups, such as Risk, Compliance, and Legal, were responsible for GRC. In other words, the company had disconnected risk. The chief audit executive analyzed the results to understand the disparity and the need to implement integrated GRC. The company needed a system to implement GRC for SOX compliance and anti-corruption certification processes.

SOX compliance is mandatory for financial results and for risks such as environment and health & safety.

Let's look at how to create a basic access request in GRC.

You enter the reason for the request and the request type, based on SPRO configuration, such as New Account, Change Account, or Delete Account; the Request For option can be Self or Other User. Also, you can provision users for firefighter IDs using access management. Select a business process and function area. You need to assign the system and roles, if more than one GRC system is connected. You can create a request for more than one system, and each system can have different roles. (If you have third-party access management, it is difficult to manage roles. In GRC, you can use different roles.) Select the role type as Single or Composite, with give a role name such as g_abc. These roles need to be configured in GRC Business Roles Management (BRM).

There is an option to perform a simulation prior to the risk-violation check. The risk-violation check executes the actual analysis based on the simulation steps. In the IMG configuration, you can specify that options such as risk analysis are mandatory or non-mandatory. Based on the SPRO configuration settings, you can run the risk analysis.

Once the access request is created, the next step is to approval.

CASE STUDY 2: LEADING ENERGY COMPANY

A large SAP implementation partner deployed the ARA standard rule set for a client's existing custom rule set and EAM with a proof-of-concept configuration for UAM and BRM. In as little as six to eight weeks, the client achieved fully operational risk reporting and audit-compliant UAM.

The client was one of the UK's largest energy companies. Energy is subject to public oversight and regulations. For its internal processes, the client depended heavily on SAP to manage demand and supply, financial obligations, and personnel and contractors:

- It had a longstanding concern relating to SoD being adequately reflected and enforced within SAP.

- It aimed to resolve the concern with an approach that minimized impact and risk to business processes already in operation.

- The resolution had to be achieved in a cost-effective manner in the short term, leaving a sustainable solution in place for the future.

- In order to manage the process effectively, the client chose to acquire and deploy a tool that allowed specific user profiles to be constructed efficiently and that facilitates identification and management of potential SoD issues.

The approach was as follows:

- Implement ARA for business processes, Finance, Procurement, Order to Cash, Human Resources, and Basis.

- Review and implement comprehensive SoD rules, including all customer-specific transactions.

- Implement EAM, enabling authorized superuser access in a controlled and auditable manner.

- Test plans and controls built in SAP GRC, following an automated email and workflow.

- Develop a remediation plan (Quick Start + option).

The benefits were as follows:

- Delivery of a simplified and integrated GRC applications framework

- Improved business performance and predictability by enabling detection of SoD conflicts in real time

- Comprehensive and flexible library of SoD rules

- Auditable records maintained for future reference and audit trials

- Reduced risk of potential fraud, errors, and misappropriation due to inappropriate allocation of privileges

- Reduced risk of inability to demonstrate compliance with audit and self-certification requirements through reporting and monitoring of risks

The value proposition for the client was as follows:

- Fixed-price implementation, providing peace of mind, value for the money spent, and flexibility through the partner's template GRC offering

- Partner implementation approach that used cost, quality, and resource scalability advantages to deliver all developments

- SAP GRC SMEs who engaged in consulting and transforming organizational needs

Performing Risk Analysis Every Day in the Background

Risk analysis can be user-based or role-based. SoD can be run at a transaction code level. Sometimes, as with the mass creation of vendors, this risk type can be defined by the company as a critical transaction. Even basic transactions, such as deleting customers, can be critical and flagged as high risk; this can be analyzed in the Compliance Calibrator Cockpit.

Risk reports can be generated at the object level or authorization level, with a detailed risk description for the roles selected. You can schedule daily reports to analyze risks introduced to the system. Typically, auditors use these reports for compliance. You can run scheduled jobs in the background to analyze risks on a daily basis.

CASE STUDY 3: UPGRADING SAP GRC 5.3 TO GRC 10.1

A client requested an upgrade from SAP GRC 5.x to GRC 10.x, in order to benefit from the functional improvements. The implementation team faced significant challenges in the upgrade project, because user management and authentication failed after the upgrade. This was primarily due to the fact that there was an SAP NetWeaver (NW) technology platform change: SAP migrated its GRC suite in 5.3 based on NW Java to NW ABAP in GRC 10.1. So, we had to remediate the GRC 5.3 custom application version for compatibility in GRC 10.1, and re-test. The automated and customized workflows powered by the Business Rules Framework (BRF) with additional functionality gave the end users many options they did not have previously.

Concluding Remarks

GRC is the foundation of an organization. Gone are the days of no transparency to customers and shareholders; they know your balance sheet, because they are watching closely. SAP's GRC software helps customers gain transparency for governance, risk, and compliance management, as discussed in the case studies. It eases the pressure on top management and auditors by auditing risks on a daily basis; hence it is a proactive approach to assessing corporate performance, rather than being reactive.

SAP GRC is a simple, easy-to-use tool that lets auditors predict and proactively measure risks through compliance metrics, reporting, and scheduled jobs. It helps you to optimize risk analysis by integrating that analysis across departments and meeting your financial reporting and statutory compliance requirements.

■ ■ ■

CHAPTER 19

Introduction to SAP Enterprise Mobility

The advent of enterprise mobility applications has led to SAP developing a robust, innovative, breakthrough mobility platform for enterprise solutions. It addresses issues in design and implementation with a simple user interface. SAP offers Fiori licenses for application developers with a packaged set of preconfigured mobile applications. These assets can be used or customized for specific solutions, depending on client requirements. Today, the world revolves around mobility and harnessing data as analytics, and SAP helps its customers implement enterprise mobility applications using Fiori.

This chapter includes an overview of the SAP Fiori mobile application platform and its features, discusses the implementation methodology, and offers a real-time case study of implementing SAP Fiori apps. Prior to examining an SAP Fiori implementation project, let's look at the basics of Fiori apps and implementation.

■ **Note** SAP Fiori gives users an enhanced and personalized user experience (UX), using key design principles. The UX interface is natively designed for SAP S/4 HANA and Simple Finance, keeping in mind future evolution in HANA.

SAP Fiori Overview

Every time we implement a project, we admire SAP's voluminous intelligence software and the visionary product ecosystem that has evolved from R/3, to ECC, to HANA. Today, mobility and analytics are the core focus areas. In simple terms, mobility helps you achieve ERP on mobile. Whether it's production plan data, customer data, or supplier data, it's available on mobile device. And the next age of enterprise mobility applications are evolving. I wouldn't be surprised to see a CEO or CFO sitting at their ranch home and deciding corporate strategy based on real-time analytical data on their mobile device via SAP HANA.

You can implement custom mobility applications developed for Android, iOS, or Google OS and run them seamlessly on the Fiori platform. Fiori can help transform your organization into a mobility enterprise with lightning data speed to help your clients, respond to suppliers, and so on. Distance and location no longer matter—you can service clients worldwide.

Traditionally, enterprise software has been based on transaction processes. But the SAP Fiori UX breaks from this approach and focuses on users and their goals. By using disaggregate transaction processes, SAP Fiori shows users only the tasks and activities they need to do their jobs. The UX is designed with applications that are easy to use and role-based, such as navigating with your smart phone. The design guidelines specify how Fiori reflects visual design, information architecture, colors, and interaction patterns. By focusing on users, you can improve productivity, increase adoption, and decrease training costs, so your business can run more efficiently and effectively.

An app reference library enables you to explore, plan, and implement Fiori; it includes key information for each app, including the technical data you need for installation and configuration. From a simple time sheet, to leave or travel approvals, to helping agents track purchase orders from their mobile device, Fiori can help you access them easily.

For all SAP Fiori apps available today, you can

- View data for previous app versions

- Show aggregated installation and configuration information for a selection of apps

- Navigate directly to related resources, such as app documentation, a product availability matrix, and a maintenance planner

Why Do You Need Fiori?

Traditionally, SAP applications have been perceived as complex and not user-friendly because of the complexities of the navigation path. However, with Fiori, the image of SAP has transitioned from shop-floor-based software to enterprise mobility software with ease of access to enterprise applications from mobile devices anytime, anywhere. The key benefits to customers are as follows:

- Enhanced, easy-to-use UX that users can personalize

- High-speed access to enterprise applications on mobile devices with accurate information

- Scalability of mobile applications for current and the future needs

- Applications that are easy to implement, enhance, and maintain across all mobile devices

- Productivity improvements in workflow approvals, service lookups, and so on

- UI evolution with UI5

- Enable customers to have an enhanced user experience

Fiori provides a consistent look and feel across all apps. It offers a collection of preconfigured scenarios out of the box, such as Employee Leave Requests.

Architecture

The Fiori architecture is shown in Figure 19-1. As you can see, mobile devices access SAP applications via SAP NetWeaver Gateway.

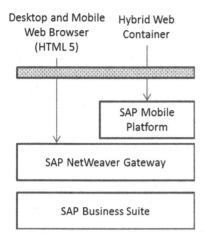

Figure 19-1. *High-level architecture*

Figure 19-2 shows key areas of the Fiori implementation, with back-end SAP implemented for FI/MM, HCM, and procurement solutions.

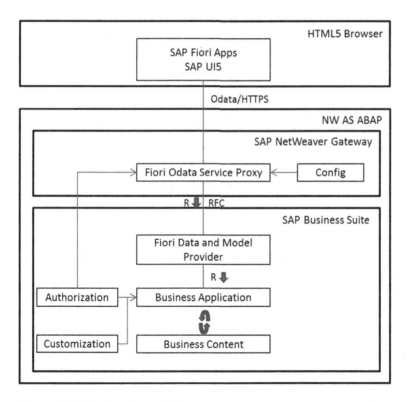

Figure 19-2. *Fiori implementation*

The SAP NetWeaver Gateway acts as an interface between the front-end UT (HTML5 browser) and the back-end ERP with authorization and customization options; it also comes with a Solution Manager. Once you deploy the ABAP stack, the Gateway is the abstraction layer, with the UI as the front end and the back-end SAP application suite. Roles and responsibilities are determined through Gateway services. You can also use OData to create new scenarios from scratch.

In terms of deployment, you can have multiple ERP systems with one central hub with a front-end UI. The back end has an add-on to communicate. In a second scenario, the Gateway can be on the ECC system, instead of deploying the ABAP stack as an embedded deployment. The primary objective is to use your current SAP landscape infrastructure without additional investment.

Let's look at an implementation case study.

CASE STUDY: SAP FIORI IMPLEMENTATION

Client Background: The client is one of the world's largest conglomerates and a Fortune 500 company with businesses across numerous industry verticals, such as hydrocarbon exploration and production, petroleum refining and marketing, petrochemicals, retail, and telecommunications. It is the largest producer of polyester yarn and fiber in the world.

The Challenge: The client used an SAP roadmap on UI5 technology in its wide array of HR processes. This system allowed business users to access these processes only on desktops. Each process took 20 to 25 screens to complete and was time consuming—and there were about 40 business processes in the HR, sales order, and purchase order tracking functions. The company needed to streamline this functionality and make it easy to access and work with from anywhere. The client had implemented SAP five years earlier and wanted to maximize the benefits from its SAP infrastructure and investments without having to change the back-end systems due to front-end app development.

The Objectives:

- Cycle-time reduction for overall HR business processes such as employee time sheets and leave approvals, with a robust solution that is extensible for the sales order and purchase order tracking process

- Ability to access processes with multiplatform, multidevice compatibility

- Increased efficiency, productivity, and scale of output

- Remote access to easily manage data

The Solution: The client approached us with this problem, seeking a solution that would iron out all these bottlenecks. Our team of highly experienced, seasoned professionals and architects had expertise in solving such problems. After examining a step-by-step process flow at the client's end, we suggested a hybrid model with the following scenarios:

- Scenario 1: Sales order creation

- Scenario 2: Spending analysis to compare the budget versus actual spending

- Scenario 3: Purchase requisition approval process

The Approach: We followed a very clear and modular approach toward the objective, as shown in Figure 19-3.

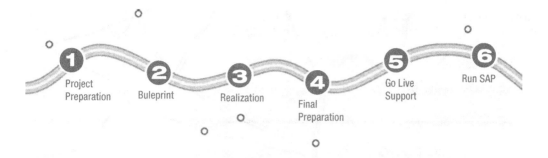

Figure 19-3. *Modular implementation approach*

Project Preparation

We discussed our plan with the business SMEs and employees who were directly interacting with the current system's owners. Further, we collected information regarding every process at a micro level:

- Types of processes
- Frequency of usage
- Type of data used
- Data load
- Business functions impacted
- Type of output
- Scale of output/process

Blueprint

The entire team along with management analyzed and brainstormed. We needed to compress the process timelines while optimizing output with minimum use of resources. We conducted multiple workshops with business users to identify an optimum solution for this situation.

Realization

Based on our analysis, we created mock-ups of the Fiori-enabled system. Using a hybrid model, an onsite team and an offshore team worked in tandem to implement a custom development and testing phase in the client systems. We also enhanced the existing system with Fiori technology; it supports multiple platforms with cross-device support and shorter cycle times, and it is remotely accessible.

We discussed options for the standard SAP UI5, including developing Fiori applications with minor modifications to the theme and incorporating an additional user administration app using custom Fiori to keep the look and feel across all apps simple and consistent.

We included the three critical business scenarios:

- Create Sales Order
- Create Purchase Order
- Approval process

And we created role-based scenarios for the following users:

- Manager

- Employer

- Sales representative

- Purchase agent

Design Considerations

Users are accustomed to specific characteristics in enterprise software like Twitter and LinkedIn. SAP has applied these aspects into Fiori, which has a consistent look and feel regardless of the device you're using to access SAP enterprise applications. Fiori comes with 25 preconfigured scenarios such as leave requests, purchase requisitions, and so on, so existing customers can quickly enable Fiori without changing their back end.

The standard Fiori out-of-the-box design has a series of tiles, each describing a specific business scenario such as Approve Purchase Orders, Approve Leave Requests, Approve Purchase Requisitions, and so on.

Each of the tiles is fully customizable, such as adding role-based ESS capabilities. You can also use the Fiori Designer to modify some of the look and feel and branding. You can use Fiori to create services and make the UI design look like other Fiori apps, using Eclipse or another platform.

The UI5 framework helps SAP customers access SAP across devices and again uses the same look and feel. Let's look how Fiori is deployed: Figure 19-4 shows the architecture.

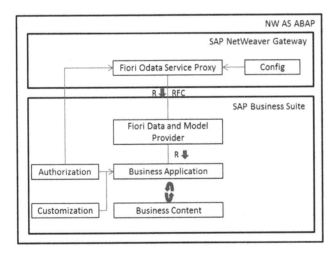

Figure 19-4. *SAP NW Gateway architecture*

SAP UI5 is an extension of the HTML libraries available in the SAP service marketplace. OData is standard; you can change or create new scenarios as you need them for customers. There are two ways to deploy Fiori applications, as shown in Figure 19-5.

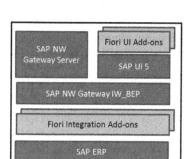

Figure 19-5. *Fiori app deployment options*

You can have multiple ERP systems with one hub to represent data from the back-end or CRM system. The back end uses add-ons to communicate with Fiori apps. Using the SAP NW Gateway infrastructure, instead of deploying an additional NW ABAP stack for Fiori, you can use the existing ECC infrastructure, thus reducing your upfront investment.

Let's look at the steps involved in creating the three scenarios mentioned earlier (creating sales orders, comparing budgets with actual spending, and approving purchase requisitions). Here are the steps to create an order:

1. Log on from a mobile or desktop device. Enter your user ID and password as you'd do in the SAP GUI.

2. The home screen displays different tiles representing scenarios based on your how your profile has been configured.

3. Select the Create Sales Orders tile to open the window.

4. Choose the customer for whom you'd like to create a sales order. If there is a preexisting sales order, it appears on the next screen.

5. In this example, let's choose sales order SO 14489 and select the Products option. This navigates to the product list, where you can identify products to sell to this customer; it includes details about materials, plants, divisions, and product hierarchies. You can add products to the shopping cart shown in the upper-right corner.

6. Next is the delivery schedule. You can change it for the products selected.

7. Once you are happy with the delivery schedule, you see a summary of your order.

8. Click Checkout.

9. In the next step, you can review the shipping options.

10. To review your shipping choice, click Review Shipping.

11. Review your order by entering the purchase order number.

12. If you need to enter specific shipping instructions, such "Ask Mr. Will Smith for monitor," you can do it on the next screen. Finally, review the order.

13. Click Place Order. You get a confirmation from the SAP back end with an order number.

14. From the home screen, you can use the Track Sales Orders tile to track your order.

Now, let's look at the second scenario: comparing budgeted spending with actual spending. You can pull some interesting order reports from the SAP back end. Follow these steps:

1. Navigate back to the home screen, and choose My Spend.

2. You can check spending by various departments for a given time period in the My Spend app.

3. This information can help you analyze the allocated amounts and actual spending. You can also analyze procurement details.

For the third scenario, let's look at the purchase requisition approval app. Follow these steps:

1. On the home screen, select the Approve Purchase Requisitions tile.

2. Review the requisition details, such as material, quantity, and cost, with G/L account assignment if completed.

3. Click Approve to approve the purchase requisition.

So far, you have seen how to use the standard Fiori applications. Now, let's look at a customized app developed for user administration.

You can change the look and feel of Fiori applications. To do so, you use the Theme Designer.

CASE STUDY, CONTINUED

Dry Run and Cut Over

We successfully performed dry runs 1 and 2, with sanity checks, and finalized the cut-over plan.

Final Prep and Go Live

We prepared the system for Go Live after the two dry runs. Finally, we achieved a successful Go Live.

Conclusion and Benefits:

- The number of users of the enhanced system increased substantially.

- One significant achievement was digitizing the entire HR process, end to end, thus reducing paperwork and the manual approval workflow.

- We extended flexibility via multi-device and cross-platform support.

- We reduced the cycle time for processes such as employee travel plans, leave management, and time sheets.

- We provided support for regular maintenance and roadblocks.

Implementation Methodology

This section analyzes the implementation methodology of Fiori APPS. To use Fiori apps, you need to install the necessary front-end components and the SAP Gateway services to configure a connection to the back end. We recommend separating the business logic and the back-end data from the UI layer, because doing so offers strategic advantages.

Decoupling the life cycle of the UI apps from the back end, especially apps that also run on a database, has these advantages:

- Faster iterations for the UI apps

- Ability to change the UI without needing development authorizations in the back end

- Single point of maintenance for UI issues, such as browser support and updated versions of SAP UI5 libraries

- Central place for theming and branding Fiori apps

To separate back-end and front-end components, set up the SAP Gateway using the Central Hub Deployment option. This means you must install the SAP Gateway independent of consumer technologies in a standalone system, either behind or in front of the firewall, depending on whether you want to enable users to consume the Fiori apps only internally or also externally.

Typically, Fiori implementation is rapid, using RDS methodology, as shown in Figure 19-6.

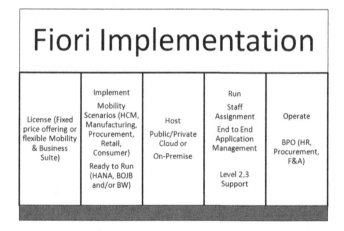

Figure 19-6. *SAP Fiori mobility implementation methodology*

The SAP Fiori client is a mobile application runtime for Fiori; it is designed around the Apache Cordova architecture, where device APIs and custom functionality are added through Cordova plug-ins. You can download it from the public app stores for iOS, Android, and Windows devices. The SAP Fiori Client overcomes limitations in the mobile browser by providing a reliable asset-caching mechanism for Fiori application assets; it also provides device APIs (such as camera, barcode scanner, and geolocation) to Fiori apps.

Prepackaged SAP Fiori Apps

The packager is a Node.js application delivered with the SAP Mobile Platform Hybrid SDK. It enables you to package existing Fiori apps as hybrid apps hosted in a native container for iOS or Android. The packaged apps are presented as tiles in a local launchpad. The packager uses the SAP Mobile Secure cloud build service API to drive a Cordova-style build. Apps can be distributed to mobile devices and users through SAP Mobile Secure and SAP Mobile Place.

The packaged app contain JavaScript and HTML assets (plus images, message strings, and so on) as local resources that are loaded directly into the app's web view. This delivers a more robust user experience, because the only network traffic required is business data. Packaging also allows certain Fiori apps be used in offline mode. In this case, SAP Mobile Platform initializes the creation of the local offline store and provides the offline OData service that periodically synchronizes the business data between the back end and the client offline store.

Implementation Planning

From the range of Fiori apps, you can choose those that are most relevant for your business. SAP guides you through the implementation. This section provides an overview of tools you can use for planning purposes.

Discovering SAP Fiori Apps with Innovation Discovery

Innovation Discovery is a self-service tool that simplifies your search for new SAP functionality (enhancement packages, support packages, add-ons, and improvement notes). SAP thus bridges the gap between business needs and technical information regarding innovations. An *innovation* can be one or several product features. Innovation Discovery contains only SAP Business Suite innovations.

Innovation Discovery relates to other tools, if available, as follows:

- If Maintenance Planner information is available for a Fiori app, you can access it from Innovation Discovery.

- If an app is available in Innovation Discovery, you can access it from the Fiori app reference library.

You can access Innovation Discovery at https://apps.support.sap.com/innovation-discovery/ Information.

■ **Note** For more information, see the Innovation Discovery help.

Planning the System Landscape with Maintenance Planner

Maintenance Planner is a graphical tool on the SAP Support Portal to help you plan and prepare the maintenance of systems in your landscape. Using Maintenance Planner, you can do, for example, the following:

- Select and install new systems for Fiori apps

- Choose the target version for the installation

- Understand the impact of planned changes in a system landscape

- Download the consolidated stack XML and push all the required archives to the download basket

You can access Maintenance Planner at `https://apps.support.sap.com/sap/support/mpInformation`.

■ **Note** For more information, see the SAP Help Portal at `http://help.sap.com/maintenanceplannerInformation`.

The matrix in Table 19-1 shows the existing Fiori roles available in the SD application and the assigned Fiori apps. Fiori apps can be used in baseline processes and can replace an existing process step. It is important to understand that Fiori apps can replace only single process steps, and not a complete process. In other cases, Fiori apps offer functionality to enhance existing processes.

Table 19-1. *SD Applications and Assigned Fiori Apps for Field Sales Representatives*

Fiori App	Description	Mapping to Scope Items	Fiori App Type
Check Price & Availability	Price check and availability of products	107 Sales Processing 109 Sale from stock 110 Free of charge Delivery	Transaction
Create Sales Order	Create a sales order	107, 109, 114: Sales Process	Transaction
Change Sales Order	Modify or display a sales order	Change the shipping address on SO Item level.	Transaction
Track Sales Order	Check open or in-process orders and delivery schedules	Check sales order tracking status.	Transaction
My Sales Contacts	Customer information	You can use this app with baseline master data.	Transaction
My Sales Quotations	Generate quotations	112 Sales Quotation.	Transaction

Benefits Summary

- Implementing Fiori apps is agile and easy to use with benefits listed below: Updates the most broadly and frequently used common business functions, based on extensive user research

- Provides a simple, easy-to-use experience across devises

- Enables customers to use existing SAP investments

IMPLEMENTING SAP FIORI APPS

This case study involves configuring a Fiori app for a simple SD sales process.

Business Purpose

Instead of using the back-end transaction VA21 to create quotations, you can use the Fiori apps. If you want to use the My Quotations app to create a new quotation, you need to be able to copy from an existing one. Therefore, it makes sense to have a quotation in the back end for the related master data, shown in Table 19-2.

Table 19-2. *Master / Org Data with Values*

Master / Org. Data	Value
Order Type	QT
Sold-to-Party	100000
Sales Organization	1000
Distribution Channel	10
Division	10
Material	H1

Procedure

Follow these steps:

1. Launch the Fiori system via the appropriate URL, and log on with your user ID and password.

2. On the home page of the application, choose My Quotations. A list of quotations is displayed.

3. Choose Sort By to sort the quotations by Expiring Date, Net Value, Status, or Creation Date, and by Ascending or Descending order.

4. Choose Filter By to filter quotations by Expiry Date: Expired; Not Expired; or Expires in the Next [selected] Days (select a number of days by scrolling). You can also filter quotations by Status: Open; Being Processed; or Completed.

5. Choose a quotation from the list, or use the Search field to find and choose a specific quotation (search by customer name or quotation number). The header and item data for the chosen quotation are displayed.

6. To save this quotation as a tile on the home page of the application, choose Save as Tile (in the lower-right corner).

7. To maintain notes, choose Notes. You can add a new one by writing in the appropriate box.

8. To attach documents, choose Attachments. A list of quotation attachments is displayed, and you can open them or add new ones by clicking the plus button.

9. To add data to or change data from the selected quotation, choose Edit. A screen appears with header and item data. You can edit the header information as shown in Table 19-3.

Table 19-3. *Mandatory Fields*

Field name	Mandatory
Street/House No	Yes
Postal Code/City	Yes
Country	Yes
Customer Reference	Yes
Valid from/to	Yes
Delivery date	
Discount	

Regarding item data, you can add or delete items in the quotation; and for each item, you can edit the following information: Quantity, Requested Delivery Date, and Discount. To create a new quotation, you have two options: create an entirely new one or create a new one by copying an existing one.

To create an entirely new quotation, follow these steps:

1. Choose the + sign. A pop-up appears with a list of customers.

2. Choose a customer, and click OK. A screen listing all the available materials for the customer is displayed.

3. To add materials to your quotation, choose them. Then fill in the Quantity field and choose Add to Cart. You can repeat this action as many times as you need until all the desired materials are added to the quotation.

4. Choose the shopping cart symbol (upper-right corner). A Review and Create Quotation screen is displayed, where you can edit all the header and item fields.

5. Click Save. The quotation is created.

To create a new quotation by copying from an existing one, follow these steps:

1. Choose from the list of available quotations the one that should serve as a model, and then click Copy. The Review and Create Quotation screen is displayed.

2. Edit all the header and item fields.

3. Choose Save. The new quotation is created.

Configuration for Baseline Scope Items

Assign the necessary back-end role for the My Quotations app in the ERP system to the user used for the launchpad logon (see Table 19-4).

Table 19-4. *Back-end role for the My Quotations app*

Fiori App Name	Field Name	Entry Value
Quotations	System Alias	<system alias of ERP>
	External service name	Load_my_quotation_srv

Refer to Table 19-5 for the service name for Quotation Field app.

Table 19-5. *Service name for Quotation Field app*

Field App Name	Service Path	Service Name
Quotations	SAP ➤ OPU ➤ OData SAP-bc-ui5-sap	Load_my_quotation_srv SD_myquotes

■ **Note** See SAP Note # 854390. The quotation needs an assignment to a sales representative in the quotation header partner functions.

The sales representative is assigned. You can see this in transaction VA23, Display Quotation in the back end. All quotations for which this assignment has been made appear in the My Quotations app. Customers for the quotation-creation process can only be selected if the sales employee is assigned as a partner in the related customer record.

■ **Note** See the following link for more information: `Help.sap.com/fiori`.

Concluding Remarks

SAP Fiori applications can help your organization step into the enterprise mobility space. The case study in this chapter demonstrates the implementation techniques and use of Fiori apps. It is essential to configure mobile apps correctly and avoid a failed configuration. SAP provides mobility apps ready for deployment for each of the functional areas, such as the logistics, finance, and analytics. Carefully assess and test the usage of the apps you want to deploy; then you can venture into deploying enterprise apps for all areas of your business.

■ ■ ■

CHAPTER 20

Implementing SAP Analytics, Powered by HANA

Organizations want to ensure that up-to-date, accurate information is available in real time. As you've learned in the previous chapters, SAP has evolved from R/3 to ECC to HANA and has a vision of real-time access anytime, anywhere. SAP also has a concept of big data as an integrated platform for analytics. In this chapter, you see how you can benefit by using SAP's analytics solution.

Common pitfalls in implementing analytics are insufficient knowledge about the software used and a lack of defined goals for the solution. A decade ago, software vendors developed data warehouses containing terabytes of data and had increasing numbers of data marts to support growing business needs. But how reliable was the data, and how many businesses could harness the data to analyze it? The result was data marts and warehouses with no ROI.

Today, businesses are opening mobile Internet sales and marketing channels for order processing and customer interaction in real time, to provide value to customers. It's all about consolidating and harnessing data to increase sales, retain customers, and enhance predictability using social media. The SAP analytics solution can help your business by providing a suite of easy-to-implement, easy-to-use applications, powered by the SAP HANA database, which lets you collaborate effectively and uncover new opportunities. This chapter covers SAP analytics, the evolution of SAP Business Warehouse (BW) to HANA for analytics, BW data warehouses, and best practices for implementation.

■ **Note**   SAP HANA analytics provide a solution to harnessing data for the enterprise. They offer advanced in-memory techniques that further enhance your real-time capabilities, thus transforming data marts into a reliable analytical engine for quick access to the enterprise-wide data.

Better Analytics, Smarter Decisions

The SAP software ecosystem integrates seamlessly with your business applications as a single unit. This chapter focuses on the analytics solution powered by an advanced in-memory database technology called HANA. SAP provides a wide range of business intelligence (BI) tools to help users gather detailed information from different sources. It helps businesses perform detailed analyses and make decisions based on facts in real time with amazing speed.

Many organizations today have trouble analyzing data effectively because of the large volume of data being produced. Every day, the amount of data increases tremendously. However, the challenge is not storing data, but how to access it in real time. IT expectations have increased; organizations want to analyze data rapidly so they can make decisions as opportunities arise. They need a mechanism that can handle large volumes of data, analyze it instantly, and do reporting in real time. Let's see how SAP analytics solutions help businesses become agile.

SAP Analytics Solution

The SAP analytics solution is primarily used for the following, to provide intuitive analytical capabilities:

- *Analytics reporting*, such as online analytical processing (OLAP), which enables end users to analyze data with fast query and calculation performance. Users can easily navigate multidimensional drill paths. This capability spans a variety of data architectures (relational or multidimensional, such as NoSQL) and physical architectures (such as disk-based or in-memory, like HANA).

- *Interactive visualization*, which displays numerous aspects of data using charts and pictures instead of rows and columns. It is used for process-driven BI projects, allowing all stakeholders to understand the workflow through an intuitive visual representation.

- *Predictive modeling and data mining*, which help you make predictions based on variables such as BI reports, dashboards, and analysis using mathematical techniques.

- *Scorecards and heatmaps*, which display metrics on a dashboard, such as KPIs with a strategic objective. These scorecard metrics are linked to the related reports for further analysis.

To work with SAP analytics, you must understand the emerging big data stack shown in Figure 20-1.

Figure 20-1. *Big data stack*

It is not uncommon for today's social networking, social media, and high-data-volume companies to collect terabytes of data per hour. IT is challenged to store and analyze this data, and at the same time there is an emerging need for innovative ways to extract value from the data which in turn leads to new business models and new ways of doing things. SAP BI provides the following options for presenting analytical information:

- Reporting and dashboards let you publish mobile reports with intuitive interactive information such as dials, gauges, sliders, check boxes, and traffic lights.

- Ad hoc queries enable you to ask your own questions of the data, without relying on IT to create reports for remote analysis.

- Search-based BI, such as search indexes, analyzes both structured and unstructured data sources and maps them into a classification structure.

- More and more customers are relying on field sales with enhanced real-time reporting, using dashboard content on mobile devices such as smartphones and tablets. The irony is that mobile computing and dashboard formatting are different from desktop and laptop computing and have advanced interaction features based on the device mode, such as tapping, swiping, and so on.

SAP provides the following analytics solutions:

- Business intelligence

- Predictive analysis

- Enterprise performance management / commercial performance management (EPM/CPM)

- Governance, risk, and compliance (GRC)

- SAP Lumira data-visualization tools

- SAP BusinessObjects (BI dashboards, Explorer)

- SAP Crystal Reports

Now, let's deep dive into SAP BW.

Introduction to SAP BW

SAP Business Warehouse is an end-to-end solution for enterprise extraction, transformation, and loading (ETL) and operational reporting needs. Let's look at why you need a data warehouse and why SAP BW is the best fit.

Organizations need accurate data to understand how business is going and to make decisions that can accelerate commerce and reduce costs. Using a data warehouse system, you can organize and make the best use of your business data. Data warehouses provide the flexibility to store, stage, maintain, and manage data. Many data-warehouse systems are available, provided by different ERPs. The difference between SAP BW and other data warehouse is that SAP BW is an end-to-end reporting solution; without it, customers have to buy a separate ETL tool for data warehousing and an additional reporting tool. SAP has an ERP system called SAP Enterprise Core Component that provides an integrated system with various applications to support the business needs of customers.

Online Data Processing

OLAP refers to the ability to report sales data in real time. For example, you may need real-time sales data from all stores, reported online. The SAP ECC system is an *online transaction processing (OLTP)* system that runs daily business transactions. Business data is classified as *master* or *transactional* data and is stored and maintained in an ECC system as *operative* data. Master data can be organizational, customer or business data. Transactional data consists of daily business transactions. See Figure 20-2.

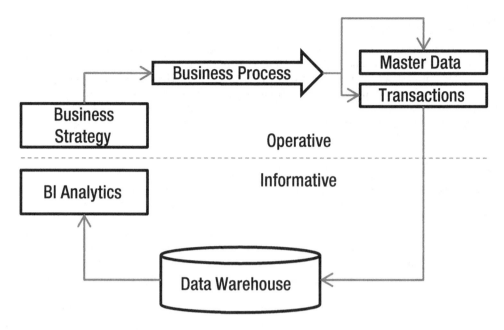

Figure 20-2. *Operative and information data store*

Standardized Solution

SAP follows best practices for an optimal BW implementation. It provides standard business content in terms of data sources, information sources, transformations, data-store objects, InfoCubes, multiproviders, roles, reports, and so on, which help organizations implement the business solution more quickly and reduce costs. SAP BW also supports extraction of data based on the custom creation of data sources as per business requirements, from the SAP ECC system and also SAP systems like CRM and APO, flat file, XML, and other third-party systems. Enterprise data can be stored in different layers in different formats after applying business logic. After the enterprise data is transformed to business data, it is available for reporting. SAP tools like SAP Business Explorer (BEx) and BusinessObjects let you build and analyze data.

Implementation Methodology

Successful projects follow a robust implementation plan. This section discusses the *accelerated systems application and products in data processing* (ASAP) methodology suggested by SAP. It is a single, pragmatic, standardized methodology that follows a sequential approach and it has been proven and developed over many years of experience. It is also cost effective, with common expectations and manageable scope. It supports best practices by using preconfigured tools and documents.

The phases of the ASAP methodology are as follows:

1. Project preparation

2. Business blueprint

3. Realization

4. Final preparation

5. Go live and support

Project Preparation

This is the first phase of the ASAP methodology. The purpose of this phase is to prepare a project platform, including an organized planning team and a high-level project plan listing objectives to be achieved. The initial planning for the project should be in terms of what to do, how to do it, when to do it, and where to do it. Key stakeholders are identified, and you decide who will communicate with them to determine the project requirement. Each team and team member is assigned a predefined role so the entire team is well-informed for discussions and meetings.

Business Blueprint

In this phase, the team puts together the as-is information collected from the business in the form of documents providing the details of the implementation project. This results in a detailed document called the *business blueprint*, which includes information gathered through interviews, meetings, and workshops and defines a detailed to-be process. Based on the communication that takes place during initial discussions, you can take feedback into consideration and make changes as needed. User profiles and user-specific roles are generated, and areas are identified where training will be provided to educate users and help them in their daily work. The business blueprint also includes process flow diagrams and diagrams depicting the business landscape.

The business blueprint document will be the primary document from this point on. It defines functional areas based on which functional specification documents will be prepared.

Realization

In this phase, the implementation is carried out as per the business blueprint. Technical specification documents are prepared based on the functional specification documents. The project team performs activities such as developing the solution as per the technical specifications, unit testing, integration testing, and preparing the solution for transport to the quality system. Security and authorization roles and profiles are created and tested for end users, superusers, and power users. Once these deliverables are tested in the quality environment, they are ready to be moved to the preproduction system for end-user acceptance testing, per the training strategy.

Final Preparation

Now deliverables are moved to the preproduction system for user acceptance testing. This is considered a rehearsal for the go-live phase. A mock cutover is performed, just as in the go-live plan, to check preparedness and identify and fix any critical open issues. Based on the feedback, changes can be applied to the final go-live plan. End users are provided with job role profiles, and training is provided for end users, superusers, and power users. Users are asked to test the system and confirm whether the deliverables are as expected. If any bugs or issues are identified, they are fixed and resubmitted for testing. Finally, there is sign-off on the deliverables.

Go Live and Support

This is the final phase of the ASAP methodology. After the successful completion of the mock cutover and user acceptance testing, the solution is deployed in the live environment and made available for real-time use. Objects are moved from preproduction to production, as per the go-live plan. The project team prepares an organizational chart and performance-management system for ongoing and continuous improvement of the system, and a help desk is set up to assist end users.

Next, let's analyze the best practices for SAP BW analytics and the recommended approach to avert disaster.

Best Practices

Now, let's see best practices help avoid pitfalls.

SAP Recommended Architecture

SAP has a recommended Layered Scalable Architecture (LSA and LSA++), which is based on the nature of the system and project requirements. Note this is not mandatory; the architecture can be customer-specific. But it is in interest the customer's interest to provide an optimum solution, to accelerate the implementation of analytics. These architectures are explained next in terms of when to use each one, and the layers are examined in detail.

Layered Scalable Architecture

SAP suggests LSA to its customers as an integrated solution. Maintaining and running a data warehouse is challenging; to ease this task, SAP provides the layered LSA architecture, which helps optimize the SAP BW implementation. LSA++ is specific for the implementation of SAP BW on the HANA database; HANA provides more flexibility and options for meeting business requirements. Operational and flexible data has been added as a special service in the LSA++ architecture (see Figure 20-3).

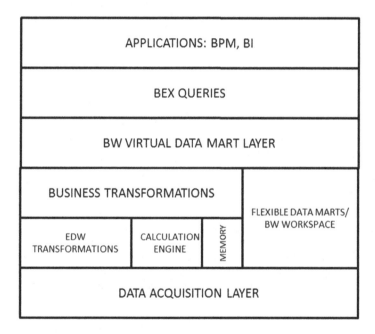

Figure 20-3. *LSA++ for SAP BW on HANA*

Open ODS Layer

The data acquisition layer is the primary layer in the LSA architecture, where the data source is integrated with the SAP BW system. This layer offers flexible options for data integration, including consuming, combining, and physically integrating data sources. Consumed data sources can be combined with SAP BW modeling objects, InfoObjects, or BW InfoProviders through composite providers. Data sources can also be generated on Open ODS views: a new modelling feature provided by SAP BW 7.4. SAP BW reporting can be done in these views without storing data in BW. These data models can be located externally in HANA schemas that are not managed by SAP BW. Using HANA Smart Data Access, the data models can be located in other databases connected to HANA.

Corporate Memory

This layer is used to stage extracted data in the SAP BW system. It is used for restructuring without having to access the source system repeatedly. It is similar to the data acquisition layer: the data is unchanged, and the difference lies in the permanent storage of historical data.

EDW Propagation Layer

Data is consolidated and stored in a granular form in this layer. The data can be further distributed and reused. This layer is important because reporting can done on data store objects (DSOs). With SAP BW 7.4, DSOs and InfoCubes are HANA-optimized by default. This provides several advantages: faster activation and loading times, easier data modelling, and data that is available in detail.

Architectured Data Marts

This layer consists of InfoCubes or DSOs. Depending on the scenario, any InfoProvider can be used. With LSA++, the data-propagation layer has HANA-optimized InfoCubes and HANA-optimized DSOs.

HANA-optimized InfoCubes have the following advantages:

- Dimension IDs (DIMIDs) are not required, so data loading is faster.

- Data modeling is simpler because there is no multidimensional modeling required, which can affect performance. Aggregates and DB indexes are also not required.

- The data model can be changed more quickly because it does not contain any data. Reporting can be done on the propagation layer on top of DSOs; the architecture data mart and its InfoCube are rarely used for reporting. There are, however, a few instances in which reporting on InfoCubes is helpful: when the InfoCube has a subset of data from the DSO, when the InfoCube has data that is only available in the DSO, and when no additional data checks (referential integrity) happen upon loading into the InfoCube.

Virtual Data Mart Layer

This layer is where reports are built for the analysis of business data. InfoProviders in this layer have only report-specific data elements. SAP provides various InfoProviders that can be used for reporting. They combine data using joins and contain data such as multiproviders and composite providers. Data can also be read from the HANA database for querying through a composite provider and the Open ODS view. This layer includes all persistence layers and is flexible. SAP BEx tools and SAP BusinessObjects tools can be used for reporting.

Roadmap of SAP Analytics on HANA

The roadmap of the SAP analytics solution is powered by HANA, with the HANA business suite as the topmost layer (see Figure 20-4). It is transformed into a robust platform for SAP big data with a Hadoop extension.

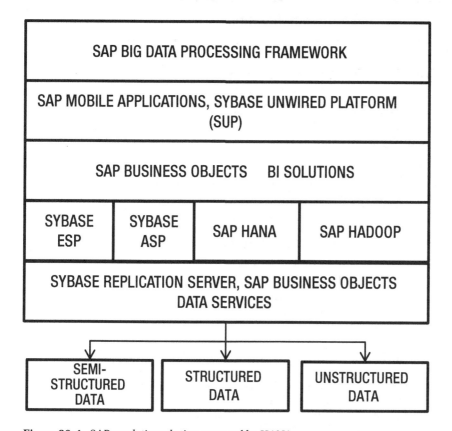

Figure 20-4. *SAP analytics solution powered by HANA*

SAP provides the HANA sidecar scenario to accelerate existing business transactions: this scenario serves as a first step to deal with critical business requirements for analytics. It supports real-time operational analytics of current business data. The SYBASE unwired platform (SUP) provides a platform for mobile interface. The advantage of this scenario is that it gives faster insight into business transactions with modeling flexibility, as shown in in Figure 20-5.

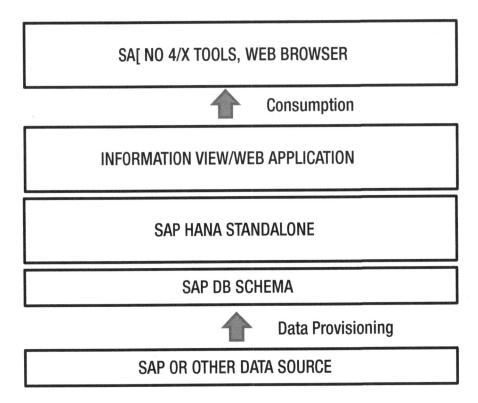

Figure 20-5. *SAP DB Schema for Analytics*

As you can see, there is no application server. HANA as a modeling platform can be combined with HANA as a programming platform. In this scenario, data from the SAP system or any other source systems with traditional databases can be moved to HANA using the data provisioning provided by either HANA or traditional ETL tools; it depends in whether data is moved to HANA raw or transformed using ETL tools. Once data replication is done, development can be performed in terms of data/information models or applications with greater flexibility. Special HANA features like in-memory storage, multicore parallel processing, and column-wise storage can be used to handle and access data with amazing speed. At this stage, data is ready to be consumed for analysis using SAP BusinessObjects or any client web browser.

Agile Data Mart for Analytics

HANA provides an environment in which rapid prototyping of data models is possible. The agile data mart is based on analytic data models. In this type of data mart, data is not in its original state: data is transformed before loading into the HANA database. Business needs determine the level of detail. Traditional ETL tools are used to load data into HANA. The SAP context extractors use Direct Extractor Connection (DXC), as shown in Figure 20-6.

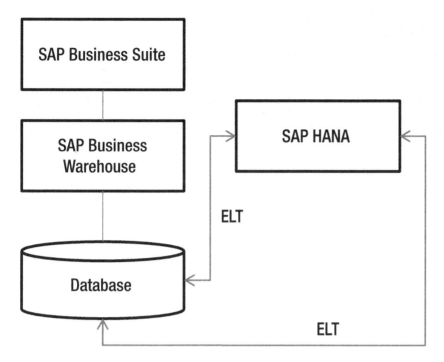

Figure 20-6. *Agile Data Mart*

Implementation Guidelines

Here are some implementation guidelines:

1. Load the tables into HANA. Transform the data first, using standard ETL tools.

2. Create a HANA-specific data model in the attributes view for the master data.

3. Create a HANA-specific data model in the analytic view to combine the master data with the fact-table data.

The data is now ready to be consumed for analytics using SAP BO or any other reporting tool.

Operational Data Mart for Analytics

HANA is best suited for operational data marts. Operational data is detailed in nature and not based on analytical models. Operational data marts report directly on operational data. Data remains at the required detail level while loading to HANA; there is no data transformation while loading. Real-time replication of data is possible with SAP Landscape Transformation (SLT). HANA-specific information models calculate data for queries in real time, so you can do real-time reporting.

The next section explores in-memory computing, which is a core feature of HANA for large-volume data processing at high speed and which is revolutionizing the industry.

In-Memory Computing

HANA uses in-memory technology to manage and handle huge volumes of SAP ERP data, analyze the data with greater speed, and provide access to real-time data for analysis. The HANA database's advanced in-memory techniques run queries 3,600 times faster in terms of analytics applications with real-time access to the transaction data. This technology is a combination of software and hardware that integrates a number of SAP components, including the HANA database, SLT, DXC, and BW. HANA supports both row-wise and column-wise storage and combines them. Table 20-1 outlines HANA's high processing capabilities.

Table 20-1. HANA DB performance

HW Technology Innovations	SAP SW Technology Innovations
Multicore architecture	Row and column store
Massive parallel scaling	Compression
64-bit address space: 1TB in current servers	Partitioning
	No aggregate tables
	Insert only on delta

With in-memory technology, all operations are performed in memory. The highlight of HANA is that the entire read/write operation is performed in memory, which indicates the merger of OLAP and OLTP into one database—meaning you no longer need data marts or warehouses. HANA can help you process transaction data as well as read data as an analytical engine. It performs multiple tasks as a multipurpose engine, ready for transactions and reporting. When all operations are performed in memory, it is easy to optimize the database engine. If you want a multipurpose engine, it should be able to crank out data at high speed. Hence, the hardware capacity should comply with core minimal specifications for best performance. This is the HANA appliance, as recommended by SAP.

Parallel Processing

HANA benefits from multicore processing. The HANA architecture has multicore CPUs, multi-CPU boards, and multi-server boards with massive memory set up for parallel processing:

> Multicore CPUs: 10 cores/CPU
>
> Multi-CPU boards: 8 CPUs/board
>
> Multi-server boards: 4 boards
>
> Memory setup: 2TB/server

Queries are split and spread across multiple CPUs and multiple server instances. You have the option to add CPUs as needed to make any operation run in real time. Data is spread across multiple blades, which allow work to be done on a smaller set of data. The column-wise table store makes the data highly compressed. You can thus run large queries on a huge volume of data in real time, much more quickly than is possible with traditional databases.

HANA has components such as a row store, a SQL parser, and advanced data-fetch options, and the column store has code derived from the SAP BWA TREX engine. Developers can use tables either row-wise or column-wise and can change from one to the other as needed. Table 20-2 highlights the importance of column-wise compression; the following sections explain the differences between row-wise and column-wise storage techniques.

Table 20-2. *HANA DB Column-Wise Compression Techniques*

Custom	Country	Product	Amount
100	DE	1	100
100	DE	1	110
200	US	1	120
300	US	2	130

Row-Wise Storage

In general, row-wise storage is used in traditional database systems. The difference between HANA and a traditional database is that all the records are stored in-memory rather than on a hard drive. The advantage of row-wise storage is that data is easier to insert and update. Table data is stored in a sequence of records, each of which contains the fields of one row. When reporting is required on all of a table's fields, then row-wise storage is suggested. If not, restructuring an entire row is expensive for column-wise store operations; often, a secondary index must be created to search the rows' record numbers.

Criteria for using row-wise table storage are as follows:

- When a table has few records (such as metadata tables)
- When all the fields in a table are required for reporting
- When there are more unique data records in the source database
- When there is no scope for search or aggregation of records

Column-Wise Storage

As mentioned earlier, column-wise storage is derived from the SAP BWA TREX engine. This is a salient feature of the HANA in-memory database. In this type of table storage, data records are stored in columns and are highly compressed. Data types are stored together, and same length columns makes compression much better. Partitioning is also supported in this type of table storage. Only a few columns are searched. Because records are stored in columns, every column is an index, so there is no need to create a secondary index.

Here are a few suggestions for when to use column-wise table storage:

- When a table has a large number of columns
- When a table has a large number of rows, but only a few columns are required for reporting
- When read access is required
- When there are not many unique keys

HANA Data Provisioning

This section analyzes HANA data provisioning, which refers to the data-replication techniques in HANA:

- SAP Landscape Transformation for real-time data replication
- SAP Data Services to extract data from SAP or non-SAP systems
- DXC to extract data from the SAP business suite of systems and Flat File to extract flat-file data

Figure 20-7 shows an operational data mart. This data model reflects the level of data detail in the application. There is real-time replication of real-time data (SLT) and real-time reporting on operational data.

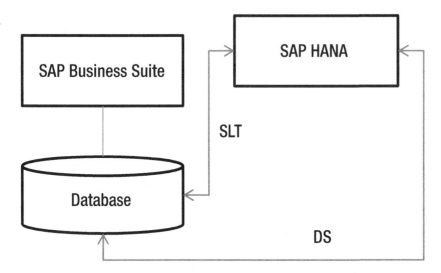

Figure 20-7. *Operational data marts*

Follow this procedure to implement an operational data mart:

1. Load the tables into HANA. The data is unchanged before loading. Use HANA data-provisioning methods.

2. Create a HANA-specific data model in the attributes view for the master data.

3. Create a HANA-specific data model in the analytic view to combine the master data with the fact-table data.

The data is now ready to be consumed for analytics using SAP BO or any other reporting tool.

SAP Business Suite on HANA

The SAP business suite is a set of integrated applications such as Sales, Manufacturing, Finance, and so on. It gives organizations an end-to-end enterprise solution. Even the SAP BW data-warehousing solution is part of the application suite. The business suite follows best practices for industry-specific solutions.

In the past, customers suffered from slow OLTP systems and batch processes. With traditional databases, issues were analyzed a day or more after their occurrence, with old data. There was always a demand for a technology platform that combined layers, reduced the time difference, and supported analysis and reporting in real time. HANA combines OLTP and OLAP and allows real-time interaction with the system: real-time planning, execution, reporting, and analysis of operational data. As mentioned earlier, HANA uses the power of in-memory technology, parallel processing, and column-wise store to store massive amounts of information and perform complex analyses with amazing speed. There is not scope for data duplication, because transactions and analytics are on the same platform, as shown in Figure 20-8.

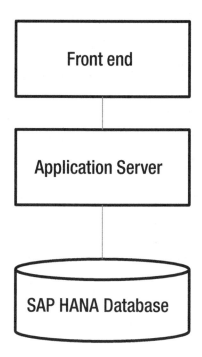

Figure 20-8. *HANA as the primary database*

The three-tier architecture combines the database layer, application layer, and presentation layer. The database layer consists of your ERP system and SAP BW system powered by HANA. No change is needed for the application server; the existing functionality still works. (Changes can be made if needed, but they aren't required.) All the data-intensive logic is pushed down to the HANA database to use its special features and accelerate the process. Data can be consumed using SAP BO or other reporting tools.

SAP BW is rich in OLAP functionality. When by powered by HANA, you will see amazing results:

- All major data-intensive logic and data-warehousing tasks are taken care by HANA.

- BW's object-based modeling approach and HANA's SQL-oriented approach reduce complexity and combine the strengths of these technologies.

- Data loading and reporting happen at amazing speed.

- Query performance is excellent, resulting in faster analytics.

- You can plan more quickly using HANA's in-memory capabilities.

- Layers of data persistency are reduced.

- With SAP BW 7.4, HANA-optimized InfoCubes and DSOs are available. Data activation happens in HANA.

- BW InfoProviders can be integrated with HANA views using the new composite provider.

- External data sources can be used for reporting and analytics without persistence, using BW Open ODS views.

- You can integrate big data scenarios like HADOOP using smart data access and BW.

- BW can use procedures written in HANA's ABAP Managed Database Procedures (AMDP).

- You can perform predictive analytics on BW using the HANA analysis process in SAP BW 7.4, as shown in Figure 20-9.

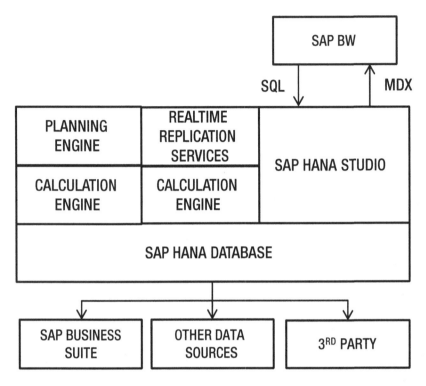

Figure 20-9. *SAP BW powered by HANA*

IMPLEMENTING SAP REAL-TIME ANALYTICS

Case Study 1

This case study illustrates the power of analytics for your business. A large oil and gas enterprises implemented an SAP ECC system to manage its enterprise operations, such as sales, finance, and plant Maintenance, with a back-end database for ECC. A critical aspect of the core operation was financial reporting, which was used for financial planning every year.

Primarily, this financial report was used for analyzing accounts receivable; it was developed in SAP ECC using ABAP programming. It gave information about customers who had not paid by their due date, as well as details such as profit center, region, and customer time aging (1 to 15 days overdue, 16 to 30 days overdue, and so on). Key business users ran the report to analyze the amount due for a specific region and profit center. The report ran for 45 minutes to an hour, depending on the selection criteria. Although real-time reporting was possible, the time constraint was a big problem. Imagine the frustration for a key end user who had to wait after requesting information.

The key pain points were as follows:

- Lack of quick, real-time output

- Overall performance implications to the core ERP system

- Limitations in the legacy database architecture, leading to performance issues

To overcome the time constraints, we decided to use the SAP BW data-warehousing tool. It is supported with the standard data extractors from the core SAP ERP (ECC) system. These extractors have business logic applied and help with fetching data from base table of the ECC system. Extracted data is loaded into BW system, further refined, and made available for consumption. The SAP BEx report was developed along lines similar to the accounts receivable report.

Here are the advantages of this approach:

- The report displays output in less than a minute.

- The report fetches data from InfoProviders in the BW system rather than ECC base tables.

- There is no impact on the source ECC system performance.

Case Study 2

This case study involves a leading energy enterprise that specializes in transmission and distribution of electricity and natural across a region that covers a vast area of dense forest. This organization needed an analytical solution to help the business run more smoothly and increase its business competence by monitoring electrical distribution using real-time analytics and analyzing data when required (both real-time and historic) to prevent accidents due to faulty transmissions.

The challenge was to safely transmit and distribute electricity without affecting other natural resources. The forest is prone to fires, and there have been painful experiences in the past. Such incidents are a huge loss to the ecosystem; and if an organization's infrastructure causes a fire, the company is subject to a huge penalty. The objective was to keep a close watch on company infrastructure—transformers, poles, conductors, and so on—and maintain a zero defect count. Faulty products needed to be identified, replaced, and monitored. The company was using a third-party analytics system that didn't help much; the key issue of real-time analytics was keeping the business at risk.

The pain points were as follows:

- Real-time analytics were needed to maintain a zero count of defective equipment.

- The company needed faster access to accurate data.

- Immediate corrective or preventive measures needed to be applied, based on reports.

Although the organization had implemented SAP ECC as the core ERP, there was no data-warehouse solution to analyze real-time analytics. Hence, we implemented SAP BW powered by HANA as an analytical solution. A BEx analytical report called a fire-mitigation count was created to identify equipment status and check details of defective equipment for timely maintenance and prevention of fires. The incident report highlighted faulty equipment with respect to functional location based on transmission and distribution categories.

The advantages of this solution were as follows:

- Real-time analytics to avoid incidents

- Faster access to accurate data for maintenance and analytics

- Ability to generate reports based on current and historic data

Concluding Remarks

SAP analytics is a core solution in today's growing enterprise in terms of real-time data availability, thanks to the invention of the back-end HANA database. This chapter has examined SAP analytics solutions (BI/BO) on HANA, including case studies, a roadmap, and implementation techniques. You now know the best practices to help your projects succeed.

■ ■ ■

CHAPTER 21

SAP Estimation Best Practices

One of the common pitfalls is a lack of robust estimation techniques. Underestimating the project in terms of required hardware, software, and efforts for design, development, testing, and Go Live support can lead to implementation failures. If you're unable to size the complexity of the project at an early stage by using adequate due diligence and a solution-oriented approach, you'll face a lot of challenges in the project implementation. I recommend a proof-of-concept study in niche areas of implementation to demonstrate critical business process implementation, prior to the actual realization. This will help you uncover the majority of unknown risks to mitigate. It is essential to size complexities based on critical business processes to develop or enhance, and then customize and test with required cycles, based on your past experience.

This chapter covers SAP estimation best practices for custom development, FRICE object types, and analysis of hardware requirements to ensure that you'll be able to accurately estimate project efforts. The chapter also provides an overview of SAP Quick Sizer. A good estimate can be the difference between making money and losing money!

■ **Note**   Project estimation is a science based on the organization's experience and industry benchmark standards. It will help you achieve the organization's and client's goals of delivering projects on time, on budget, and on target.

Project Estimation Overview

SAP project estimation forms an integral part of your proposal. This estimation is an application of scientific methods, combined with past experiences of a similar project or line of business (LOB). Let's look at an overview of the estimation process. The objective is to create a reliable estimate by following ground rules, and to develop a high-quality estimate for a successful implementation. Why do you need to do sizing? It is a crucial step that provides the following:

- Top-down estimation (single application size is required)

- Bottom-up estimate (task-level sizing is useful)

- Productivity measurement

- Baseline estimates

- Benchmarking estimates by comparison with industry standards

- Tracking progress of the project

- Measuring progress vs. milestone targets (earned value!)

Figure 21-1 shows an estimation workflow.

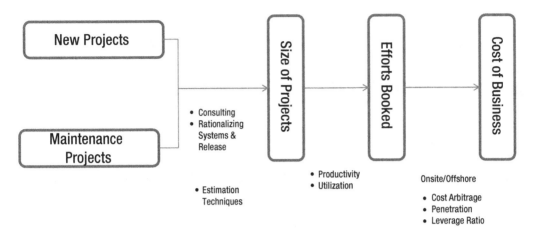

Figure 21-1. *Estimation workflow*

As you can see, the estimation is triggered by a new or a maintenance project requirement. Once a request is received, the team analyzes scope and risks, and estimates the size of the project. During the realization of the project, the project manager monitors the effort's burn ratio to identify the gross profit margin, leading to the overall cost of the project. The PM has levers to increase or reduce the on-site: offshore ratio as per the project requirements and risks.

In a functional specification, estimations are done throughout various stages of the project life cycle, as illustrated in Figure 21-2.

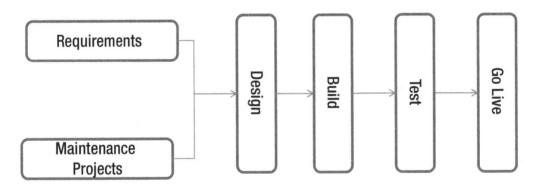

Figure 21-2. *Estimation phases*

The scope of the project is determined during the initial requirements stage. During the design phase, each of the assumptions is validated and the scope is finalized. Each phase might induce additional changes, which should be handled without altering the overall schedule. In a typical SAP implementation, you can leverage SAP best practices (RDS) with a baseline estimate of configuration, and an anticipation of changes up to 20%. If you're following Agile methodology, you must be cognizant of the acceptable scope changes in every release cycle. Once you plan the baseline and final estimates by the end of blueprint phase, you should be able to follow through the phases with the standard estimates. Figure 21-2 illustrates requirements gathering to Design, Build, Test and Go Live phases.

The estimation levers are managed during every stage of the project. For example, the testing requirements will be higher during the functional unit and integration test phases, while the development and/or functional configuration tasks will be minimal. The project manager has the levers to manage efforts during the respective phases. It is good to estimate for each phase, and to break down the estimates to the activity level to ensure that you have the required resources for each phase.

Table 21-1 lists various types of estimation techniques. SAP has evolved into a FRICE component-based estimation technique. It is good to understand other estimation techniques used in the industry, as you've focused mostly on custom development, specific to the customer business process.

Table 21-1. *Estimation Techniques Pros and Cons*

Estimation Technique	Description	Pro	Con
Function point count	Based on FP count	Industry standard.	Expensive
. Use- case point count	Based on number of use cases	Industry standard	Cannot benchmark
Component (FRICE) model	Based on FRICE objects	Accurate for ERP implementations	N/A
Source code	Based on the source code	N/A	Legacy, not suitable for ERP

A SAP implementation follows a simple component model (FRICE) for custom development.

Now, let's look at the key tenets of estimating SAP implementation projects.

Key Steps

Before you estimate the project work, you must be aware of these key steps:

- Determine whether you have enough information to create an estimate (scope, budget, schedule, key risks, and so forth).

- Identify the right estimation team with solid SAP implementation expertise.

- Use a solid work breakdown structure (WBS).

- Handle assumptions and prerequisites carefully.

- Consider the best practices and use of accelerators.

- Combine the WBS with a high-level timeline and resource plan.

- Challenge the result and refer to past estimates, realization projects, and benchmark standards.

Next, here's what you'll do:

1. Get a list of key drivers for the estimate, such as a checklist, accelerators, best practices, additional inspection services from SAP, for example. Make Go Live functional checks, new product integration checks, SME checks.

2. Take the opportunity to request additional information from the customer, in the form of a questionnaire or workshop.

3. Gain understanding of the customer's budget

4. Collect known requirements in a structured way. Managing a project's requirements already starts during the proposal creation. Use your demo systems to build a prototype if possible, prior to finalizing the estimates.

5. Understand SAP best practices, based on the customer requirements.

6. In case of newer product implementations, rely on inputs from the product owners such as SAP HANA to ensure accuracy.

First you should focus on the problem statement, and then the solution. Using SAP best practices (such as RDS or Agile best practices), you'll be able to assess more accurately. As discussed, common pitfalls such as incorrect estimates can jeopardize your project, in terms of scope, schedule, budget, and skill. You should spend a lot of time identifying the solution and then estimate the project work, using the FRICE component model for custom developments and configuration tasks. A detailed WBS will help you identify risks, to build contingency. Finally, an unhappy customer is a lost customer, so you should be diligent during the initial phases to relieve stress from the realization team implementing the project. By performing estimates right at the beginning, leveraging best practices, obtaining the right SME talent, and gaining overall support from the product team (SAP) with additional services budged, you can avert a disaster.

In my opinion, critical pitfalls are due to lack of understanding the software, and lack of due diligence to understand customer requirements and integration issues. If a careful mitigation plan is developed, these failures can be averted. If the product is in a niche, seek additional SME support internally, or additional support from SAP safeguard services. The initial feasibility study can uncover product issues or specific customization-related issues. Also, ensure you get adequate response to the OSS message raised to SAP, through the channel partner support from SAP.

Best Practices

Use the standard SAP WBS as a starting point or at least a checklist. You must distinguish the roles and phases when you make the estimate. Other examples and structures are available at the SAP Marketplace (Solution Center).

Let's think about the deliverables that an activity will create. A bottom-up estimate is a good way to assess the scope of work accurately, with exact estimates at the task level. However, a change in the solution might impact the estimates. A good estimate should encompass a FRICE component model approach, for correct understanding of the customer requirements and integration requirements. If it is a newer product implementation, it is good to test run using a prototype or RDS configured in the demo system to asses exact custom development requirements.

As you might have experienced, scope is not always given; it will be defined along the way. As discussed in previous chapters, Agile can be a good option to mitigate risks by leveraging SAP (RDS) best practices with regular sprint releases. This means that customers can have a look at every cycle, rather than waiting for the UAT phase as one big-bang approach. This will help you prioritize customer backlogs, a.k.a. requirements, in every sprint release cycle (Agile). Alongside tools such as Solution Manager, Accelerator will help you mitigate risks by monitoring at the task level with a baseline. If there is any variance in terms of schedule or efforts, you can re-prioritize and re-estimate as required, based on the critical path. As a good practice, validate assumptions and prerequisites during the blueprint phase of the project. Ensure that risks are monitored, controlled, and mitigated as you progress.

You must gain consensus with the SAP Custom Development (CD) team prior to implementing complex changes to the standard software; this customer objects specialist team can understand the product pitfalls and suggest enhancements. Of course, this exercise would be an additional service from SAP. Any cloning (copying from the standard code standards) can malign the integrity of the system. It is a good practice to gain consensus prior to the R&D approach by copying the standards and/or implementing changes to the standard SAP software. In one of my projects, the standard software was changed to implement custom requirements, which lead to lot of integration issues. As a project manager, and/or a consultant, it is your responsibility to explain the impact due to the changes to the standard code, in case of a core modification to implement customer-specific changes. Perhaps using exits or enhancement points provided by SAP is a better way to implement changes, instead of modifying the standard code, which could result in heavy maintenance of custom code as you progress. Assuming a successful implementation, maintenance would be a tedious task for the support team, with too many changes to the standard software. As a rule of thumb, if the changes require modifying SAP by over 15% and/or 30% customization requirements, then you need to reassess scope and consult with SAP CD team. You cannot implement a product that cannot be supported. Furthermore, SAP's upgrade will modify its database, causing issues if you modify standard code. This would result in losing your critical changes; hence it becomes part of your overhead to manage modified SAP code, as SAP will overwrite your modifications.

If you're planning a SAP software upgrade or platform migration to the cloud, you should be aware of the tasks and assess past project experience to mitigate substantial risks. For example, most of your development efforts in a software upgrade will be remediation, which is code correction for release compatibility. You should assess the impact using the benchmark standards or a tool to check the custom code impacted in a release or EHP upgrade. However, platform migration could be challenging in terms of interfaces with testing requirements.

Estimation Considering Accelerators

The experience of the implementation team, benchmark standards, and accelerators can help you estimate a project accurately. The following factors are essential in project estimation:

- Consider the template solutions; reuse and capitalize on previous experiences.

- Maturity levels of the delivery approach and level of industrialization of the approach and level of required compliance to standards and tools of the customer (learning time).

- Use of tools, methods, and accelerators, with collective expert knowledge and experience to create estimates you can deliver.

Standard estimation tools should be able to do the following:

- Provide easy-to-use interface, with simple inputs, and output derived from standard metrics

- Cater to offline and local usage

- Create a comprehensive user guide document

- Creating operational flexibility— facility to override the defaults

- Deliver reporting flexibility— various views of the final estimates

- Facilitate the capturing of assumptions/background/risks

Table 21-2 illustrates the effort distribution by domain for an implementation project.

Table 21-2. *Effort Distribution by Domain for an Implementation Project*

Domain	% Distribution
Project manager	10–20%
Technical	15–20%
Development	50–60%
Testing (SIT)	15–30%
Training	10–15%
Documentation	5–10%

The overall project distribution differs depending on the type of project. If you're implementing a project, you'll have additional support requirements of installation, commission of the instances, and maintenance, from a technical support perspective. Therefore, the distribution will be slightly higher than in a typical maintenance project. The same analogy is true with an upgrade project from a development perspective, since the FRICE object development would be substantially lower for an SAP upgrade project, when compared to an implementation project. You should be aware that the distribution depends on the type of project. The training efforts are almost nil for any upgrade project, for example.

Table 21-3 illustrates effort distribution for testing.

Table 21-3. *Effort Distribution for Testing*

Domain	% Distribution
Design	10–20%
Execute	40–50%
Corrections	10–20%
Project management	5–10%

You should be able to distribute efforts within development and testing, to monitor tasks closely. Table 21-4 compares different types of projects in terms of overall effort distribution.

Table 21-4. *Effort Distribution for Various Types of Projects*

Domain	Implementation	Upgrade	Rollout
Project manager	10%	5%	15%
Technical	15%	50%	15%
Development	20%	10%	15%
Testing (SIT)	30%	15%	30%
Training	20%	13%	20%
Documentation	5%	2%	5%

This variation is predominantly due to the effort required in respective phases. An upgrade, typically focuses on code correction, so no substantial effort is required for development, and testing can be based on the impact caused by the software upgrade. In an implementation project, development and functional configuration tasks rank very high, whereas the effort of Basis is primarily commission instances, instead of an upgrade. Similarly, a rollout has additional overhead for a project manager to discuss various regional and core teams. Development efforts could vary, depending on the deviations from the standard template; however, it will be lower than a typical implementation project.

You must build contingencies for unforeseen risks such as the following:

- Scope changes (additional diligence required for Agile practices, as scope changes are part of the methodology)

- Lack of highly experienced and skilled resources in niche areas

- Lack of sufficient development models and management models

- Time lost due to lack of stable environments for development/testing, integration

- Optimistic estimates based on your organization's ability to complete realization

SAP FRICE Estimation

Now, let's look at how to estimate a FRICE component in SAP for custom developments. This is critical for the success of the project. To identify a set of guidelines this section explains complexity points estimate and work breakdown estimate to reduce the subjective nature of the decision and scientifically increase the probability of predicting the effort required for a project.

The SAP implementation project's efforts should be estimated during the project preparation and business blueprint phases. The project preparation phase estimate is expected to be +/- 40% accurate, whereas the business blueprint phase estimate is expected to be +/- 10% accurate. Effort must be estimated using the two techniques. If you have a variance of more than 20% between the estimates, you should re-estimate to find out whether there are any wrong assumptions. After comparing the two estimate values, derive the finalized estimate. Any assumptions used for the estimations should be entered under the Assumptions column.

Let's look at the benchmark to break down the total estimated effort for each management phase of a project. Table 21-5 provides a rough indication of the efforts, and the distribution of the respective phases.

Table 21-5. *Effort Distribution of Respective Phases*

Project Phases	Efforts Distribution (%)
Project Preparation	5%
Business Blueprint	20%
Realization	60%
Final Preparation	5%
Go Live & Support	10%

After understanding the scope of the project, identify the number of objects/components to be developed. Categorize them based on type of object, as discussed in the FRICE components. In order to determine the effort required for development of an object, determine complexity using data/logic parameters.

Then use the complexity points for respective object type to assess exact development hours. Most likely, your organization will have developed standard estimates with benchmark comparisons for sizing a project. You can carefully play around with various parameters to calculate the most realistic development estimates. The products of complexity points and effort required for developing a Very High complex object will need to be determined based on discussions with your development team, by carefully studying customer requirements. If you're assuming a certain complexity, it is a good practice to state that to the customer, for transparency in all early pursuits. If you're working from a fixed bid, it is essential to write the basis of your complexity for the objects.

Now, let's see how to estimate based on the component model FRICE object types for an SAP implementation project work of reference. Table 21-6 Illustrates a FRICE component-based effort estimation).

Table 21-6. *FRICE Component-Based Effort Estimation in Man Days*

Object Type	Low (Man Days)	Medium	High	Very High
Forms	2	3	4	5
Reports	1	2	3	4
Interface	1.5	2.3	3.2	4.5
Conversion	1	1.5	2.1	3.0
Enhancements	1	2	3	4
ABAP query	1.2	2	3	4

The challenge is to quantify each of these object types as Low, Medium, High, or Very High, based on data access and logic. Well, that's not rocket science if you've done a few projects. Let's try to judge each of the objects based on a few parameters, as highlighted in Table 21-7.

Table 21-7. *Form Object Complexity Analysis Based on DATA/LOGIC*

Form Object	Low	Medium	High	Very High
Data	SAP standard (no custom DB access)	Non-SAP standard (access logical DB)	Non-SAP standard	Non-SAP standard with large variance in rows processed
Logic	No need for ABAP coding required	Creating a form from scratch in ABAP	Complex form layout with intense logic	Graphics with variable layout

Table 21-8 shows an analysis of Report object complexity, based on DATA/LOGIC.

Table 21-8. *REPORT Object Complexity Analysis Based on DATA/LOGIC*

Report Object	Low	Medium	High	Very High
Data	< 5 standard tables accessed or < 1 external file	5–9 standard tables accessed or < 3 external files accessed	> 10 standard tables accessed or > 3 external files accessed from multiple functional areas	Combination of legacy DB access and SAP
Logic	Basic single-level report	Multilevel drill-down capability with calculations	Multilevel with the use of subscreens, pop-ups with authorization checks	Complex drill-down

Typically, most consulting organizations use Optimistic and Pessimistic efforts. Here, an Optimistic value would mean the minimum number of hours in which the particular phase could be completed. The Pessimistic value is the maximum number of hours the particular phase could take. The formula to estimate the total effort based on WBS is as follows:

$$Total\ Effort = ((Optimistic\ Effort + 4 \times Most\ Likely\ Effort) + (Pessimistic\ Effort)) / 6$$

The total project effort in person hours is determined as the sum of efforts for all the phases. Let's look at categorizing Interface and Conversion object types. Table 21-9 shows the Interface types.

Table 21-9. *Interface Object Complexity Analysis Based on DATA/LOGIC*

Outbound Interface Object	Low	Medium	High	Very High
Data	Data read from < 5 tables or < 2 external files	5–9 standard tables accessed or <= 3 external files accessed	> 10 standard tables accessed or > 5 external files accessed from multiple functional areas	Combination of legacy DB access and SAP
Logic	No translation of codes	Moderate translation of codes	Heavy translation of codes	Synchronous updates (Online process)

For inbound interface objects, the complexity depends on logic for BDC with number of transactions. For example, up to two SAP transactions with no reentry logic in BDC uploaded is considered a low complex inbound interface object.

Now, let's look at the conversion object types, shown in Table 21-10.

Table 21-10. *Conversion Object Complexity Analysis Based on Data/Logic*

Conversion Object	Low	Medium	High	Very High
Data	Data is pre-extracted with < 2 files/record types	Reformatting of data is required with <= 4 files/record types	Reformatting is required with > 5 files/record types	Combination of legacy DB access and SAP
Logic	Standard SAP programs	Simple ABAP custom program (single-load program)	Moderate custom ABAP with validation	Complex ABAP with validation requirements

Now, let's look at the enhancement object types shown in Table 21-11.

Table 21-11. *Enhancement Object Complexity Analysis Based on data/logic*

Enhancements Object	Low	Medium	High	Very High
Data	< 1 standard table change	2–3 standard table changes.	<5 standard table changes	Changing the standard as nonstandard available
Logic	No need for user exit	Required user exit to capture screen data. Need for function exit updates to DB.	User exit with substitution logic	Complex exit logic

The ABAP queries can be simple or complex, based on the simple data access from the infoset or logical DB access types, which is similar to the preceding estimates. It is possible to assess the scope of work based on the data/logic parameters to determine accurate development estimates in man-day efforts. Now, let's spend some time on the hardware (HW) sizing requirements for running your SAP instance. Often your IT department will use standard sizing templates for arriving at the right HW for a SAP landscape.

Let's try to understand the basics of SAP HW sizing using the SAP Quick Sizer tool for HW evaluation, with an example. While designing your SAP landscape, one of the obvious questions is the estimated sizing requirements of your hardware, which indicate the CPU capacity, hard disc space, and memory requirements based on the load capacity and concurrent users.

SAP Quick Sizer and Design Guidelines

Now that you're familiar with sizing the project effort for SAP implementation, how about the required hardware? It is easy to size required HW by using SAP Quick Sizer. The goal of sizing is to plan hardware expenditures required to run SAP software (required CPU processing power, projected disk growth, memory, and network for WAN connections). As you know, most production systems run 20% of all transactions and account for 80% of the capacity requirements. The SAP sizing guidelines take this ratio into consideration; the Quick Sizer and its related guidelines help you transform information about your most important business processes into high-level requirements for CPU, memory, and disk.

You can use the Quick Sizer to estimate hardware requirements. This online application on the SAP Service Marketplace consists of a questionnaire and provides two sizing methods: user sizing and throughput sizing for customers and partners. If information about your planned SAP implementation is limited and you do not have more than 200 concurrent users, we suggest user-based sizing.

For example, in the course of a standard Sales & Distribution (SD) process as defined in the SAP SD standard application benchmark, the following business objects are created and thus can be sized in the Quick Sizer: customer order, delivery note, goods issue, and billing document. Each sizing element is associated with particular hardware, such as CPU, memory or disk. Table 21-12 illustrates this example of hardware sizing done using SAP Quick Sizer.

Table 21-12. *SAP Hardware Requirements for a Production System*

Production Systems	# of Instances	CPU (SAPS)	Disk Space (GB)	Memory RAM (GB)
ECC	4	4000	600	32
Solution Manager	1	2000	400	16

■ **Note**   A hardware-independent unit of measurement of CPU power for SAP applications, 100 SAPS is equivalent to 2,000 fully processed order items per hour. The redundancy at each hardware level should be considered adequate to avoid any SPOF. High Availability has been configured for ECC for PRD in the Primary Data Center SAN in Primary Usable 3TB 2200GB 2200 PRD/QAS/DEV (3 System Landscape) for ECC Backup. Each physical server is to be virtualized using virtualization software, with 1 backup in the physical server and the remaining in tape drives.

Based on these parameters, it is easy to determine hardware requirements for DEV and QAS instances, with similar disk space requirements. However, the CPU (SAPS)/RAM could be low for DEV/QAS. It is a good practice to keep QAS as close as possible to PRD to avoid any performance bottleneck, while DEV can be lower in terms of RAM / hard disc capacity, as it is intended for development and unit testing.

■ **Note**   For more details about sizing, see `http://service.sapc.om/quicksizing`.

Concluding Remarks

The key to a successful implementation is to size a project accurately. You've read through the chapter to adopt best practices of SAP estimation for custom developments using the FRICE component model. A project that's started well will end well! As you adopt the best practices to size a project in terms of hardware and software requirements, you'll be able to implement projects successfully. Project estimation is a science based on your organization's enormous expertise in the delivery of complex projects. You'll need to be innovative in finding ways to do things smartly to help customers achieve their goals. Finally, estimating your project correctly will lead to a successful implementation with minimal risks.

■ ■ ■

CHAPTER 22

A Day in the Life of an SAP Project Manager

Well, you've donned the hat of managing the most complex SAP implementation project. Now what? It is time to set the ground rules and execution strategy, and pull the team together to assess its strengths. There are a few key rules that you'll need to follow in this complex SAP landscape, as it demands technical, functional, and business process expertise and a 360-degree view of the software package.

Let's explore some of the common challenges faced by an SAP project manager during implementation projects. This chapter guides you through some of the common pitfalls to avoid—such as a lack of robust project management methodology, a lack of a communication plan, and lack of reporting—which can lead to a failed implementation. A project manager is a leader who drives people, processes, and technology to succeed in the endeavor.

■ **Note** SAP project management is the art of transforming the impossible into the possible, by helping clients succeed in their endeavors. With the tools, accelerators, and methods provided by SAP, there is no room for errors. If you follow the simple rules of the game with due diligence, right actions, and product support, your implementations will succeed. The SAP ERP package software can work well if done right, or can become maligned with too many customizations and integration issues if not following the basic principles. Success or failure depends on the project manager, who leads the team from the front.

Life of a SAP Project Manager

The SAP project manager is the key person responsible for driving a successful implementation. Undoubtedly, the PM is the captain who can successfully navigate the ship to the shore. As an SAP PM, you're responsible for managing the key processes, people, and technology, while also managing the scope, budget, and schedule.

The following ASAP methodology is a standard SAP method for implementing projects. As a PM, you'll be responsible for setting up the ground rules of using templates, delivery guidelines, and metrics to demonstrate success in every milestone achieved. Let's look at a day in the life a PM by analyzing every phase of SAP methodology and how you'd manage it diligently. Above all, the implementation expertise that you provide to the customer as a solution architect and trusted advisor is the most critical element. Often PMs are considered merely administrative leads, which is not true when managing SAP implementation projects. A PM is a trusted advisor who understands the 360-degree view of the product and takes necessary corrective actions to reach project goals that help customers achieve a successful implementation using the ASAP methodology.

Let's review how a project manager spends time in the following ASAP phases:

1. Project preparation

2. Blueprint

3. Realization

4. Final preparation

5. Go Live support

6. Operation

PMs spend most of their time in meetings, which have to be crisp and to the point with action items. Instead a PM should spend more time on solution design, evolution, and implementation planning, as execution can follow. If you're working with offshore team in a global delivery model, for example, ensure that the right metrics are in place—such as cost performance index (CPI) and schedule performance index (SPI)—to measure the quality of deliverables and timeliness, because often offshore delivery centers are a black box and not perceived by the client. The on-site project manager has the additional responsibility of ensuring that offshore work packages are shipped on time, with high quality, and measured as part of the overall project performance. This can be achieved only through process rigor, quality metrics, and KPIs defined for the overall project, including the offshore component. The handoff between on-site/offshore should be planned on a daily basis to ensure close communication between on-site/offshore teams. This is essential to evaluate risks, monitor progress, and control and mitigate steps through the project phases. On-site and offshore PMs have different responsibilities: for example, an on-site PM might be responsible for managing key stakeholders at the client site; meeting business SMEs; overseeing the project scope, schedule, and budget; and reviewing the solution design and status reports on a daily basis; whereas an offshore PM might be responsible for deliverables such as quality, overseeing meeting scope, and appraising an internal committee of the delivery organization. Today, most delivery organizations are global, so it is imperative to understand the roles of an on-site or offshore project manager, who is pivotal in driving a successful implementation project. As more and more projects are aligned to the global delivery model, it is imperative that PMs understand this model and its global delivery tasks. Let's take a look at the foundation of global delivery management, outlined in Table 22-1.

Table 22-1. *Global Delivery Management*

PM Phase	Purpose	Global Delivery Tasks
Initiating	Define objectives of the project. Evaluate costs, benefits, and approach.	Define project. Evaluate ROI and total cost of outsourcing. Engage global delivery with on-site/offshore SMEs.
Planning	Determine how projects will be delivered, and plan all aspects of the project, including detailed WBS.	Evaluate and modify knowledge acquisition and KT templates, and team and project charter. Define scope, budget, and schedule with risks baseline.
Executing	Plan the work, with assurance of high-quality deliverables.	Establish SLAs and WBS task execution, and monitor with metrics that measure the agreed-upon scope of work delivered.
Controlling	Continuously measure project performance to determine variance against the plan.	Use delivery dashboards, earned value management (EVM), and balance scorecard with toll gates.
Closing	Final handover with metrics, reports, sign-off from stakeholders, and archive project deliverables.	Sign off project, validate SLAs, confirm deliverables, and confirm customer acceptance.

What is more important is that most corporate IT departments do not operate at Capability Maturity Model (CMM) level 5. As a PM, you must ensure compliance in order for your implementation projects to succeed. On average, companies that are less mature in PM KPIs miss scheduled targets by 40%, and the cost of implementing SAP projects increases by 15–20% in less mature organizations. In a global delivery model, it is important to leverage standard tools, accelerators, and methods to consistently deliver projects successfully. The advantages of using a global delivery model include help in accessing SMEs across the globe, in offshore centers at locations such as India, China, and Buenos Aires. This model provides an opportunity to leverage the benefits of local delivery combined with global experience. One of the companies that I've worked with, Big Blue, pioneered the art of managing projects through global delivery centers located near the client or offshore-centric delivery, delivering consistently by utilizing a factory-mode approach. A global delivery manager should understand the challenges of working in different places and be sensitive to various cultures; work allocation in countries such as Japan is different from that in the United States. . In a conservative society such as in the MENA region, a lot of sensitivity is required while dealing with clients and global delivery employees; you need to be especially aware of work schedules and religious sentiments. Each of these aspects can help you succeed as a global delivery manager.

Typically, an on-site SAP project manager's calendar is filled as follows:

- Discussions with client stakeholders— 10%%

- High-level solution review and design—PMs should emphasize the solution for business-critical scenarios to prioritize to deliver a robust product – 15%.

- Detailed review discussions with the client business process SMEs—10%

- Daily status reviews, dashboards, and discussions with client stakeholders to review the plan. Brainstorming sessions with the team, evolving technical discussions such as architecture planning—10%

- Consolidating responses to the client— 5%

- Planning ahead, building rapport with SMEs, risk mitigation, project plan activities such as initiation, monitoring activities, quality management, administrative tasks, efforts burn ratio (contribution margin), budgetary issues, timelines, plans, status reporting—25%

- Spending time with the key SMEs across the organization, socializing with the key stakeholders to understand the political environment—5%

- Team building, motivating, and setting up KPIs for the team—5%

- Managing client escalations with corrective actions and socializing with the client project managers and business leads – 5%

- Managing change requests (CRs) and scope negotiations from time to time- 5%

- Handling conflicts within teams and with the client – 5%

Responsibilities of an offshore PM include the following:

- Solution design, development, and review, jointly with on-site PM

- Administrative responsibilities such as hiring new resources, training, on-boarding resources, mentoring, seat and asset allocation

- Delivering product as per defined standards

- Conducting interviews, team appraisal, performance review

- Delivery guidelines, development of code, testing, quality gate reviews

- Liaison with internal center of excellence (CoE) teams to ensure high-quality product delivery

- Use of delivery accelerators (tools, methods), metrics finalization, and standards as per customer requirements

- Collecting project metrics, monitoring success of achieving milestones

- Supporting on-site PM to monitor scope, schedule, and budget

- Delivery dashboards for reporting to the internal committee and external client stakeholders

SAP Project Manager Activities

To drive successful projects, you must modularize work packages in simple, measurable work units. A detailed WBS at the task level with measurement criteria is critical for a successful implementation. A project manager's job is to deliver the project within the various constraints that have been agreed upon. As a critical step in implementing projects, you should understand the proposed technical solution, overall implementation plan and implementation approach and discuss these with the client to gain consensus. In the preparation phase, the project manager sets up the project framework. Most important, in a global delivery (GD) model, you should network with different groups and COEs to collaborate effectively, as often the advantage of the GD model is knowledge across the board to support projects' success. Because SAP implementations are skill based, there is no time for training; hence the COEs come in handy in supporting your project implementations. Another advantage is to support projects with SMEs in niche areas of implementation, such as SAP transport management, Fiori, or HANA implementation projects. These SMEs can guide the rest of the team to succeed in the project implementation. You should liaise with SAP Active Global Support (AGS) to leverage their expertise, align with SAP's product strategy such as the cloud, HANA, or enterprise mobility and remain nimble in aligning your organizational strategy with SAP's product evolution.

The project manager considers the high-level goals for the project and what must be achieved. What are the key critical success factors? Project management tasks are intense during the initial stages, to set up the guidelines and the process. Once the framework is set up, the PM's focus is on monitoring and completion. The PM's responsibilities will increase during the final preparations and Go Live stage to ensure successful implementation of the project. A few essential competencies are required for a global delivery manager, as described in Table 22-2.

Table 22-2. *Essential Global Delivery Competencies*

Core Group	Global Competencies
Human Resources	Team building Rewards and recognition
KPIs	Define, track, measure, and improve KPIs. Collaborate with respective teams and service providers to resolve escalating issues.
Effective Decision Making	Understand the individual, team, and corporate dynamic; Determining key stakeholders to effectively resolve key issues.
Management	Ensure SLA adherence, establish processes and procedures to manage service levels.
Cognitive	Analytical thinking, collaborate with supplier to improve global delivery effectiveness.
Organizational Effectiveness	Flexibility, cultural awareness.

Now, let's look at the ASAP phases and key responsibilities of a PM.

Project Preparation

Project preparation is the initiation stage of a project. This stage includes setting required project goals, creating a team, and determining infrastructure requirements. Typically, a PM spends a lot of time in supporting administrative tasks such as interviewing the "A" team; requesting infrastructure setup, tools, and accelerators for connectivity; system access; and environment for development. Let's review key tasks accomplished during the project preparation phase:

- High-level business requirements completed

- Ensure that a high-level project plan is done with WBS breakup of tasks

- Workshop calendar—To plan your daily and weekly activities with the business SMEs, as client organizations are highly process oriented, and to publish the relevant topics to discuss with the client and ensure that you stick to the plan.

- Timely status—Agree on a standard status format, such as daily, weekly, and monthly reporting. Also ensure one-on-one discussions with the respective managers to avoid any gaps. Include all stakeholders to the plan, to keep them informed.

- Communication plan—Pay attention to on-site/offshore communication planning.

- Access requirements such as network connectivity to the offshore VPN, SAP system access, security and security soft tokens, and access to the remote desktops (RDP), as often remote connectivity takes longer. Also, onboarding formalities, space requirements, and workstations should be planned in advance to avoid delays in the deliverables.

- Assess required tools to implement for effectively managing the project, such as Microsoft Project plan, SAP Solution Manager to monitor status of the respective tasks by date.

- Finally, ensure that metrics are planned to measure the success rate of deliverables.

Blueprint

The blueprint is the most critical part of the project. Half of your problems will be solved, if you can define the solution, mapping the client's most critical business process. In my view, most teams rely on a sales pitch, rather than the real solution. Every niche area of implementation, such as enterprise mobility, must be done in a proof-of-concept (POC), to uncover most hidden risks in the project. The entire plan must be based on the POC done in a sandbox environment. This would set realistic goals that are simple, measurable, and achievable as you drive through the lanes of the realization phases. You can reevaluate the baseline estimates, schedule, and scope to set realistic goals:

- Business blueprint completed. You've understood most critical business scenarios and defined a solution in SAP. Well done.

- Ensure that business requirements are captured and validated with the respective SMEs.

- A detailed process overview discussion is required. It is essential to organize your discussions with the respective business teams such as OTC, P2P, and RTR. This will help you assess the most critical business process and pay attention to the critical processes first. Understand the client's business in order to talk in the language that they're familiar with.

- Ensure availability of the respective environments in the landscape to plan development and testing activities (for example, sandbox, development, test, production.

- Plan change management activities, such as organization change management for training and technical change management for managing changes to the production and support track in the landscape, if this is an existing landscape.

Realization

The PM must ensure that milestones are achieved with well-defined stage gates. Unless the work packages delivered for offshore are measured at regular intervals, there is no guarantee of a successful code package delivered to the customer. Hence, agile methods are gaining prominence, as you showcase the product at regular intervals to client stakeholders, without having to wait until the UAT phase. The integration points of the project are crucial for a successful delivery. The PM must spend time with integration leads to understand the complexity, with a timely assessment of risks to monitor and control.

- Ensure that the team success rate is measured and KPIs are achieved such as quality and deliverables on time.

- The development should encompass a detailed functional/technical specification, custom development (forms, reports, interfaces, conversion programs, and enhancements: FRICE) completion status with unit and integration tests completed.

- If there is an additional requirement of automated regression, considering test options such as manual functional testing and performance testing should be part of the overall test strategy.

- Design, develop, and implement test cases for the project as soon as the development activities are done.

- Record risks, and control and monitor risks,

- Implement the core business process.

- Test the implementation.

Final Preparation

The final preparations are crucial, as you're near the critical phase of the project. All your hard work implementing the solution is almost done. Now it's time to Go Live in production. In this stage, you should pay specific attention to the cutover plan, as well as the rollback plan to ensure business continuity and drive a successful Go Live in production by getting technical, functional, and business SMEs together in the war room. Let's review the tasks performed during the dry run and cut-over phases.

- During the dry run, watch out for potential errors in external interfaces. Capture every artifact of the dry run such as downtime in an upgrade or challenges faced during the new installation, in case of an implementation project. The cutover plan should have tasks captured for monitoring processes every hour to ensure a successful Go Live phase.

- Start of production cutover.

Go Live Support

Now, let's analyze the most critical phase of the project, which is the Go Live phase. As a PM, you're responsible for all the cutover activities, communication planning, and discussions with respective stakeholders. As a matter of fact, a major pitfall is lack of communication with the stakeholders, which could lead to a delayed Go Live. Ensure that all stakeholders are apprised of the situation, review the cutover plan after the dry run, and then involve SAP AGS support for a functional Go Live check to ensure that there are no anomalies prior to the Go Live. Also, as a PM, you're responsible for a transition plan to the support team with deliverables such as technical and functional operating manuals. Let's review the critical tasks performed during the go live support phase.

- Ensure that the entire team is geared up for the Go Live; the SMEs, cutover lead, and PM should fasten their seat belts to ensure a successful Go Live.

- Achieve a successful Go Live.

- Complete handover.

Operation

You must plan the transition to ensure that the support team can handle the post-implementation and hypercare support period. Once you deliver a successful Go Live, you must ensure that the required support manuals are complete and up-to-date, with a training plan for technical and functional teams to follow critical processes to ensure a smooth transition. Once you hand off, get a sign-off from the respective business SMEs and the SLAs for post Go Live support. Let's see handover tasks below:

- Ensure a handover to the support manager with all project artifacts and support during the hypercare period for a period of two to three months to ensure a successful post Go Live support without major incidents.

- Support a resolution of incidents as per SLAs, compliant with ITIL processes in service delivery.

Key PMO Startup Activities

Let's look at key project management office (PMO) activities to accomplish. A PM should spend adequate time in each of these specific areas and set up KPIs to achieve successful implementation.

- Identify key stakeholders: You'll need buy-in from all relevant stakeholders in the projects. If there is any difference in the understanding of the project scope, it should be sorted out early on, prior to the sign-off of the blueprint. The blueprint's sign-off indicates you're complying with the scope, schedule, and budget as stated in the statement of work. Hence, there could be conflict at a later stage, if your stakeholders do not agree. For example, a stakeholder responsible for integration might see activities relevant to interface testing as your responsibility, whereas you might think the interface test requirements should be completely done by the respective interface team. You should be prudent and ask questions early to sort out any differences. You should send out a standard report to ensure that all stakeholders are on the same page and aware of any ongoing issues in the project. Also, a regular monthly meeting scheduled to discuss outstanding issues is a good way of keeping the stakeholders aligned.

- Build a high-performing team: All right, you've focused enough on the customer side, requirements, scope, budget, and schedule. However, you don't yet have a high-performance team, which is going to deliver the project. You have to assess each individual on the team for technical capabilities, because SAP projects are primarily skill based. You cannot manage a low-performing team and/or have underskilled workers or trainees. As a general rule of thumb, you must ensure that you have the right people, who are highly skilled and able to deliver the project. A word of caution: I don't mean a consultant, who can answer questions. Instead, you should have individuals who are capable of understanding the business requirements and of mapping them into SAP with good technical and functional expertise, and with similar experience in the line of business (LOB) to deliver the project. You cannot afford to have a mix of high- and low-performing individuals. You must ensure that every individual is adept in responding to the business requirements and able to map to SAP. Above all, a periodic review of individuals to measure performance with metrics will help you succeed.

- Develop a robust project charter: In order to start the work, you'll need an official document signed off for legal purposes such as a statement of work (SOW). The project charter is your bible for the project. You'll define scope, technical implementation strategy, assumptions, and deliverables charted out with a resource strategy.

- Develop L1, L2 project plan: The project plan outlines the implementation, including the infrastructure plan and schedule of every activity. Typically, we use an MS Project plan to list all the tasks with an assigned priority. The plan also helps to measure a unit of work by the respective resources. You'll evolve from the baseline plan to the realization plan after your proof of concept (POC) phase, as you experience the risks and critical path. A robust project plan consists of all activities, including the critical path and task relationships charted out with resource requirements. It defines the milestones. Since the project plan provides the overall roadmap, PMs typically spend a lot of time analyzing the dependencies and the critical path with a start/end date of every activity. The plan should be reviewed on a daily basis to accommodate schedule delays and to reprioritize activities based on availability of the core SMEs from the business side. If the plan is good, realization will be as simple as following the roadmap.

- Develop the work breakdown structure (WBS)): A detailed WBS helps you identify tasks individually. How much time is required for every single task, and how many resources? What type of schedule is required to complete a unit of work? This level of detail will help you monitor the task through completion and compare the actual utilization with the planned. A burn chart indicates the utilization of resources, which will help you assess the partner organizations' gross profit.

- Develop a detailed schedule plan at task level with dependencies and critical path.

- Develop a communication plan: There is a lot of communication overhead in the GD model, as your delivery teams are located across the globe. The communication plan should be clear in terms of a set agenda with details of key participants and action items to cover.

- Develop a QM plan: We talked about the need for a detailed quality plan; every project should encompass a detailed QM plan during the blueprint phase, with the appropriate quality metrics to measure throughout the project to ensure high-quality deliverables.

- Develop delivery metrics: It is imperative to measure performance in terms of cost, schedule, and quality. As noted previously, critical metrics such as CPI and SPI are measured based on earned value metrics. It is important to review metrics at every milestone.

In most organizations, the preceding activities are sets of tasks to complete with tools and standardized templates. You must adhere to the industry standards to ensure that these key startup activities are completed, prior to proceeding to the realization phase.

Realization Tasks

In the realization phase, you'll need a high=performing team, stakeholder communication, and support from time to time, analyzing the overall performance of the project by using appropriate delivery measurements. Above all, the PM should monitor cost, time, and scope, and should analyze risks with control measures. A good project deployment follows project management best practices combined with tools, accelerators, and methods. Tools can help in implementation, which makes a difference by accelerating development and testing phases. In a similar context, metrics can prove that something is right or wrong, but it is up to a PM to study the outcome in every phase, and reorganize tasks as required to bring the project back on track. The main pitfalls to avoid during realization are a lack of process controls and measurement. If there is a variance in schedule or cost, the respective PM must ensure additional controls, or bring the issue up to the steering committee to ensure that appropriate control measures are implemented to avert a major disaster. As the PMI states, most projects fail during the initial phase of design and development. Typically, a PM spends a lot of time strategizing, planning, and communicating with key stakeholders during the prep and blueprint phase. Once you draft the roadmap in the form of a robust project plan, realization can be achieved easily. A PM must provide a good critique to ensure a good understanding of the product ecosystem, as common pitfalls such as lack of product knowledge will lead to failed implementations. A PM must communicate rigorously during integration scenarios to ensure that interface scenarios works with all critical integration points, including non-SAP software.

As discussed, a PM must anticipate risks up front and control problems before the client escalates a problem. Every risk should be controlled before it occurs. You should study the probability of occurrence, the frequency with impact to the business, to be able to monitor and control risks before they escalate into issues.

Another point is that to handle escalations, it is imperative to understand issues and bring them to the table in the steering committee. Often partner organizations hide these potential risks under the carpet, with an assumption of handling them later. As a word of caution, many stakeholders have called off projects because of a lack of communication. This is one of the major pitfalls in project implementation. Every problem has a solution. You must research into the problem to find a viable solution by collaborating with respective stakeholders, solution architects, along with SAP product SMEs that can help in every phase to monitor and control project risks. These services from SAP can guide you throughout the implementation, with services such as Go Live functional checks, or upgrade checks that will avert a major project failure. I recommend a rapid prototype model using agile methods to implement projects. RDS is a new concept in SAP for rapid deployment using SAP best practices that are preconfigured scenarios; however RDS varies from customer to customer, with changes and requirements. In case of RDS implementation, ensure understanding of the product and its capabilities aligning to the business scenario.

Closure

The project lessons learned are one of the most important aspects of what you've done so far. If the results are good, try to benchmark your project to benefit the delivery organization. If the results are bad, document the lessons learned the hard way. Either way, you will have an example of pitfalls to avoid. Some lessons are bitter, as you may end up with a failed implementation project due to product integration issues or client requirements with an unrealistic scope, or even a lack of skills or resources. There are apparent issues in every project. Therefore, due diligence is required throughout the project phases. If your case study becomes a success, reward the team for the good work, and ensure it is part of the project catalog, so that the sales team can use it as a success story. The tools and accelerators that you've used can become part of the standard accelerators package. Further, you can customize the solution for the specific LOB to demonstrate your leadership. Above all, you've gained experience and the team has gained expertise and become more skilled. Perhaps you can use templates for the solution, creating a standard tool suite for similar customers and promoting reusable assets to benefit the organization. If you're able to demonstrate leadership qualities, leading by example from the front, your team will be constantly motivated. A real success is not a one-time endeavor; you'll want to cherish the present moments by working with customers and teams, solving problems with absolute professionalism and ethical responsibilities. If you're demonstrating ethics, your team will follow!

Concluding Remarks

Now, you have a 360-degree view of the SAP project manager's role and responsibilities. It is an exciting and responsive role, and the challenge is to lead your team to ensure a successful implementation project. SAP leadership skills combined with your technical and functional skills will help the team to succeed. If you're able to nip risks in the bud, they can be mitigated early, before escalating. It is an essential attribute of a SAP project manager to anticipate problems in terms of product challenges, integration issues, and skills required. The SAP PM should be diligently aware of upcoming issues, based on studying the project artifacts. Above all, good client leadership, support from stakeholders, and accurate report metrics can guide you to a successful implementation project.

CHAPTER 23

■ ■ ■

Approach to Writing Effective SAP Proposals

Let's start with five key questions. You should be able to answer these questions prior to writing an effective SAP proposal:

- What are you going to do?

- Why is this work important/significant?

- How are you going to complete this project?

- How long will it take?

- What are the outcomes/intended results?

One of the common pitfalls in a SAP implementation project is due to lack of diligence in architecting a solution in the deal: projects fail because of an undersized bid in terms of resources, schedule, and lack of clear scope itself. Once you promise a customer to complete all customizations, even without a deep-dive analysis, it becomes a commitment to deliver. I believe that if the due diligence is done earlier, you can avert a major disaster. Because of increased competition, most organizations are participating in complex proposals with a competitively priced bids, without realizing the overall solution and complexities in the landscape, thus leading to a failed implementation project. It is imperative to deliver what you've promised a client, as honesty is the best policy. Most of these projects fail to deliver as promised due to the aggressive sale, thus compromising the quality of services, with risks to delivery. If you're diligently discussing the project with the client and conducting workshops, you can understand the dynamics of the organization prior to submitting a proposal.

■ **Note** The key aspect to winning a proposal is putting together a solid solution and implementation plan as per the benchmark standards. You need to contemplate the customer's key issues and come up with the best possible solution that addresses the customer's key concerns or problem areas.

Key Tenets

The proposal writer should clarify what it is he wants to do, why and how he wants to do it, and then present that proposal in the manner and time frame proposed. Once the solution is approved post internal review, provide a written contract between the client in the form of a statement of work with detailed activities, and a RACI matrix with scope, budget, and schedule.

What Is This About?

The Introduction to the project provides a general presentation of the phenomena or issue of interest, and is usually contained in one to two pages. The issue or problem under investigation is described, and background and/or context for understanding the nature of the issue is provided. In writing this section, the bid manager should provide answers to two main questions:

- What is the project all about?

- Why is the project important or worthwhile? The Introduction also typically concludes with a brief description of the structure of the remainder of the document.

You should include key characteristics, as highlighted in Table 23-1, for reference.

Table 23-1. *Key Characteristics*

Principles	Description
Effective collaboration	Client, employees, suppliers, and business partners have the ability to integrate closely, at one time to deliver a solution with greater value to the client.
Data knowledge & content integration	Timely, contextual access to real-time data and content are critical elements of a proposed solution, to help in timely decisions.
Process standardization	Deploy solution using industry best practices.
Agile & flexible	Leverage industry-standard architecture and integration capabilities (ESA).

Solution Approach (How Am I Going to Solve Your Problems?)

Every project must state a detailed understanding of the customer constraints or a statement on the intent of the project. This statement includes several smaller questions nested in the larger one. The solution approach and the understanding of the key customer constraints are two required elements of all proposals. The connections between the two must be obvious.

This section is the key to winning a proposal, as you'll demonstrate your expertise. For example, SAP implementation project phases are standard, but you should assess the scope of each activity relevant to the customer. In any SAP upgrade project, you need not have an extended blueprint phase, so the strategy is to conduct an impact analysis during the initial stage of the project. Typically, an implementation project follows the standard ASAP or Agile-ASAP combined approach, depending on the specific constraints. Perhaps you'll evaluate an RDS combined approach to build prototypes. In the case of a rollout, you must explain the different rollout approaches for each country for which the solution is being rolled out. You should explain the solution in brief in this section.

Also, it helps to explain your tools and accelerators that will mitigate risks in the project with your delivery capabilities. The project scope subsection explains the key components, such as those highlighted in Table 23-2 for mapping business requirements.

Table 23-2. *Mapping Business Requirements*

SAP Module	Business Requirements
Accounts Receivable	Credit and collections, dispute resolution, electronic bill presentment and payment, managing security deposits, payment processing, returns processing and reconciliation
Sales & Distribution	A/C processing, billing, product listing, consignment, compliance, contract, credit-memo, delivery, in-house, invoice, order, quotation, service orders, service contracts, custom product sales, pricing, credit check, commission and output processing
Materials & Inventory Management	Inventory, services and parts, batch management and parts, inventory related to tank maintenance
Analytics	Operational planning, inventory and sales planning, sales cockpit and tracking

You should indicate the customization complexities with the total number of FRICE components to develop. Where the constraints appear in the proposal is something each writer must decide. The constraints could appear in the introduction; they could follow the introduction or the background, or they could appear within any of the preceding sections. Just don't leave them until the reference section!

Implementation Project Methodology (How? Who? Where?)

This section must make sense within the context of the document and be linked to the sections preceding it. In this section, provide a clear, explicit, and thorough description of how you will complete your project and the schedule for completing each step—for example, ASAP implementation methodology, or ASAP-Agile or even RDS, depending on the customer situation. It is the writer's responsibility to ensure that the proposal is clear about what is being proposed, with whom, where, and when. Approximately one to two pages is suitable for this section, with an appendix describing the tools, methods, and accelerators.

You must elaborate ASAP phases with activities as highlighted in Table 23-3.

Table 23-3. *SAP ASAP Activities with Deliverables*

Phase	Activities	Deliverables
Project Prep & Blueprint	Project management, establish phase-specific tasks, PMO and design phase, organizational change management, communication plan, training plan and risk management	Key business process document with mapping scenarios
Realization	FRICE development, testing (unit, integration, and UAT), and implementation	Functional specifications, FRICE technical plan Cutover plan
Final Preparations & Go Live	Training execution Cutover plan and execution Dry run and Go Live	Training plan
Operate	Transition plan and execution	Transition document, incident report

Tools, Methods, and Accelerators

Describe your proprietary tools and methods to accelerate the development phase, and explain how you intend to mitigate risks in the project. If you're leveraging an offshore delivery center, describe your plan for regular communication and issue resolution, or work packages assigned to the offshore components, with a QA plan. If you're using additional licensed tools such as MS Project, indicate the usage with quantifiable benefits to the client, and how it will mitigate risks. Additional SAP consolidation and upgrade remediation tools are available in the market to accelerate the remediation phase and/or functional consolidation. You should also indicate the QA services provided by SAP, if required, at an additional cost to mitigate risks. Tools such as SAP SLO can be handy for functional consolidation, and data migration tools provided by SAP can ease migration from legacy database to SAP database.

Effective Strategy to Win SAP Proposals

One of the daunting tasks for any organization is to consolidate a solid proposal in front of the customer within the stipulated time. Most organizations rely on standard estimation guidelines, a solution approach, and in-house capabilities to demonstrate the skills available to complete a project on time, on budget, and on target. However, the real challenge is to consolidate the information required within the organization, because of multiple departments' involvement in the project their relevance to the customer. When you draft a proposal, you must comply with the guidelines described by the customer. Since most customers compare bids, in order to have an optimized solution, you should compare your solution approach to the proposed budget based on the benchmark standards. Also, you must evaluate your in-house capabilities, with the real intent of solving the customer's problems. An effective questionnaire, workshops, and/or interview is required to assess the scope and is imperative to understand key constraints of a customer. The solid foundation of the technical proposal response should be based on the key constraints and how you address these constraints in the solution.

Do not overpromise and underdeliver. That would malign your reputation upon delivery with poor standards or perhaps a delayed delivery. You should promise what you can deliver based on your strengths. It is better to conduct a detailed demo/walk-through of the intended solution, with options to deliver—for example, phased vs. big bang with pro's and con's. Once done, gain consensus and draft a proposal based on the agreed-upon approach. It will be better if you're able to articulate one key constraint of the customer, such as the P2P process, and explain how your solution would remedy the situation with a detailed walk-through. Often delivery teams have no clue about what was promised during the sales pursuit. Proposal teams should work closely with and engage the delivery team leads during the pursuit.

▪ **Note**   While it is good to build a template proposal based on respective geography, *do not* copy and paste content from another proposal. Every proposal should be based on the individual customer and project complexities. A winning proposal in one case won't necessarily be another winning situation, as every client situation will vary based on various parameters.

Developing a Detailed Solution Approach

The key to a robust proposal is to understand customer requirements and the problem statement prior to proposing a viable solution. The solution approach should be tailor-made, specific to each customer, by understanding the business requirements to provide the right solution. The approach should be extremely clear. The estimation guidelines and use of accelerators have to be well-defined with quantifiable benefits. The bid manager should be able to consolidate responses based on input from the delivery teams, and the solution architect should be able to define the solution with critical reasons for the approach.

A well-written proposal must include a detailed solution approach, methodology, and the team's capabilities to the extent required without including unnecessary content copied from any other proposal. Every proposal must be started over again, specific to the customer and the project situation. For example, the following is a list of requirements:

- The key aspect is to understand customer requirements and how you intend to leverage technology to address customer constraints. Most project implementations fail because of a failure to understand customer requirements.

- Understand the real intent of the project: business optimization and/or improve services.

- Build an effective strategy based on the customer constraints and inputs gathered during the interview sessions.

- Demonstrate excellence in use of best practices, tools, accelerators, and the ROI benefits to the customer.

- Develop a robust solution approach, methodology, and project management capabilities.

- The customer would like to implement an ERP solution to enable automation of the end-to-end operations. In this case, you must assess the scope of full-blown or partial implementation based on the ROI to the customer.

- You must provide the ERP implementation questionnaire to understand more about the customer project details and organization. This step can help you fine-tune the solution.

- Develop a prototype and workshops with the client, to demonstrate your understanding of the specific constraints with the proposed solution.

- Workshops are key to understanding these constraints. You'll be able raise few questions and understand the client's working dynamics and business model.

- Describe your quality enablement. How do you measure defects and quality of deliverables by using standard metrics?

If you're able to address the key constraints and explain how implementing your solution will help a customer benefit, this is the key to a winning proposal. Each proposal is different depending on the customer geography and project requirements. A customer in the MENA region might want to understand the cost, strategy, and timeline, whereas a customer in the EMEA or NA might want to understand the mitigation plan for risks. You'll need to alter the plan depending on these customer-specific constraints.

Now, let's look at how to describe a specific process in the proposal that addresses a customer's key constraints. The proposed SAP Accounts Payable screen should map to the business requirements, such as the client's accounts practices and the year-end closing procedure. Once you study the accounts payable practices, you should be able to map them to the SAP standard solution and then explain the solution with a detailed flow chart.

Figure 23-1 indicates the accounts payables in a client situation, starting from the vendor master to the postings. This is one of the critical process flows. Once you start breaking down the complex business scenarios into SAP standard processes, it's easy to assess the scope of the required configuration of the client's business. Additional customization can be discussed in workshops, while demonstrating every process flow. These workshops should include a detailed discussion with the business and end users to collect requirements.

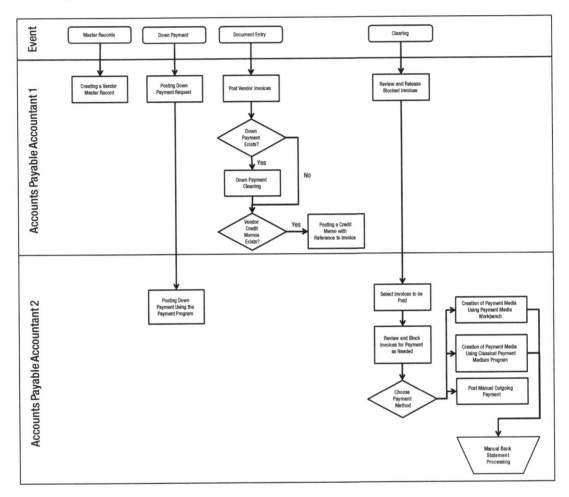

Figure 23-1. *A/P process flow*

This A/P flow highlights the triggered-by events such as document entry, followed by the sequence of activities such as account postings. An effective executive summary should highlight the customer problem and the proposed solution that addresses these constraints. It is an opportunity to set the context right at the beginning and to follow through with the response document. Each section should illustrate these key constraints and how you intend to tailor the solution, specific to the client. Once you demonstrate understanding of the customer constraints, you need to provide a solution that will be understood by the client business experts. In SAP, the technical approach carries the weight. For example, your proposal is evaluated based on a simple percentage factor as follows:

- Understanding the key constraints—10%

- Providing a solution that addresses the constraints—20%

- Demonstrating skills in similar project implementations, case studies, references—30%

- Demonstrating differentiators such as use of tools and accelerators to mitigate risks—10%

- Demonstrating expertise in relevant domain skills—15%

- Demonstrating consulting expertise in the respective geography—10%

- Providing thought leadership and innovation by going the extra mile to support customers—5%

Also, in today's competitive market, your capability to provide enhanced delivery offshore can help you win projects, as well as implement them successfully. Figure 23-2 shows offshore work packages that have been outsourced to stay competitive in the market in a SAP implementation project. The chart shows the percent of offshore work packages in the respective phases. Knowing these percentages can help you determine the best strategy for an improved delivery model.

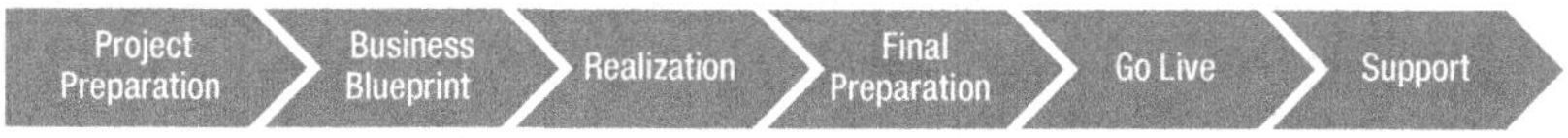

	Project Preparation	Business Blueprint	Realization	Final Preparation	Go Live	Support
Percent of Project	3%	20%	40%	15%	10%	12%
Offshore Component	0%	0%	70%	5-%	50%	70%

Figure 23-2. *Onsite, offshore work packages by phases*

CASE STUDY: USING RDS METHODOLOGY

If you're using RDS, explain the benefits to the customer via a detailed list of deliverables. The following table highlights a standard SAP rapid deployment and implementation methodology of Start, Deploy, and Run.

SAP RDS Activities and Deliverables

	Phase	Activities	Deliverables
1.	Start	Project management, kickoff workshop, and system landscape check.	Delivery guide Project schedule WBS, service delivery model, roles and responsibilities Templates, process-flow documents, kickoff presentation, consumption guide, pre-delivery requirements, and checklist
2.	Deploy	Solution realization, master data load, refinement workshop, and refinement realization, KT to key users	Install guide, solution documentation, SolMan content, best practice content (preconfigured), configuration activities, and implementation content
3.	Run	Performance tests, end-user training, sign-off solution, Go Live prep and Go Live, post Go Live support and activities, improvements and roadmap workshop	Test cases, delivery acceptable forms, training materials, and Go Live checklist

EXERCISE

1. Write an effective executive summary describing your solution at a high level and including the key constraints of the client.

2. Explain the technical solution approach in detail, with illustrations for different project types such as an implementation, a technical upgrade, and a rollout project.

3. Write an effective project management strategy, including project phases and activities, risk management, and change and scope management.

4. Demonstrate your organizational skills, tools, and accelerators to mitigate risks.

Concluding Remarks

Every proposal is a customer story. The story should help achieve a win-win situation for both the client and the implementation partner. As you saw in the preceding case study, a lot of due diligence is required, before discussing the key constraints and the proposed solution. If you're able to convince the client of your organization's ability to succeed in the endeavor, with an effective written proposal, the project is all yours!

CHAPTER 24

■ ■ ■

Enhancing Your Consulting Skills

Unfortunately, implementations sometimes fail due to a lack of skill or—most important—a lack of good attitudes, integrity, and teamwork. In most cases, remembering that "honesty is the best policy" could alleviate many challenges: the person who raises their hand during turbulent times, states problems clearly, and offers a proposed solution, is a leader. Today, technology has become a driving force for organizations, offering enhanced capabilities to expand business opportunities and venture into new areas of products and services. In essence, technology is now the brain of any industry. As a technology consultant or project manager, you're a brand ambassador for SAP and the organization. Hence, your actions should be bound by ethics, and you should go the extra mile for the organization for your team.

This chapter examines common traits of successful consultants and how you can hone your skills. As a consultant, you must ensure that you obtain, master, and demonstrate the necessary skills. If you're a project manager, you must manage your team, maintain the clientele relationship, and ensure a successful implementation. It is your responsibility as an SAP project manager to ensure that you have the right skills for the project, or as an SAP consultant to broaden your skill set as a quick learner with a passion to excel.

■ **Note** Attitude matters if you want to succeed. The right attitude will help you achieve a long and rewarding career.

Building a Rewarding Career

The market is expanding in specific domains such as retail, automotive, insurance, banking, pharmaceuticals, clinical trials, utilities, and manufacturing. It's difficult to precisely, but the market expectation is that you will have strong technical and functional domain expertise, especially if you're a project manager. You should plan your core area of expertise with expanded functional and/or technical strengths. If you're switching jobs frequently—say, more often than every three years on average—you should plan to stay longer and build your core skills in domain-specific areas. You may start as a consultant, but somewhere along the line you can choose a specific path based on your passion. Being a Jack of all trades but master of none won't work, especially in SAP: the market needs professionals who are aligned with emerging markets. You cannot sell your profile as a plain SAP SD and/or SAP MM consultant and/or project manager; you need areas of specialization such as SAP SD, CRM, or MM/PP/WM with knowledge of SAP HANA to excel in the competitive market and sell your credentials as a consultant. If you've mastered ABAP, try Web Dynpro, or venture into SAP mobility using Fiori. It is not how much you know in the broad areas of SAP but rather how well you can focus on a specialization and move into niche areas such as analytics.

Figure 24-1 illustrates how you should build your skills, which requires planning. You should not let the company drive your skill development, or you may become redundant. I don't want to overgeneralize, but the emerging trend across growing organizations is to hire a skill instead of cross-training employees. The IT team has to be dynamic and able to re-skill itself. If you're planning to stay five to ten years on one good career path and grow your skills, then you need to decide now to control your future.

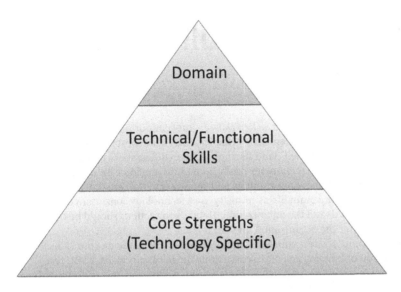

Figure 24-1. *Career pyramid*

First, you should choose your technological area of expertise. Assuming SAP is your focus area, narrow it to an SAP technical or functional topic based on your past experiences and interests. Let's say you have SAP SD or SAP Basis as your core area. You should specialize: SAP Basis can lead to HANA, which is the emerging trend; and SD can lead to CRM. In addition, focus on secondary skills such as supply chain or analytics.

Leadership is no longer just a nice skill to have; it is a mandate that you demonstrate to the hiring manager that you have leadership skills in your technical, functional, and domain areas. Ensure that you understand all the relevant areas and can provide detailed project artifacts and references.

Maintaining Your Skills

I suggest building a profile on social media such as LinkedIn and other job portals and keeping it up to date. You could build a Facebook page with all your project specifics and restrict access to hiring managers. If you have at least one SAP certification, it will help prove that you're a leader in the role you're applying for.

Gone are the days when hiring managers looked at your resume and thought of questions to ask. Nowadays, it is easy for them to research your history on LinkedIn. In addition, they have a set of questions to ask about the skills they need, to test your basics. It is a good idea to test your knowledge and get re-certified with BrainBench.com or similar. As your career progresses, you may lose focus on your career path; I recommend staying at a job long enough to gain your footing regarding organizational dynamics, functionality, and domain-specific skills. Remember, the market is too narrow for generic skills. Unless you're an SAP professional with certifications and relevant domain skills, your resume will not even be shortlisted for SAP project manager and/or program manager leadership roles. If you're contemplating an offshore career, such as delivery manager, be sure you have additional certifications such as PMP, agile, PRINCE, CMMI, and quality certifications, as well as sufficient knowledge to demonstrate your project-management capabilities and understanding of the nuances of budgeting and estimation techniques. There are freelance options as well, but pursuing them depends on your interest in travelling globally and your willingness to take risks to succeed in your career.

If you're applying for a management role, you need expertise in managing people, conflict resolution, appraisals, and performance management. Human resources principles will help you position yourself as a leader. *Do not* apply for any position without reading the job description and understanding the requirements. Examine the company's background and ask yourself how well you would fit and whether you qualify. Doing so will save time on both ends. If you're applying for the services industry, indicate your relevant credentials to the hiring manager and focus on those areas. If you have strengths from working for a manufacturing company, such as implementing core logistics in SAP, focus on what the hiring company needs by projecting yourself into the interviewer's place and preparing accordingly. Share information that makes sense to the hiring team and the organization. Be very specific and polished with your responses.

You are human, and you cannot fit into every role in the industry. You should match your interests with the business. If you fail at an interview, learn from your mistakes and move on. For example, consider A. P. Abdul Kalam, an atomic scientist who hailed from a poor family in India. He failed to qualify as a fighter pilot, but this eventually helped him achieve greater heights in a career as a rocket scientist—and he eventually became president of India. You can succeed if you put in enough effort and persevere, while remembering that you cannot control every parameter. For example, you may have family constraints that limit your ability to relocate, which may reduce your flexibility and opportunities. For this reason, you should plan for at least five years of your career and keep a reserve to sustain yourself and family if you experience a downturn. You need a good contingency plan to safeguard your finances, because our lives are increasingly dependent on market conditions. Plan your finances such that you minimize risk and optimize spending, and remember the value of saving.

The world has shrunk into one global village. The United States is a huge market for SAP professionals, the EMEA has been stable, and APJ is also a decent market, although offshore jobs are not very client interactive at times, depending on the role and organizational profile. Due to rapid globalization, countries like China, India, and the Philippines provide employment opportunities with abundant growth. If you're part of a service organization, you'll primarily support the clientele on site; if you're part of a captive center, you have the opportunity to grow with the client and enhance your domain expertise. You're responsible for your career, so you should keep your roadmap in mind and take interim steps to help you achieve your goals.

Remember that switching careers for immediate benefits may not help you in the long run: your legacy is erased every time you change jobs. Switching technologies too often also is not a good idea, because you cannot build solid expertise that way. There are obvious differences between a solid ten years of SAP expertise and five years of SAP plus five years of Java. It's better to emerge as a leader in one of the areas and build your career path on the specific technology.

Play It Smart, and Work Hard

There is no point in being political. Politics will give you heartburn and sleepless nights and not help you in any way. If you're on the emotional side, it's time to take a course on managing your emotions; I've seen projects fail because teams are caught between personalities. Such organizational conflicts are mainly due to egoistic attitudes, which are often misconstrued as leadership traits. It is good to challenge each other for the benefit of the organization, to help brew innovative ideas; but be diplomatic. Do good work and do it to the fullest, and help your team.

For example, I consulted for a few years with Target in Minneapolis, Minnesota, in the United States, and I was amazed by the teamwork and dedication of employees from retail to the distributor network to the back office IT operations. Even when people excelled as individuals, they attributed the success to the team. I also had the opportunity to learn about industry best practices in strategy, consulting, and project management with absolute integrity at IBM. Above all, my association with SAP (GD) taught me best practices in SAP's product strategy and implementation.

I understand that businesses may sometimes place less value on ethics, due to the competitive environment, but my view is that your core values should be based on ethical values, regardless of the organization's culture. Being competitive doesn't mean you should flaunt all the rules and ethics while managing contracts and implementing projects. Your financial reports should be accurate, because they may have global impact as consolidated data is passed to leadership, and from there to the steering committee, board members, and stockholders. In many service organizations, marquee client projects are crucial for stock valuation, which is based on quarterly financial results; and your project may have an impact on the quarterly closures.

I admire companies such as IBM for their ethical values and culture. If you abide by simple values such as honesty, you can walk an extra mile and achieve success. Success is not just about money: it also includes the satisfaction derived from what you're doing. Harness your energy for team building, helping others with technology, or even providing counseling or training. Dr. Abdul Kalam taught his whole life; when someone asked him, "What would you want to be called?" he said, "I want to be known as a teacher," despite being an esteemed rocket scientist and former president of India.

I believe in being creative; writing poetry is my passion. If you keep both the logical and creative parts of your brain active, you'll be happy and feel content. Sometimes, writing poetry helps me solve complex technical and/or functional issues. If you're only competitive, you'll eventually be like a robot! Suppose you've had a terrible experience and failed to deliver a project or had a bad interview. So what? It's not the end of the world. Relax and find a way to get past the problem. Be honest with your manager and/or client. Issues with a project will be exponentially multiplied if you aren't honest, whereas simple truth can alleviate them. In addition, you've learned from the experience and are stronger than before. For example, consider Sylvester Stallone. You may be surprised to learn that the script Stallone wrote for the movie *Rocky* was rejected for years, but he didn't give up. He worked hard to demonstrate the quality of the script and his interest in acting in the film, which eventually became a blockbuster that won three Academy Awards. The next time you fail, remember that the sum of your failures will eventually help you achieve a grand success. Microsoft was started in a dorm room, and Apple began in a garage. A group from IBM started SAP AGS, which is now the Everest of ERP technology. The same is true for Flipkart, Amazon, Google, and many other companies that have reached the epitome of success!

Similarly, if you have a bad boss, why not get to know with the person and socialize with them? Learn from the experience without taking things personally. Accept the challenge of observing and accepting the situation as is, and grow from it. If the situation becomes unbearable, try other alternatives; the entire horizon awaits you.

If issues arise, do not single out employees; address the entire team and work through problems as a team. If you're a manager, promote teamwork. You're responsible for the team and the employees representing the organization: keep it simple, stick to the rules, and help provide a positive experience for every employee. For instance, Abraham Lincoln was one of the most admired presidents of the United States. After his election, when someone in Congress called him the son of a cobbler, he stated that it was his responsibility to serve people as his father did: with integrity. Be a good leader rather than a dictator. Bad leaders can force things to happen, but in the end they fail. On the other hand, a silent and humble man like Mahatma Gandhi led India to independence from the British government.

Breathing exercises and other relaxation techniques can help calm your mind and focus your attention on your work. As I've said, success is not just about money; it encompasses a holistic view of life. A good life means living it to the fullest.

Top Ten Desirable Traits of an SAP Consultant

All of the following are important for achieving success during your career:

- *SAP skills:* As an SAP consultant, you're the solution provider who sees the 360-degree view of the product and provides a solution to your clients. It's imperative that you talk from a business perspective and map it to the relevant modules. Implementation projects fail all too often due to a lack of integration. Know the interface points, assess risks during the blueprint stage, and give due attention to the interface scenarios.

- *Integrity:* An SAP Global Risk & Compliance (GRC) implementation is all about risk governance and mitigation for enterprises. As an SAP consultant, you're responsible for behaving with integrity, adhering to policies, maintaining professional communications, and understanding conflict. If you're an implementation partner, ensure that your data-driven estimates match your actual capacity to delivery, and maintain CMM global standards to deliver with adequate data security and privacy.

- *Effective client management:* You must understand the working dynamics of your clients and support business users throughout the project. Don't try to force-fit a solution that is not possible in SAP; in such cases, honesty is the best policy. An SAP consultant should provide simple solutions to complex business problems in a timely manner.

- *Good presentation, communication, and correspondence skills:* You need to be able to explain functionality succinctly in emails, presentations, and business SME discussions. Difficult end users will ask basic questions about the technology, and you must explain the SAP processes and how they will help users transact their business. A detailed training plan to help them understand how business processes are mapped in SAP can help you avoid pitfalls resulting from users' lack of understanding.

- *Good documentation skills:* You're responsible for documenting scope, creating a configuration plan, and gaining consensus with the client as part of the deliverables in every milestone. If there is a change requested or scope creep, you should report to the project manager to trigger a change-management process with documentary evidence of the agreed baseline. Otherwise the project may go haywire, if multiple requests from the client lead to significant scope changes.

- *Functional and technical skills:* Functional consultants should understand the business requirements and translate them into configuration documents and functional specifications on how to use SAP. You also need good technical knowledge to guide the technical team as they write the technical specifications for customization.

- *Effective teamwork and mentorship:* Teamwork and mutual learning can help you implement projects successfully. Just as Target rewards teamwork, SAP implementations are about working together as a unit in a global delivery model, respecting each member of the team.

- *Knowledge of SAP Solution Manager:* Most projects use Solution Manager, so it is imperative that you have sufficient knowledge to expedite SAP implementation projects using Solution Manager accelerators.

- *Attention to details:* Listen, listen, and listen to end users and business SMEs, and dive into the critical factors and pain points. As a consultant, you must demonstrate leadership in your business area and use technology as a tool to help customers succeed. You are not there just to do the configuration; you're there to help the customer achieve business goals.

- *Flexibility:* There are different ways to fly from the East coast to the West Coast of the United States. A good SAP consultant determines the best possible ways to reach the destination through sound knowledge of the map, rather than customizing a trip that doesn't serve the purpose. Step back, assess the requirements, map the issues, and do not shy away from confronting your customers' views. You need to provide the best possible solution, not just bend the software to achieve whatever the customer wants, which may lead to implementation failure.

Interview Tips

If you're applying for a job as a newbie, an experienced consultant, or a professional, there are a few key points you need to understand. First, believe in yourself. Then, keep the following in mind, to ensure that you have the right skills for the project:

- You should have adequate client-facing skills and hands-on configuration skills in a similar and/or complex environment.

- You should have performed well in a target- and time-based environment in a similar project in similar LOBs.

- You should have good communication skills, be able to articulate business processes to end users, be able to explain process maps in SAP with good functional mapping skills, and have a 360-degree view of the product ecosystem.

- You should have good problem-solving skills, with demonstrated expertise in past projects, and the ability to answer scenario-specific questions.

Your resume should be succinct and include a list of key accomplishments. Don't repeat the same points to an interviewer: speak from your experience. Know the interviewer and the job description, and ask how you'd be a good fit. You must demonstrate a good attitude, honesty, and expertise. Don't inflate your resume or yourself. What is the point of getting into a job that doesn't suit your interests and specific skills? If you determine during the interview that the job is not your cup of tea, say so, and tell the interviewer that you'd be interested in being part of a team in the organization that better suited you. There is nothing wrong with being up-front and honest.

There are two key SAP questions to prepare for:

1. Explain an end-to-end business scenario and how you mapped it in SAP.

   I have been asked to draw a business process such as Order to Cash (OTC) on a board and then explain to the interviewers how it was mapped. I also had to explain the specific problems faced by the customer and how an SAP implementation helped them succeed. If you're an SAP SD/CRM consultant, be very specific; explain what you've done beginning with the basics, so interviewers can gauge your knowledge of the business scenarios and your capacity to use SAP to resolve issues. Don't use jargon—be simple. You're not teaching the interviewers, you're demonstrating your expertise. Ask the interviewer questions if you're not clear on any points.

2. Explain the quality/delivery metrics used for measuring performance in a project.

I have been in some funny situations, such as trying to explain the Earn Value Management (EVM) Cost Performance Index. Brushing up on your metrics skills prior to the interview. The questions can be a little strange, depending on the individual interviewers.

Rehearse what you're going to say. If you're being interviewed for a CRM implementation, the interviewer will want to know your credentials in marketing, sales, and service areas with core and extended capabilities in terms of industry knowledge and SAP. Always try to explain from a simple business perspective, and work up to complex scenarios if the interviewer is interested. Remember, interviewers will ask you to rank your core module expertise, and their questions will be based on the areas in which you ranked your skills as excellent.

Gaining Skills

After you land a consulting job, the first six months are crucial to proving your skills to the organization. Try to be innovative in your approach as a key differentiator and align yourself with the organization/ project goals. You'll be measured on KPIs for the department. Be aware of your department goals and your manager's KPIs to ensure that you are supporting the global picture. Understand where you stand in the organization and how you can create positive growth. It is important to know the values, culture, and network within the organization. Survey growing and emerging market trends, and align your skills accordingly. As you're able, expand your skills in the domain areas aligned with the organizational goals; this can help you achieve your KPIs more quickly.

If you are contemplating a lateral career move at some point, your focus should be on core business processes with skills as a backdrop; the opposite is true if you're planning for a global consulting SME type of job. Assess your skills every two to three years against global emerging technology trends. If you grow into leadership, it is imperative to build your people skills and management skills and obtain a PMI type of certification. It is good to renew your certifications in SAP and/or PMI to ensure that you stay current in the job market. Actively network with professionals, participate in SAP TechEd, and socialize with technology experts on social media. This will help you in times of need. I even recommend gaining citizenship or work permits in emerging markets such as the United States, EMEA, and APJ, to secure a consulting space in the extremely competitive future market. As you reach mid-career, be prudent and stay in place as long as possible, because job hunting can be strenuous. The grass may look greener, but it may not be when you get there!

Navigating Turbulent Times

It is essential for a leader to stay in place. Every project is an ordeal filled with challenges. There are two ways to think about it: as a risk or as an opportunity. Every risk indicates an opportunity to grow and excel in your career. You aren't expecting a job without challenges, right? When you're challenged, you learn. If you're a fighter pilot, you learn to fly through the highs and lows and be prepared to face critical situations. Facing challenges will help you grow personally and professionally.

As Figure 24-2 shows, these are the key drivers to grow through turbulent business situations:

- Building a vision

- Flexibility and leadership

- Team spirit

- Challenging the obvious!

Figure 24-2. *Key drivers of success*

Global Behavioral Traits

In addition to the traits mentioned earlier that are important for all SAP consultants, the following characteristics are required to work amid rapid globalization:

- *Cross-cultural awareness:* Particularly if you're working with a client in the MENA region, you need to be culturally sensitive. Study client responses and learn how to deal with the client regarding things such as timing, religious sentiment, and so on.

- *Flexibility:* At times your expertise may be required to support the client beyond normal working hours. Be flexible, if such requests are not too frequent.

- *Networking:* You should know how to network with global and local COEs, discuss solution strategy, and use best practices from prior implementations.

- *Global delivery awareness:* It is essential to be aware of the working dynamics of global delivery, because most clients work with this approach. Teams should understand these dynamics and support each other.

- *Timing:* Respond to client requirements in a timely manner, attend meetings on time, and be at work during the client's office hours.

- *Communication and escalation:* Following client escalation, use the required communication protocol. Information passed to the client must be accurate. If you're a partner, follow the correct escalation procedures with regard to personal or official issues.

- *Responsive, professional consultant:* As a professional consultant, you are responsible for the solution implemented. Plan your work, and assess the scope of risks in all tasks prior to implementation. Provide accurate information to the client, and if there are risks, say so up front. You must wear the hat of a business consultant on the client side to provide an SAP solution.

There is an acute shortage of business consulting skills in the industry due to lack of training. As an SAP ERP consultant, you should be able to demonstrate understanding of specific business processes, help clients by providing necessary knowledge, and configure client business processes in SAP while adhering to standards.

The project manager is responsible for planning, scheduling, and handling conflicts within the team and/or the client. By providing transparent reporting, escalating issues in a timely manner will help you succeed as a team. If you're working with large teams, follow industry standards, tools, and accelerators, and set ground rules. I have seen projects begin per normal procedures but then die due to lack of control measures and a persistent approach. There are intangible risks such as client holidays, which can derail your progress, especially if you're expecting client business consultant support. You must be aware of these risks well in advance in order to raise them with stakeholders.

I believe honesty as the best policy in any culture. You are empowered to innovate with freedom of thought, while having fun at work. Be bold and honest, and work as a team to deliver projects using the right skill mix without compromising quality or scope.

As you grow beyond cultural barriers, be aware of global cultural challenges. Dealing with clients and employees in any part of the globe with equanimity of mind and without aversion to specific cultures. Above all, it is essential that you have a mentor in the workplace or outside the organization whom you can ask for guidance as a trusted advisor to help you grow in your career. Your career is in your hands. Review your professional goals to assess where you stand and how to achieve new milestones. You should find what you're passionate about—and I believe SAP is your passion. Go for it!

Concluding Remarks

Thanks for your patience as you have read this book and come to understand the pitfalls you should avoid in SAP implementations. It has been a wonderful journey, expressing my thoughts to help you grow in your career by mastering the art of implementing SAP for complex business scenarios. Last but not least, I would like to wish you good luck and success in all your endeavors!

Index

Get the eBook for only $5!

Why limit yourself?

Now you can take the weightless companion with you wherever you go and access your content on your PC, phone, tablet, or reader.

Since you've purchased this print book, we're happy to offer you the eBook in all 3 formats for just $5.

Convenient and fully searchable, the PDF version enables you to easily find and copy code—or perform examples by quickly toggling between instructions and applications. The MOBI format is ideal for your Kindle, while the ePUB can be utilized on a variety of mobile devices.

To learn more, go to www.apress.com/companion or contact support@apress.com.

Printed in the United States
By Bookmasters